THE UNITED NATIONS IN THE POST–COLD WAR ERA

DILEMMAS IN WORLD POLITICS

Series Editor

George A. Lopez, University of Notre Dame

Dilemmas in World Politics offers teachers and students of international relations a series of quality books on critical issues, trends, and regions in international politics. Each text examines a "real world" dilemma and is structured to cover the historical, theoretical, practical, and projected dimensions of its subject.

FORTHCOMING TITLES

Gareth Porter and Janet Welsh Brown
Global Environmental Politics, second edition

☐ ☐ ☐

Bruce E. Moon
Dilemmas of International Trade

☐ ☐ ☐

James A. Caporaso
Challenges and Dilemmas of European Union

☐ ☐ ☐

David S. Mason
Revolution in East-Central Europe, second edition

☐ ☐ ☐

Thomas G. Weiss
Humanitarian Action, Intervention, and World Politics

THE UNITED NATIONS IN THE POST–COLD WAR ERA

■ ■ ■

Karen A. Mingst
UNIVERSITY OF KENTUCKY

Margaret P. Karns
UNIVERSITY OF DAYTON

WestviewPress
A Division of HarperCollins*Publishers*

Dilemmas in World Politics Series

Published in 1995 in the United States of America by Westview Press, Inc., 5500 Central Avenue, Boulder, Colorado 80301-2877, and in the United Kingdom by Westview Press, 12 Hid's Copse Road, Cumnor Hill, Oxford OX2 9JJ

Library of Congress Cataloging-in-Publication Data
Mingst, Karen A., 1947–
The United Nations in the post–cold war era / Karen A. Mingst, Margaret P. Karns.
p. cm. — (Dilemmas in world politics)
Includes bibliographical references and index.
ISBN 0–8133–2260-X (HC). — ISBN 0–8133–2261–8 (PB)
1. United Nations. I. Karns, Margaret P. II. Title.
III. Series.
JX1977.M54 1995
341.23'09'049—dc20 95–5657
CIP

The paper used in this publication meets the requirements of the American National Standard for Permanence of Paper for Printed Library Materials Z39.48-1984.

10 9 8 7 6 5 4 3 2

Contents

Tables and Illustrations

Tables

Boxes

Figures

Photographs and Cartoons

Illustrations

Acknowledgments

This book represents our first effort to reach undergraduate students and members of the informed public, although our collaborative work on multilateral institutions now spans a decade. We offer special thanks to George Lopez, editor of the Dilemmas series, and to Jennifer Knerr of Westview Press for encouraging us to write such a book and for providing critical feedback. Lawrence S. Finkelstein and two anonymous reviewers helped us sharpen our ideas. Thanks also to Nelson Messone from the University of Kentucky, who assisted with research.

Addressing the dilemmas confronting the United Nations and analyzing the reforms necessary to equip it for greater effectiveness in the post–Cold War world lead us to dedicate this book to the individual futures of our children—Ginger, Brett, and Paul—and to the collective future of the planet.

Karen A. Mingst
Margaret P. Karns

Acronyms

ACP	Africa, Caribbean, and Pacific
ACUNS	Academic Council on the United Nations System
AIDS	acquired immune deficiency syndrome
ASEAN	Association of Southeast Asian Nations
CPC	Committee for Program and Coordination
CSCE	Conference on Security and Cooperation in Europe
CSD	Commission on Sustainable Development
CSW	Commission on the Status of Women
DAWN	Development Alternatives with Women for a New Era
EC	European Community (also known as European Economic Community, or EEC)
ECLA	Economic Commission for Latin America
ECOSOC	United Nations Economic and Social Council
EPC	European Political Cooperation
EPTA	Expanded Programme of Technical Assistance
EU	European Union (previously referred to as EC or EEC)
FAO	Food and Agriculture Organization
FMLN	Frente Farabundo Martí para la Liberación Nacional
GATT	General Agreement on Tariffs and Trade
GEF	Global Environmental Facility
GNP	gross national product
G-77	Group of 77
IAEA	International Atomic Energy Agency
IBRD	International Bank for Reconstruction and Development (also known as World Bank)
ICJ	International Court of Justice
ICPD	International Conference on Population and Development
IDA	International Development Association
IFC	International Finance Corporation
IGO	international governmental organization
ILO	International Labor Organization
IMF	International Monetary Fund

IMO	International Maritime Organization
INSTRAW	International Research and Training Institute for the Advancement of Women
LDC	less developed country (also referred to as the South)
MIGA	Multilateral Investment Guarantee Agency
MINURSO	United Nations Mission for the Referendum in Western Sahara
NAFTA	North American Free Trade Agreement
NATO	North Atlantic Treaty Organization
NGO	nongovernmental organization
NIEO	New International Economic Order
OAS	Organization of American States
OAU	Organization of African Unity
OECD	Organization for Economic Cooperation and Development
ONUC	United Nations Operation in the Congo
ONUCA	United Nations Observer Group in Central America
ONUMOZ	United Nations Operation in Mozambique
ONUSAL	United Nations Observer Mission in El Salvador
OPEC	Organization of Petroleum Exporting Countries
PDD	Presidential Decision Directive
PLO	Palestine Liberation Organization
PRC	People's Republic of China
PrepCom	Preparation Commission
SWAPO	South West Africa People's Organization
TNC	transnational corporations
UNAMIC	United Nations Advance Mission in Cambodia
UNAMIR	United Nations Assistance Mission for Rwanda
UNA/USA	United Nations Association of the United States of America
UNAVEM I, II	United Nations Angola Verification Mission
UNCED	United Nations Conference on the Environment and Development
UNCHE	United Nations Conference on the Human Environment
UNCLOS	United Nations Conference on the Law of the Sea
UNCTAD	United Nations Conference on Trade and Development
UNDOF	United Nations Disengagement Observer Force
UNDP	United Nations Development Program
UNDRO	United Nations Disaster Relief Organization
UNEF I, II	United Nations Emergency Force
UNEP	United Nations Environmental Program
UNESCO	United Nations Educational, Scientific, and Cultural Organization

UNFICYP	United Nations Force in Cyprus
UNFPA	United Nations Fund for Population Activities
UNGOMAP	United Nations Good Offices Missions in Afghanistan and Pakistan
UNHCR	United Nations High Commissioner for Refugees
UNICEF	United Nations Children's Fund
UNIFEM	Voluntary Fund for the United Nations Decade for Women
UNIFIL	United Nations Interim Force in Lebanon
UNIKOM	United Nations Iraq-Kuwait Observer Mission
UNIMOG	United Nations Iran-Iraq Military Observer Group
UNITA	National Union for the Total Independence of Angola
UNITAF	Unified Task Force on Somalia (also known as Operation Restore Hope)
UNMIH	United Nations Mission in Haiti
UNMOGIP	United Nations Military Observer Group in India and Pakistan
UNOMIG	United Nations Observer Mission in Georgia
UNOMIL	United Nations Observer Mission in Liberia
UNOMSA	United Nations Observer Mission in South Africa
UNOMUR	United Nations Observer Mission in Uganda and Rwanda
UNOSOM I, II	United Nations Operation in Somalia
UNOVEN	United Nations Observer Mission to Verify the Electoral Process in Nicaragua
UNPROFOR	United Nations Protection Force (in the former Yugoslavia)
UNSCOM	United Nations Special Commission for the Disarmament of Iraq
UNTAC	United Nations Transitional Authority in Cambodia
UNTAG	United Nations Transition Assistance Group
UNTSO	United Nations Truce Supervision Organization
UNUMOZ	United Nations Mission in Mozambique
WCED	World Commission on Environment and Development
WEU	Western European Union
WFP	World Food Program
WHO	World Health Organization
WID	women in development
WTO	World Trade Organization

ONE

□ □ □

Challenges and Dilemmas of the Post–Cold War Era

Students hammer down the Berlin Wall. President Mikhail Gorbachev descends the plane in Moscow after the abortive coup. Chinese tanks roll into Tiananmen Square, and Iraqi tanks cross the desert into Kuwait. Live television cameras cover the bombing of Baghdad and missiles striking Israel. Prime Minister Yitzhak Rabin and Chairman Yasir Arafat embrace on the White House lawn. A new flag is raised over a democratic South Africa. These events defined the end of the Cold War as the world had known it for forty-five years, the end of the ideological, political, economic, and military conflict between East and West, between communism and democracy. They produced a fundamental change in the very structure of international politics, which had been defined by the bipolarity generated by two superpowers and their competing alliances.

Less familiar but equally as potent are another group of images. A United Nations official raises the flag for the newly independent Namibia. UN tanks stall on a snowy mountain pass leading to Saravejo. UN doctors and nurses work to save a starving Somali child. UN monitors observe El Salvador's and Nicaragua's elections. A dynamic President Nelson Mandela addresses the UN General Assembly, thanking the body for its support and pleading for development funds. These events illustrate the variety of new activities for the UN in the post–Cold War era.

Indeed, the Cold War's end found the United Nations in greater demand than ever before to deal with peace and security issues as well as environment and development issues, population growth, humanitarian disasters, and other problems. UN peacekeepers have been called on to play roles in defusing conflicts, disarming combatant forces, organizing and monitoring elections, monitoring human rights violations, and overseeing humanitarian relief in many post–Cold War problem areas. In fact, the UN's enforcement powers have been used more in the post–Cold War era than at any previous time.

The United Nations and its secretary-general in particular have become quasi-independent actors on the world stage. But the organization continues to reflect the interests and concerns of its member states. It is therefore constrained by their willingness to work through it in dealing with specific problems, to comply with and support its actions, to provide peacekeeping contingents (military or civilian), and to pay for its regular operations and special programs. Increasingly, the UN seeks to work with regional organizations such as the North Atlantic Treaty Organization (NATO), the Organization of American States (OAS), and the Organization of African Unity (OAU). But with the UN in greater demand than ever to deal with needs that are very different from those it faced at its founding in 1945, reform in the UN's structure and operations has also become a major issue.

Understanding the role of the UN in the post–Cold War era requires exploration of three dilemmas that are products of global changes: the tension between state sovereignty and the reality of its erosion, between demands for global governance and the capacity of both the UN and states to fulfill commitments, and between the need for leadership and the diffusion of power in the international system. Let us turn first to a consideration of these dilemmas that are shaping the UN's ability to address increased demands in the post–Cold War era.

DILEMMAS IN THE POST–COLD WAR ERA

Sovereignty Versus Eroding Sovereignty

The first dilemma derives from the long-standing principles of state sovereignty and nonintervention in states' domestic affairs and the reality of increasing multilateralism, humanitarian intervention, and the erosion of sovereignty. Article 2 of the UN Charter acknowledges the basic principles of states' sovereignty and equality. Historically, **sovereignty** and equality have empowered each state, regardless of size and resources, to govern all matters within its territorial jurisdiction. Sovereignty has also meant that states as political units do not recognize any higher authority. **Nonintervention** is a related principle that obliges other states and international organizations not to interfere in matters within the internal (domestic) jurisdiction of a sovereign state. **Multilateralism** involves the conduct of international activities by three or more states in accordance with shared general principles. The UN and other **international governmental organizations** (IGOs) are multilateral institutions that have been designed to protect states' sovereignty, territorial integrity, and interests as well as make up for their inadequacies.

Yet in reality sovereignty has eroded on many fronts. Global telecommunications and economic interdependencies, international human rights, election monitoring, and environmental regulation are among the developments infringing on states' sovereignty and traditional areas of domestic jurisdiction. IGOs and **nongovernmental organizations** (NGOs)—private associations of individuals or groups engaging in political activity such as human rights advocacy or environmentalism—have grown in numbers, eroding the centrality of states as the primary actors in world politics. For example, Amnesty International and the International Commission of Jurists have been central to expanded efforts to promote human rights, sometimes exerting more power than states themselves. In the environmental area various expert groups composed of scientists, engineers, policy specialists, and government officials have been instrumental in forging shared understandings of environmental problems and in identifying policy options dealing with such issues as ocean pollution, ozone depletion, and biodiversity. **Transnational corporations** (TNCs) or industry groups such as paper, oil, or shipping are important players in trade negotiations, some having more resources than states.

How is sovereignty eroded by these developments? Global telecommunications and economic interdependence diminish the control governments can exercise over the information their citizens receive, the value of their money, and the health of the country's economy. These developments have also aided the growth of TNCs, which by their very nature as transnational entities are not under the control of any one government and which benefit from communications technologies and lowered barriers to trade and investment. NGOs can exercise influence on legislators and government officials both from within countries and from outside through international networks and access to the media. International norms and rules established through particular IGOs set standards for states' actions, and often states themselves accept commitments to uphold these standards, commitments they may or may not take seriously. IGOs, then, provide forums where states' violations of human rights or of trade agreements can be subjected to scrutiny and criticism. This may, in turn, influence governments and erode states' sovereignty.

Although multilateral institutions in theory take actions that constitute intervention in states' domestic affairs only with their consent, there is now a growing body of precedent for humanitarian intervention.[1] **Humanitarian intervention** has emerged as a new norm to justify UN actions to alleviate human suffering during violent conflicts without the consent of the "host" country. Desert Storm halted the Gulf War short of invading Iraq, but subsequent efforts by Western allies under U.S. leadership to protect the Kurdish people in northern Iraq clearly constituted intervention without Iraq's consent. In Somalia, for example, there was no central government to give consent to the UN in 1992 for humanitarian food relief and efforts to reestablish civil order. The UN's long campaign to end apartheid—South Africa's domestic policy of racial segregation and discrimination—gave further credence to the erosion of sovereignty even before the term *humanitarian intervention* was coined. Pressures exerted by the multilateral community are largely responsible for these changes.

Increasing multilateralism, humanitarian intervention, and the erosion of sovereignty clearly link to part of the second dilemma: demands for global governance.

Demands for Governance Versus the Weakness of Institutions

The second dilemma addresses the increasing demands for **global governance** versus the weakness of the United Nations as an institution and the increasing reluctance of states to commit the resources to support new programs. The United Nations and other multilateral institutions are increasingly faced with new demands, from both established and new states as well as NGOs, for peacekeeping and peace-building operations, for international regulation to halt environmental degradation, for programs to promote environmentally sustainable development, and for the promotion or protection of women, indigenous peoples, and human rights in general. These are demands for global governance—not world government, but the pieces of governance represented in rules, norms, and organizational structures to address problems that states acting alone cannot solve.[2]

These demands require states themselves to provide troops for peacekeeping, funds for development programs, reformed judicial and police institutions for the protection of human rights, and tighter domestic environmental regulations. Such requirements test both the capacity and willingness of states to commit themselves to international cooperation. The new states from central Europe and the former Soviet Union, like many of the small, less developed states that joined the UN in the late 1960s and 1970s, lack resources to contribute to global cooperation. Frequently they may also be unable to implement international rules dealing with environmental degradation or the terms of World Bank loans, either because their domestic enforcement capabilities are weak or because the political and social costs of loan conditions are deemed unacceptably high.

The demands also test the capacity of the UN and other international organizations for effective functioning. To what extent can the UN meet these new demands without merely adding programs? How can the initiatives be funded? How can the UN become a more effective coordinating body among various institutions, states, and NGOs? The UN's organizational structure for addressing economic development issues, for example, has become increasingly cumbersome and inefficient. The UN Charter's provisions for dealing with threats to international peace and security are designed for interstate conflicts, not intrastate or civil conflicts, yet most post–Cold War conflicts have been civil wars. Clearly the UN will have to reform to meet new demands, to provide greater capacity, and to reflect the changing distribution of power and authority in the post–Cold War era. The demands for global governance not only require the commitment of states and enhanced institutional capacity in the UN; they also require leadership. This leads to the third dilemma.

Need for Leadership Versus Expanding Numbers of Actors

The third dilemma concerns the need for leadership in the post–Cold War world versus the reality that power has become more diffused and states and other actors have proliferated. To be sure, the major powers, especially the United States, have provided leadership for UN initiatives. Multilateral institutions, however, create opportunities for small and middle powers as well as for NGOs, groups of states, and their own executive heads to exercise initiative and leadership. The UN secretary-general has become an increasingly important figure in the international arena; he is in demand for mediating conflicts and articulating international responses to a wide range of problems. Key individuals even from small states, such as Tommy Koh, the former Singaporean ambassador to the UN who brought the nine-year-long negotiations on the Law of the Sea to closure in 1982, have exercised leadership through technical expertise or diplomatic skill. Australia, Canada, and other middle powers have been influential in international trade negotiations on agricultural issues, as they have long been in peacekeeping and development issues. Likewise, within certain issue areas such as human rights, development, and environment, nongovernmental groups have not only gained voice but also provided key input for institutional and policy development.

The Earth Summit in Rio de Janeiro and the Population Conference in Cairo were notable for the thousands of people who participated in the NGO-sponsored sessions. Although one goal of these sessions was to influence the proceedings of the official conference, the multitude of voices and interests interfered with that possibility. The same is frequently true in human rights, refugee matters, and development.

Since 1989 UN membership has increased from 159 to 185, making consensus that much harder to achieve. Furthermore, these newest states are still struggling to establish their identity and integrity as sovereign entities and lack both the resources to contribute to global initiatives and the

The UN International Conference on Population and Development, convened in September 1994, drew a large number of heads of state. UN/DPI Photo by Evan Schneider.

capacity to implement international rules. Inevitably, the expanding number of actors, including states themselves, makes it difficult for any one state or actor to exercise leadership in the international arena.

With the demise of the Soviet Union, the United States is clearly the sole remaining superpower—that is, the only state with intervention capabilities and interest in many parts of the globe. Democracy and market capitalism have seemingly won the day, and only a few diehard socialist regimes, such as Cuba and North Korea, seem bent on ignoring global trends. Can the United States enjoy a new period of dominance in the world? What role will the UN play in U.S. foreign policy, and what role should the United States play in the UN?

The problem for the United States in the 1990s is meeting the demands for leadership in the UN system. The domestic politics of building and sustaining support for the UN is proving no small challenge, as Congress, under pressure to cut spending, finds UN assessments an easy target. Multilateral initiatives that cannot be controlled by Washington are also suspect for many members of Congress and the public.

The challenge is also one of others' commitment. The United States is reluctant to take on the responsibilities of UN leadership without the strong support of other states in providing people and financial resources. And leadership is not dominance. U.S. economic, military, tech-

A flag is raised for Eritrea, a new member of the United Nations, in 1993. UN Photo 183078/M. Grant.

nological, and other resources may make it "bound to lead," but the style of leadership required in a world marked by multilateralism is one geared to coalition and consensus building, active consultation, and cooperation, not unilateral initiatives.[3] For the United States as the sole remaining superpower, the challenge, then, is to formulate a new conception of its role in the world, of the role of the UN and other international institutions, and of the opportunities for leadership.

The mantle of leadership will not be an easy one for either the United States or others to accept. Two opinions capture the problem: For the United States, "the danger of the 'multilateral temptation' is that [the United States] will resort to the UN reflexively. That reduces America's unilateral or non-UN options, and could even erode its sovereignty."[4] For others, "without U.S. leadership and power, the United Nations lacks muscle. With it, the United Nations loses its independent identity."[5]

Consideration of these dilemmas requires all of us to erase the sharp line that has traditionally separated study of domestic and international systems. It requires us to explore the domestic factors that influence the ability and willingness of states to address global environmental degradation, to support UN peacemaking activities, and to commit resources to fund new programs. It also requires breaking out of the "jails" of old conceptions of world politics, coping with complexity, and understanding differing rates of change. It means examining the alternative sources of leadership and the institutional capacity of the UN to meet new demands. The three dilemmas are products of global changes that shape the arena in which the UN operates today. It is a very different world from the one for which the UN was created in 1945.

CHANGES IN WORLD POLITICS: INTEGRATION VERSUS FRAGMENTATION

Nature and Sources of Change in World Politics

Two simultaneous, yet contradictory patterns are discernible in world politics: one toward greater integration and interdependence among peoples and states; a second toward increasing fragmentation and even disintegration. **Integration** is the process by which societies or nations are economically and politically brought closer together. **Interdependence** involves the sensitivity and vulnerability of states to each other's actions resulting from increased trade, monetary flows, telecommunications, and shared interests.

The integrative trend has been facilitated particularly by the communications revolution, which historian William McNeill has termed the "central disturber of our age."[6] It has spread knowledge, images, and ideas to the farthest corners of the globe, prompting Marshall McLuhan's famous reference to the "global village."[7] Consider the fax machine's role in the 1989 demonstrations in China's Tiananmen Square, when Chinese students in U.S. universities were the chief source of information for their counterparts in Beijing. Or consider CNN's policy agenda–setting role in Somalia, Bosnia, the Gulf crisis, and Haiti. The world was brought together by the revolution of instantaneous communication.

In the late 1960s satellite technology brought us pictures of earth from outer space, making us conscious of our vulnerability and interdependence. These pictures have dramatically changed the way people view and think about the world. They have contributed to greater consciousness of global environmental degradation and to environmental activism.

Increasing economic interdependence has touched much of the world also. The integration process is most advanced among the countries of the European Union (EU), which continue to eliminate barriers among their economies and to develop common policies. The accession of Austria, Finland, and Sweden to the EU in 1995 marks yet another step in this process.

The current preeminence of two core philosophies, economic liberalism and democracy, has accelerated the trend toward interdependence. **Economic liberalism** emphasizes the role of the private sector over the state (that is, government) in economic development. The demise of communism in Eastern Europe and the Soviet Union discredited socialist economic systems, while economic difficulties in many less developed countries (LDCs) with state-dominated economies forced them to liberalize and privatize. More countries have sought membership in the General Agreement on Tariffs and Trade (GATT) and in regional trade blocs such as the North American Free Trade Agreement (NAFTA) and the Asia-Pacific Economic Cooperation Forum, changed their economic policies, opened their borders to trade and investment, and became more integrated into the global economic system.

Likewise, **democratization** spread to all regions of the globe in the 1980s and 1990s. From Latin America to Eastern Europe and the former Soviet Union to Africa and Asia, authoritarian governments have been forced to open the political process to competing political parties, to adopt more stringent human rights standards, and to hold free elections. The UN has been in heavy demand to provide observers to monitor elections in countries around the world. And in many countries democratization has been linked to adoption of the principles of economic liberalism.

These trends toward global integration and interdependence are contradicted by disintegrative tendencies. The Cold War's end clearly contributed to the resurgence of nationalism and ethnic conflict, especially in the regions formerly under authoritarian, communist-dominated governments. The result has been a further fragmentation of the state system with the creation of new states, new demands for self-determination, and a new generation of civil wars tearing apart the fabric of the former Yugoslavia, Georgia, Armenia, Azerbaijan, and elsewhere.

In Africa we see the new phenomenon of "failed states."[8] More than a decade of economic decay, devastating state policies, corruption, natural disasters, and civil wars are leading to the collapse of law and order and to the loss of rudimentary economic productivity in such states as Sierra Leone, Zaire, Somalia, Zambia, and Rwanda. As one observer remarks, "The reconciliation of these profoundly conflicting trends—the political and nationalist trends affirming state sovereignty, the economic trends forcing their wider association and the ethnically driven fragmentation trends threatening their unity—is a central task for modern statecraft."[9] One key instrument of statecraft is multilateral institutions.

The disintegrative trend is also evident in the rejection of closer European union by Danish voters in 1992 and of membership in the EU itself by Norwegian voters in 1994. It is manifested in backlash against refugees and immigrants in Germany, France, and even California as well as fears about free trade dramatized by Ross Perot and other opponents of NAFTA.

Multilateral institutions such as the UN provide processes and forums wherein there are opportunities to articulate issues and build coalitions in support of programs to address them. These institutions provide sources of information that are rooted in shared understandings. They can thus contribute to changing ideas and beliefs. They provide a means through which states may redefine their interests and open up new policy choices.

With increasing global interdependence, multilateral diplomacy has also grown as both states and nongovernmental groups have consulted more actively with one another, formed coalitions to press particular issues, and cooperated in resolving problems. Multilateral diplomacy is most visible in activities centered on formal organizations, especially those of the UN system, but it permeates regional and global efforts to address economic, social, and environmental issues as well as to control the use of force. Figure 1.1 shows the increase in the number of both IGOs and NGOs over time. Along with the the increasing volume of international treaty law, they represent the tangible evidence of the growth in multilateralism.[10]

At what point, however, do we as students, teachers, and concerned citizens recognize that changes are taking place around us and consider them significant? At what point do we begin to analyze them and consider their effects not only on the world itself but also on the theoretical and conceptual frameworks that we use to view the world?

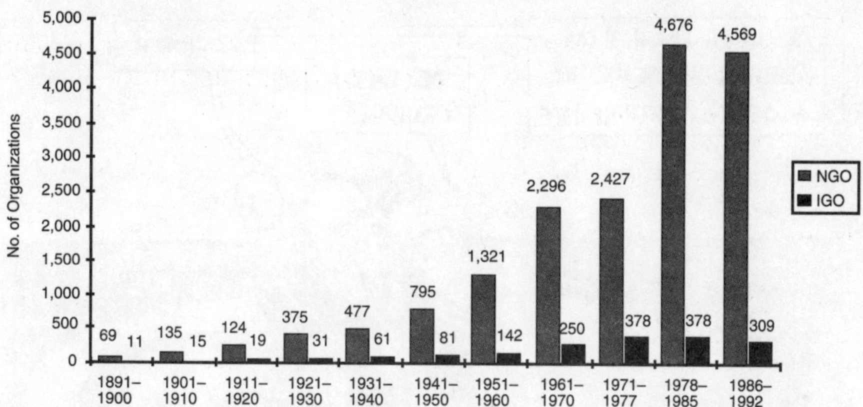

FIGURE 1.1 Growth Patterns of IGOs and NGOs (1891–1992). *Source:* Werner J. Feld, *Nongovernmental Forces and Organization 1985–86* 22d ed. (Brussels: Belgium Union of International Associates), Table 1; *Yearbook of International Organizations 1992–93* vol.1 (Munich: Union of International Associations), Table 1.

The story of international relations for 350 years has emphasized territorially based states as individual, self-interested actors. The **realist theory** of international politics, or **realism,** has traditionally argued that states are the most important actors in world politics but that their interests are fixed and that they are concerned primarily with power and security. Global changes and interdependencies are eroding the validity of this assumption.

We can now speak of many different actors, including states and multilateral institutions, and of differing definitions of interest as well as of different concepts of order. British scholar Hedley Bull has described the international system as a "society of states" whose members "conceive themselves to be bound by a common set of rules in their relations with one another, and share in the working of common institutions."[11] Within this emerging society interdependence and multilateral diplomacy are changing the way states and other actors interact with each other.

In reality, change may occur at different rates and degrees in different parts of the world and with respect to different issue areas. Structures and patterns from the past may coexist with still evolving structures, processes, and behavior patterns. Such changes are further advanced in Europe than in most other regions of the world, but they are noticeable also in Latin America, Asia, and Africa. Hence, we find a number of scholars talking about more than one "world" or "society" to capture the complexity and turbulence of the international system today.[12]

Memories of a changing world. Tom Gibb/*Altoona Mirror,* PA/Rothco.

The competing post–Cold War trends of integration versus disintegration make for a rather schizophrenic world. Although there is unprecedented opportunity for global governance, global institution building is made more difficult by the absence of superpowers to move the system. The proliferation of states makes global agendas and bargaining more problematic. NGOs and other nonstate actors do not fit easily into the traditional state-centric structures, such as the UN. The UN Charter's provisions for protecting international peace and security are not readily applicable to conflicts that are not interstate in nature but civil. The UN is pressed to address an expanding agenda of issues, yet its organizational structure has become increasingly cumbersome and inefficient, and states are increasingly reluctant to commit the resources to fund new programs. Thus, the three dilemmas shape the world in which the UN must operate in the post–Cold War era.

CONCLUSION

Subsequent chapters explore the realities behind these dilemmas. Chapter 2 outlines the historical evolution of the United Nations, including the interpretation of the Charter's proscription of interference in matters within the domestic jurisdiction of states. This chapter reviews the increasing demands for an expanded UN role in light of the proliferation of the number of states.

Chapter 3 considers the major actors in the UN system as well as the issue of the UN itself as an actor on the "stage" of world politics. It focuses on the UN as both an instrument and influencer of states and examines the role of domestic factors in shaping the capacity and willingness of states to commit. This chapter also explores the roles of NGOs, coalitions and blocs, small states and middle powers, and the United States and other major powers in putting demands on the UN system and in providing support and resources.

Given the immense scope of issues the UN deals with, we have elected to focus on two major areas: issues of peace and security and issues of sustainable development. Chapter 4 deals with the evolution of peacekeeping, the question of collective security after the Gulf War, the new challenges of peacemaking, and the dilemmas that UN action now pose for sovereignty, noninterference, leadership, and commitment. Chapter 5 reviews the evolution of thinking on development and institutional responses, the emergence of environmental issues in the 1970s, the increasing importance of NGOs, and the challenges to both international and domestic institutions posed by the need for environmentally sustainable approaches to development.

The concluding chapter, Chapter 6, focuses on the need for institutional reform within the UN to meet the increased demands of the post–Cold War era and on the issues of U.S. leadership and role. Finally, it considers how the three dilemmas may be "resolved" given the dynamics of a schizophrenic world.

TWO

□ □ □

Historical Evolution of the United Nations

Political communities throughout history have tried to establish norms and rules for interacting with their neighbors. Many of these early schemes, which date as far back as early Chinese and Indian civilizations, sought methods specifically designed to manage or eliminate conflict among differing parties. For example, Confucius (551–479 B.C.) preached moderation in interstate relations and condemned the use of violence. The Greeks sought to establish more permanent relationships, both protective alliances among the city-states and mechanisms to deal with conflict before war broke out. Yet none of these "international organizations" was in reality either an "international" entity or an "organization." Groups were limited to a specific geographical area, and organizations were generally ad hoc arrangements, lacking permanent institutionalized relationships.

More than a millennium later a number of European philosophers began to elaborate schemes for world unity. The Roman Catholic Church and its head, the pope, provided the focal point for many of these. For example, medieval French writer Pierre Dubois (1250–1322) proposed that Christian (at that time, Catholic) leaders should form political alliances against violators of prevailing norms. He even proposed that disputes over this order be arbitrated by the pope. When the European states began to challenge the mantle of religious authority, Hugo Grotius (1583–1645), an early Dutch legal scholar, proposed a new legitimacy based on international law.

The **Grotian tradition** elucidated a number of fundamental principles that serve as the foundation not for only modern international law but also for the theory behind international organization.[1] For Grotius all international relations were subject to the rule of law—that is, a law of nations and the law of nature, the latter serving as the ethical basis for the former. Central to Grotian thinking is a rejection of the idea that states can do whatever they wish and that war is the supreme right of states and the hallmark of their sovereignty. Grotius believed that states, like people, are basically rational and law-abiding entities capable of achieving cooperative goals.

What the Grotian tradition does is posit an order in international relations based on the rule of law. Although Grotius himself was not concerned with an organization for administering this rule of law, many subsequent theorists have seen an organizational structure as a vital component in realizing the principles. For example, Frenchman Émeric Crucé (1590–1648), writing at the same time, proposed a universal organization within which groups of ambassadors would hear disputes among complainants and the majority would decide how to approach the problem. Enforcement would occur through mutual military sanctions.

The Grotian tradition was challenged by the notion of state sovereignty within a territorial space. The idea of state sovereignty—that states had exclusive governing authority within their borders—became the cornerstone of European politics, as symbolized by the Treaty of Westphalia in 1648.

A tension thus arose between the **Westphalian tradition,** with its emphasis on sovereignty, and the Grotian tradition, with its focus on law and order. Did affirmation of state sovereignty mean that international law was irrelevant? Could international law threaten state sovereignty? Would states join an international body that would potentially challenge or even undermine sovereignty? Before the nineteenth century the tensions were largely intellectual, the impact on practice minimal. Two hundred years later the Westphalian and Grotian worlds were joined.

NINETEENTH-CENTURY ROOTS OF CONTEMPORARY INTERNATIONAL ORGANIZATIONS

In the nineteenth century ideas for international organizations and the practice of governments began to bear fruit. In a pioneering textbook on international organization, *Swords into Plowshares,* Inis Claude described how three major strands of thinking and practice emerged.[2] The first strand involved the recognition of the utility of multilateral diplomacy in contrast to the standard practice of bilateral diplomacy. Beginning in 1815 the Europeans participated in the **Concert of Europe.** The **Concert system** involved the practice of multilateral meetings among the leaders of the major European powers for the purposes of settling problems and coordinating actions. Meeting over thirty times in the century preceding World War I, the major powers established a "club" of the "like-minded," dictating the conditions of entry for other would-be participants. Although these meetings were not institutionalized, they solidified important practices that later international organizations followed. These included multilateral consultation, collective diplomacy, and special status for a great "power." As Claude summarizes, "The Concert system was the manifestation of a rudimentary but growing sense of interdependence and community of interest among the states of Europe."[3] Such a community of interest was a vital prerequisite for modern international organizations.

The second strand revolved around the **Hague system.** Czar Nicholas II of Russia convened two conferences in The Hague (Netherlands) involving both European *and* non-European states to think proactively about what techniques states should have available to prevent war and under what conditions arbitration, negotiation, and legal recourse would be appropriate. Exploration of such issues in the absence of a crisis was a novelty. The Hague conferences of 1899 and 1907 led to the Convention for the Pacific Settlement of International Disputes, ad hoc International Commissions of Inquiry, and the Permanent Court of Arbitration.

The Hague conferences also produced several major procedural innovations. It was the first time that participants included both small states and non-European states. The Latin American states were given an equal role, thus establishing the principle of universality and bolstering legal equality. For the first time techniques of multilateral diplomacy were utilized in the election of chairs, the organization of committees, and roll call votes, all of which became permanent features of twentieth-century organizations.

The third strand involved the formation of public international unions. These agencies were initially established among European states to deal with problems stemming from expanding commerce, communications, and technological innovation, such as health standards for travelers, shipping rules on the Rhine River, increased mail volume, and the telegraph's invention. Many of these problems proved amenable to resolution with intergovernmental cooperation. Hence, the International Telegraphic Union was formed in 1865 and the Universal Postal Union in 1874, each instrumental in its own way in facilitating communication, transportation, and hence commerce. The European states with high levels of interdependence had found it necessary to cooperate on a voluntary basis to accomplish nonpolitical tasks. The public international unions also spawned procedural innovations. Most creative was the institutionalizaton of international secretariats—permanent personnel hired from a variety of countries to perform specific tasks.

Thus, the nineteenth century essentially served as a vital precursor to the development of international organizations in the twentieth century. For the first time ideas and state action gelled. Governments established new approaches to dealing with problems of joint concern, approaches such as the multilateral diplomacy of the Concert system, the broader legalistic consultations of the Hague system, and the cooperative institutions of the public international unions. To implement the new approaches, innovative procedures were developed, participation broadened, and international secretariats institutionalized. Each has been extensively utilized during the twentieth century.

The institutional arrangements of the nineteenth century proved inadequate for preventing war, however. The balance of power among the great powers—so vital to the Concert system—broke down into two competing military alliances, which, in turn, led to conflicts. Cooperation in other areas of interest proved insufficient to prevent war when national security was at stake. Hence, the outbreak of World War I pointed vividly to the weaknesses and shortcomings of the nineteenth-century arrangements.

THE LEAGUE OF NATIONS

World War I had hardly begun when private groups in both Europe and the United States began to plan for the postwar era. These nongovernmental groups, such as the League to Enforce Peace in the United States and the League of Nations in Great Britain, were eager to develop more permanent frameworks for preventing future wars. President Woodrow Wilson's proposal to incorporate a permanent international organization within the Versailles Peace Treaty was based on these plans.

The League of Nations first and foremost reflected the environment in which it was conceived.[4] Almost one-half of the League Covenant's twenty-six provisions focused on preventing war. Two basic principles were paramount: (1) member states agreed to respect and preserve the territorial integrity and political independence of states; and (2) members agreed to try different methods of dispute settlement, but failing that, the League was given the power under Article 16 to enforce settlements through sanctions. The second principle was firmly embedded in the proposition of **collective security,** namely, that aggression by one state should be countered by all acting together as a "league of nations."

The League Convenant established an assembly and a council, the latter recognizing the special prerogative of great powers, a lasting remnant of the European council system, and the former giving pride of place to universality of membership (about sixty states at that time). Authority rested with the Council, composed of four permanent members and four elected members. It was the Council that was to be settler of disputes, enforcer of sanctions, and implementer of peaceful settlements. The requirement of unanimity made action very difficult.

Although often considered a failure, the League did enjoy a number of successes, many of them on territorial issues. It conducted plebiscites in Silesia and the Saar and then demarcated the German-Polish border. It settled territorial disputes between Lithuania and Poland, Finland and Russia, and Bulgaria and Greece and guaranteed Albanian territorial integrity against encroachments by Italy, Greece, and Yugoslavia.

The failure of the League's Council to act when Japan invaded Manchuria pointed to the organization's fundamental weaknesses. The League

Assembly, at the urging of small states, seized the initiative, though it lacked real power.

The League's response to the Italian invasion of Ethiopia further undermined the organization's legitimacy. The Ethiopians appealed to the League Council, to be met only by stalling actions for nine months. Both France and Great Britain had assured Italian dictator Benito Mussolini that they would not interfere in his operations. The smaller states (plus Russia) were horrified by the lack of support for Ethiopia. Eventually the Council approved voluntary sanctions. But without unanimity, they carried little effect and were lifted in 1936. The sanctions were clearly a case of the League acting too little and too late. Without the willingness of the great powers to support the League's principles, the institution's power and legitimacy deteriorated. Nowhere was the absence of great power support for the League felt more than in the fact that the United States never even joined the organization.

The League of Nations failed to act decisively against Italy's and Japan's aggression, let alone prevent the outbreak of World War II. Yet it represented an important step forward in the process of international organization. Planning for the post–World War II peace began shortly after the United States entered the war and involved continual high-level government participation by the Allied powers. Most important, this planning built on the lessons of the League in laying the groundwork for its successor: the United Nations. Despite the League's shortcomings, there was consensus on the importance of such an international organization, albeit one whose scope was far greater than the League's.

ORIGINS OF THE UNITED NATIONS

The Atlantic Charter of August 14, 1941—a joint declaration by President Franklin Roosevelt and Prime Minister Winston Churchill calling for collaboration in economic issues and preparation of a permanent system of security—served as the foundation for the Declaration by the United Nations in January 1942. Twenty-six nations affirmed the principles of the Atlantic Charter and agreed to draft a charter for a new universal organization to replace the League. The UN Charter was then drafted in two sets of meetings between August and October 1944 at Dumbarton Oaks in Washington, D.C. The participants agreed that the organization would be based on the principle of the sovereign equality of members, with all "peace-loving" states eligible for membership. This provision excluded the Axis powers. It was also agreed that decisions on security issues would require unanimity of the permanent members of the Security Council, the great powers.

When the United Nations Conference on International Organization convened in San Francisco on April 25, 1945, there was agreement on the major principles and structures. The delegates from the fifty states that were represented modified and finalized what had already been negotiated among the great powers. On July 28, 1945, with Senate approval, the United States became the first country to ratify the Charter. The fact that it took only three months before a sufficient number of countries had ratified the Charter indicates the high level of agreement among the member states of the new organization.[5]

PRINCIPLES AND STRUCTURE OF THE UN

Basic Principles

Three basic principles, under Article 2 of the Charter, provide the foundation for UN action. They have also posed significant dilemmas for the organization over the fifty years of its existence.

The UN is based on the notion of the sovereign equality of member states, consistent with the Westphalian tradition. Each state is legally the equivalent of every other state, and thus each state has the power to make its own decisions and the capability to control outcomes within its own jurisdiction. The principle applies, for instance, to Russia, Lithuania, China, and Burma, although each is clearly not of the same size or same political power. Sovereign legal equality is the basis for each state having one vote in the General Assembly. Yet inequality is also part of the UN framework, as the veto power of the five permanent members of the Security Council demonstrates. And over time the major powers have acquired additional powers—special positions on budgetary committees and secure, uncontested seats on the Economic and Social Council (ECOSOC). So despite the Charter's commitment to sovereign equality, voting in the separate organs and changes in practice have modified the commitment.

The second principle under Article 2(7) asserts that nothing in the Charter may be interpreted to "authorize the UN to intervene in matters which are essentially within the domestic jurisdiction of any state," again indicative of the Westphalian influence. Only international problems and issues are within the jurisdiction of the UN. But who decides what is an international and what a domestic problem? Over time the scope of what is considered "international" has broadened, but the tension between the two persists.

The third principle is that the UN, like its precedessor, is designed primarily to maintain international peace and security, as the Grotian tradition posited. For the UN's founders this meant that states should refrain from the threat or use of force, settle disputes by peaceful means, and support **enforcement measures** such as economic sanctions. However, a careful reading of the Charter suggests that a broader definition of security might evolve—one that encompasses economic and social well-being and respect for human rights. Indeed, over the life of the UN, that definition of security has been continually broadened. Expansion into many of these newer areas of security butts squarely against the domestic authority of states, conflicting with the principle of state sovereignty. The founders recognized the tension between the commitment to act collectively against a member state and the affirmation of state sovereignty represented in Article 2(7)'s reference to noninterference in states' domestic affairs. But they could not foresee the dilemmas that changing definitions of security would pose.

Structure

The structure of the United Nations as outlined in the Charter includes six major bodies. Each organ has changed over the life of the organization, responding to external realities, internal pressures, and interactions with other organs.[6] Figure 2.1 shows the organizational structure of the UN system. An abridged version of the UN Charter can be found in Appendix A.

Security Council. The Security Council has primary responsibility for maintenance of international peace and security (Article 24) and the authority to identify aggressors (Articles 39, 40), decide what enforcement measures should be taken (Articles 41, 42, 48, 49), and call on members to make military forces available, subject to special agreements (Articles 43, 44, 45). More generally, under Article 34 "the Security Council may investigate any dispute, or any situation which might lead to international friction or give rise to a dispute, to order to determine whether the continuance of the dispute or situation is likely to endanger the maintenance of international peace and security." However, the Security Council has used its enforcement powers in only seven situations, five of them since 1990. Rather, it has relied primarily on its peaceful settlement mechanisms to respond to the many situations on its agenda over the years.

The five permanent members remain the key to Security Council decisionmaking—the United States, Great Britain, France, Russia (successor state to the seat of the Soviet Union in 1992), and the People's Republic of China (PRC, replacing the Republic of China in 1971)—each with **veto** power. The nonpermanent members, originally six in number and expanded to ten in 1965, are elected for two-year terms. Following an "informal agreement" in the 1940s to allocate specific seats by region (Western Europe, Eastern Europe, Middle East, British Commonwealth), the General Assembly in 1965 adopted a resolution allocating five of those seats to Africa and Asia, two to Latin America and Western Europe, and one to Eastern Europe. This reflected the geographically based bloc representation that became a major force in the General Assembly during the 1960s.

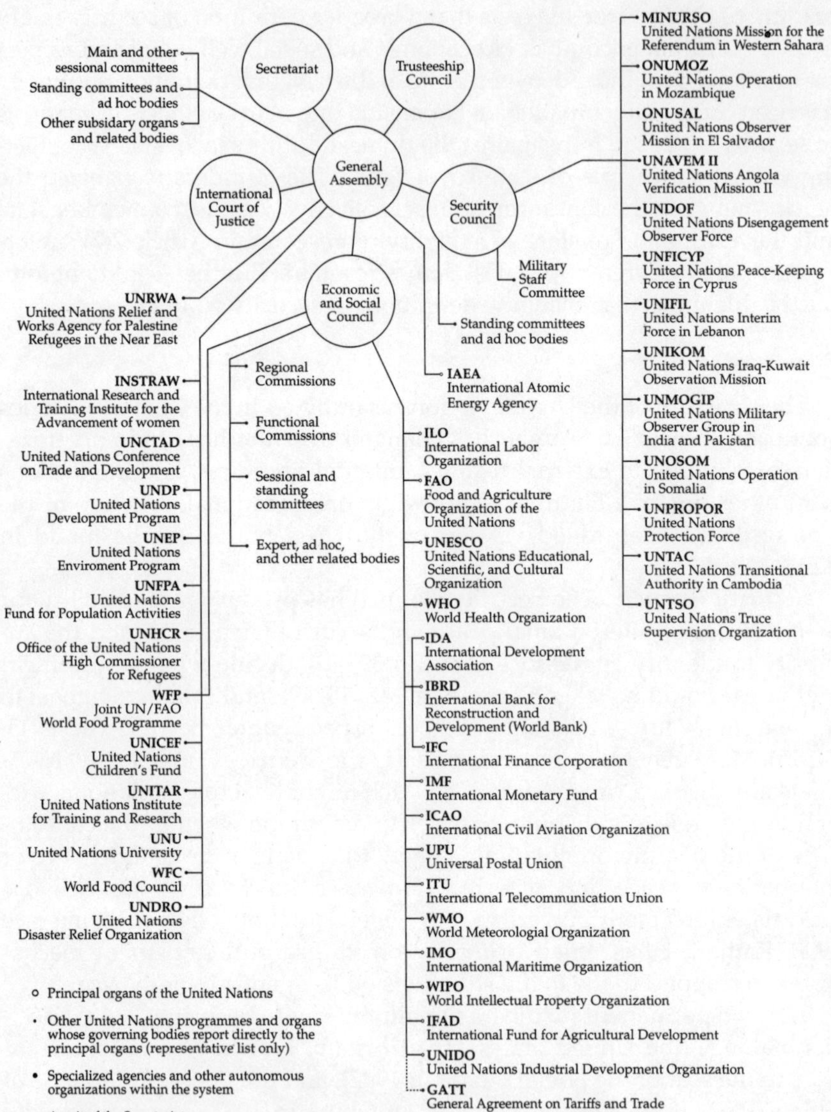

FIGURE 2.1 The UN System. *Source* : Robert E Riggs and Jack C. Plano, *The United Nations* (Belmont, CA: Wadsworth, 1994). Copyright © 1994 by Wadsworth Publishing Co. Reprinted by permission.

TABLE 2.1 Vetoes in the Security Council, 1946–1994

Time Period	*China*	*France*	*United Kingdom*	*United States*	*Soviet Union/Russia*
1945–1955	1	2	0	0	77
1956–1965	0	2	3	0	26
1966–1975	4	2	9	12	11
1976–1985	17	9	11	37	7
1986–1990	0	3	8	23	0
1991–1994	0[a]	0	0	0	1
Total	22	18	31	72	122

[a]In 1991 China abstained two times and in 1992, nine times. No other permanent member abstained.

SOURCES: Sydney D. Bailey, *The Procedure of the United Nations Security Council,* 2d ed. (Oxford: Clarendon Press, 1988), Table B, p. 209; Anjali V. Patil, *The UN Veto in World Affairs, 1946–1990* (Sarasota, Fla.: UNIFO, 1992), pp. 485–486; United Nations, *Index to Proceedings of the Security Council,* 47th sess., 1992 (ST/LIB/SER.B13.29).

The functioning and indeed the prestige of the Security Council have waxed and waned. As envisioned by the founders, the Security Council was to be the premier body, charged with the most essential security tasks and participating in organizational housekeeping chores in collaboration with the General Assembly. Indeed, during the 1940s it held approximately 130 meetings a year. But by the end of the next decade the Cold War split between East and West had diminished the use of the Security Council as an authoritative body. In 1959 only five meetings were held. The Soviet Union's frequent use of its veto power during the Cold War was a major factor in blocking Security Council action on many peace and security issues. (See Table 2.1 for a summary of vetoes cast.)

Since the late 1980s and the demise of the Cold War the Security Council's power and prestige have once again grown. Between 1987 and 1993 the number of official meetings rose from 49 to more than 171, and the number of annual resolutions passed increased from 13 to 93. Over time the Security Council has conducted an increasing amount of its work in informal, private consultations and reached more decisions by consensus than by formal voting. These processes have enlarged the council president's role. Since 1987 the permanent members have themselves engaged in informal consultations as a group, a practice that enhanced their close cooperation in the Persian Gulf conflict and other crises. Also since 1987 the Security Council has taken action on more armed conflicts, made more decisions under Chapter VII of the Charter, and spent more on peacekeeping than at any previous time. These trends reflect the absence of Cold War hostility and the permanent members' newfound solidarity.

This general view of the General Assembly shows the opening session of the 48th assembly, September 21, 1993. UN Photo 183659/M. Grant.

Only one veto has been cast since 1991. Yet this very increase in the Security Council's activity has led other members to propose changing the council's composition, as we see in Chapter 6.

General Assembly. The General Assembly, like the League's Assembly, was designed as the general debate arena where all members would be equally represented according to a one state–one vote formula. It would be the organization's hub, with a diverse agenda and the responsibility for coordinating and supervising subsidiary bodies. The assembly has important elective functions: admitting states to UN membership; electing the nonpermanent members of the Security Council, ECOSOC, and the Trusteeship Council; appointing judges to the International Court of Justice (ICJ); and appointing the secretary-general on the recommendation of the Security Council.

Like the Security Council, the General Assembly has responsibilities in the area of peace and security. Although the secretary-general is authorized to bring to the Security Council's attention any and all matters that threaten international peace and security (Article 99), the General Assembly has the right to make inquiries and studies that might trigger further action (Articles 13, 14) and to be kept informed (Articles 10, 11, 12). On the basis of the General Assembly's right to consider any matter within the purview of the Charter, the "**Uniting for Peace Resolution**" during the Korean War in 1950 established a precedent that has enabled the General Assembly to act when the Security Council is stymied by great power veto. Also like the Security Council, the General Assembly has responsibilities in the area of Charter revision. The assembly can propose amendments with a two-thirds majority; two-thirds of the states, including all the permanent members of the Security Council, must then ratify the changes. The General Assembly may also call a general conference for the purpose of Charter revision.

Meetings of the General Assembly are held for three months a year, and special sessions may be called to deal with specific problems (e.g., Financial and Budgetary Problems in 1963, Raw Materials and Development in 1974, Development and International Economic Cooperation in 1975, and Disarmament in 1978). Over time regionally based **voting blocs** emerged as member states sought to coordinate positions and build support for them, facilitating the assembly's work as its membership grew from 51 in 1945 to 184 in 1994. In the early years the Soviet Union and Eastern Europe formed the most cohesive bloc, voting together against three-quarters of the resolutions passed. During the 1980s a bloc led by the United States and including a few Western European countries and Israel frequently constituted a minority on many issues. From the 1960s onwards the newly independent states of Africa and Asia joined with Latin American states to form a cohesive voting bloc in the assembly and other UN bodies. This group, known as the **Group of 77** (G-77), dominated General Assembly agendas and voting from the mid-1960s until the early 1990s. In Chapter 3 we explore the phenomenon of blocs and coalitions further.

The bulk of the General Assembly's work occurs in the six functional committees: the First or Disarmament and International Security Committee; Second or Economic and Financial Committee; Third or Social, Humanitarian, and Cultural Committee; Fourth or Special Political and Decolonization Committee; Fifth or Administrative and Budgetary Committee; Sixth or Legal Committee. The General Assembly's activities during a typical session are sketched in Figure 2.2.

The number of resolutions passed in the General Assembly steadily increased, from about 117 annually during the first five years, to 133 in 1961–1965, 188 in 1971–1975, and more than 343 in 1981–1985.[7] Between 1989 and 1992, the number of resolutions averaged 328 per year. Throughout all these years many have been adopted with little or no opposition.

With the end of the Cold War, the General Assembly's work has been increasingly marginalized, as the epicenter of UN power has shifted back to the Security Council and a more active Secretariat, much to the dismay of the South, which would like more consultation between the General Assembly and Security Council.

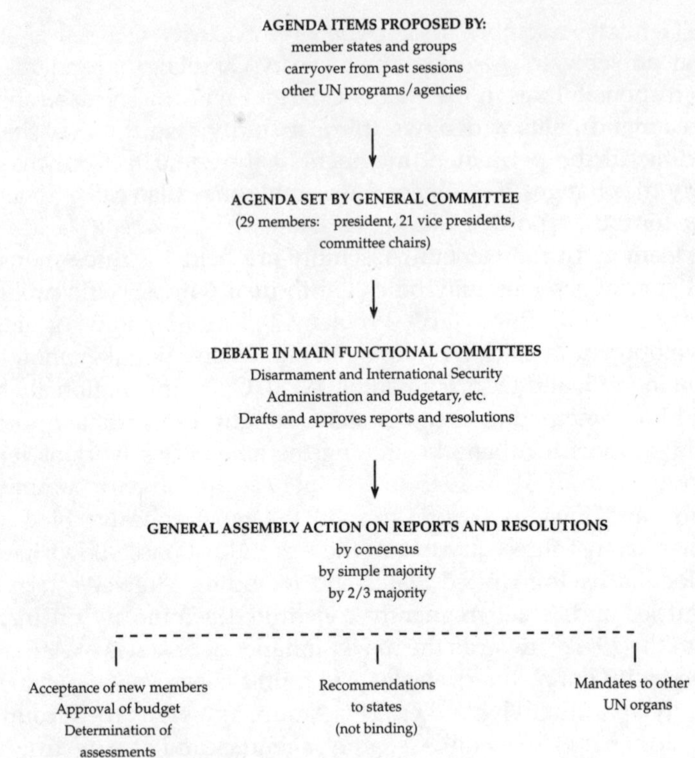

FIGURE 2.2 The Work of the General Assembly

Secretariat. Headed by the secretary-general, this body of about 14,700 professional and clerical staff based in New York, Geneva, and elsewhere around the world comprises international civil servants, individuals who, though nationals of member countries, represent the international community. Steadily increasing in number, the Secretariat has been the frequent object of criticism for lapses in its neutrality, duplication of tasks, and poor administrative practices.

The secretary-general's position has been termed "one of the most ill-defined: a combination of chief administrative officer of the United Nations and global diplomat with a fat portfolio whose pages are blank."[8] In fact, the secretary-general has several responsibilities, as stipulated in the Charter. S/he is the chief administrative officer of the organization and the official secretary to major delegate bodies. He oversees reports and studies conducted at the request of the other major organs. Although not stipulated by the Charter, the secretary-general is also a major force and spokesperson for the organization, acting as a mediator and neutral third party in numerous circumstances. We explore these roles more fully in Chapter 3.

The secretary-general holds office for a five-year renewable term on election by two-thirds of the General Assembly and recommendation by the Security Council. The process of nomination is an intensely political one, with the five permanent members of the Security Council having key input. Not surprisingly, the persons elected have tended to come from neutral states: Trygve Lie from Norway, Dag Hammarskjöld from Sweden, U Thant from Burma, Kurt Waldheim from Austria, Javier Pérez de Cuéllar from Peru, and Boutros Boutros-Ghali from Egypt. (See Box 2.1 for further information.) Each, because of differences in personality and skills, has undertaken his tasks in a different way, making his imprint on the organization.

Economic and Social Council. ECOSOC, with its fifty-four members, coordinates the economic and social welfare programs of the UN itself and the specialized agencies, such as the Food and Agriculture Organization (FAO), World Health Organization (WHO), and United Nations Educational, Scientific, and Cultural Organization (UNESCO). Specifically, those functions include coordinating the activities of various subsidiary bodies, conducting research and writing reports on economic and social issues, and making recommendations on which approach to follow. Of those tasks the coordinating task has proven the most problematic since a myriad of activities formally lie outside the effective jurisdiction of ECOSOC.

The expansion of the membership in this organ illustrates the increasing scope and importance of its activity. The original eighteen members were increased to twenty-seven in 1965 and to fifty-four in 1973. Motivated by recognition that states with the ability to pay should be continuously represented, four of the five permanent members of the Security Council have been reelected by convention. Decisions taken, reports accepted, or coordination strategies adopted are subject to simple majority votes. The expansion of UN economic and social activities, unanticipated by the founders, and often on an ad hoc basis, has left

BOX 2.1 UN Secretaries-General, 1946–1994

Secretary-General	*Nationality*	*Dates of Service*
Trygve Lie	Norway	1946–1953
Dag Hammarskjöld	Sweden	1953–1961
U Thant	Burma	1961–1971
Kurt Waldheim	Austria	1972–1981
Javier Pérez de Cuéllar	Peru	1982–1991
Boutros Boutros-Ghali	Egypt	1992–

This June 1968 view of UN headquarters in New York shows the General Assembly (foreground), the Secretariat (behind), the Council Chambers and Conference Rooms (river's edge), and the Dag Hammarskjöld Library (background). UN Photo 104713/Saw Lwin.

ECOSOC with an unmanageable task—one for which there has been a persistent call for reform.

Trusteeship Council. This council was originally established to oversee the administration of the non-self-governing UN trust territories that carried over from the League's mandate system. The council's supervisory activities include reporting on the status of the people of the territories, making annual reports, and conducting periodic visits to the territories. Beginning with eleven trusts following World War II, the council has now terminated the last trusteeship agreement: The people of the Trust Territory of the Pacific Islands voted in November 1993 for free association with the United States. Thus, the very success of the Trusteeship Council has meant its demise. To avoid amending the UN Charter, the council will continue to exist, but it will no longer meet in annual sessions.

International Court of Justice (ICJ). The World Court, with fifteen justices headquartered in The Hague, provides a forum for **noncompulsory dispute settlement** and UN agency advisory opinions. Since the court hears only cases to which all parties have agreed, the number of actual cases litigated is rather small.

Inevitably, the UN's organs have had to adapt to changing circumstances over fifty years. Post–World War II politics posed special difficulties for the organization. We turn to a brief examination of this evolution.

UN AND POST–WORLD WAR II ORDER

Cold War Politics: Peace and Security

The UN Charter ensured that no collective measures could ever be instituted against those countries with veto power. Yet rising great power disunity in the aftermath of World War II made Security Council operations extremely problematic. The foundation of UN unity—continuance of the postwar coalition—was torn asunder by the Cold War. The sanctioning of UN forces to counter the North Korean invasion of South Korea in 1950 was made possible only by the temporary absence of the Soviet Union in protest against the UN's refusal to seat the newly established communist government of the People's Republic of China. Yet the procedural innovation that authorized continuance of those forces once the Soviet Union returned to its seat and exercised its veto, the "Uniting for Peace Resolution," provided the precedent for the General Assembly to assume responsibility for issues of security when the Security Council was deadlocked by the veto. This procedure was used subsequently to deal with crises in Suez and Hungary (1956), in the Middle East (1958), and in the Congo (1960). In all, nine emergency special sessions of the assembly have dealt with threats to international peace when the Security Council was deadlocked.

To deal with the problem of the breakdown of great power unity, yet respond to regional conflicts, the UN developed what came to be called **peacekeeping.** It has been defined as

> the prevention, containment, moderation, and termination of hostilities between or within states, through the medium of peaceful third party intervention, organized and directed internationally, using multinational forces of soldiers, police, and civilians to restore and maintain peace.9

The Charter does not mention peacekeeping. Because the permanent UN military forces envisioned by the Charter were never created, ad hoc military units, drawn from the armed forces of nonpermanent members of the Security Council (often small, neutral members), have been used to prevent the escalation of those conflicts, to keep the great powers at bay, and to keep the warring parties apart until the dispute is settled.

Peacekeeping was a creative response to the breakdown of great power unity and the spread of East-West tensions to regional conflicts. First developed to provide observer groups for conflicts in Kashmir and Palestine in the late 1940s, peacekeeping was formally proposed by Canada's secretary of state for external affairs, Lester B. Pearson, at the height of the Suez crisis in 1956 as a means for securing the withdrawal of British, French, and Israeli forces from Egypt, pending a political settlement.

UN peacekeeping forces were used most extensively in the Middle East and in conflicts arising out of the decolonization process during the Cold War period. A total of thirteen operations were deployed from 1948 to 1988. Peacekeeping's advantage during the Cold War period was its usefulness preventing the superpowers from getting involved in conflicts tangential to their interests.[10] We discuss the UN's peacekeeping experience during and after the Cold War in Chapter 4.

UN Role in Decolonization and Emergence of New States

At the close of World War II few would have predicted the end of colonial rule in most of Africa and Asia. Yet the UN Charter called for friendly relations among nations based on "self-determination" of peoples and self-government or independence. This was a far cry from the League's mandate system, in which colonies and territories were "sacred trusts." Twenty-five years after the UN Charter's signing, independence in most of the former colonies had been largely accomplished and with relatively little threat to international peace and security. The number of members of the UN increased from 51 in 1945 to 184 in 1994, as shown in Figure 2.3. The United Nations played a significant role in this remarkably peaceful transformation.

The Charter endorsed the principle of **self-determination** for colonial peoples. Already independent former colonies such as India, Egypt, Indonesia, and the Latin American states used the UN as a forum to advocate an end to colonialism and independence for territories ruled by Great Britain, France, the Netherlands, Belgium, Spain, and Portugal. Success added new votes to the growing anticolonial coalition, which was supported strongly by the United States, despite its alliance ties to the Western European colonial powers.

By 1960 a majority of the UN's members favored decolonization. General Assembly Resolution 1514 condemned the continuation of colonial rule and preconditions for granting independence (such as lack of preparation for self-rule) and called for annual reports on the progress to-

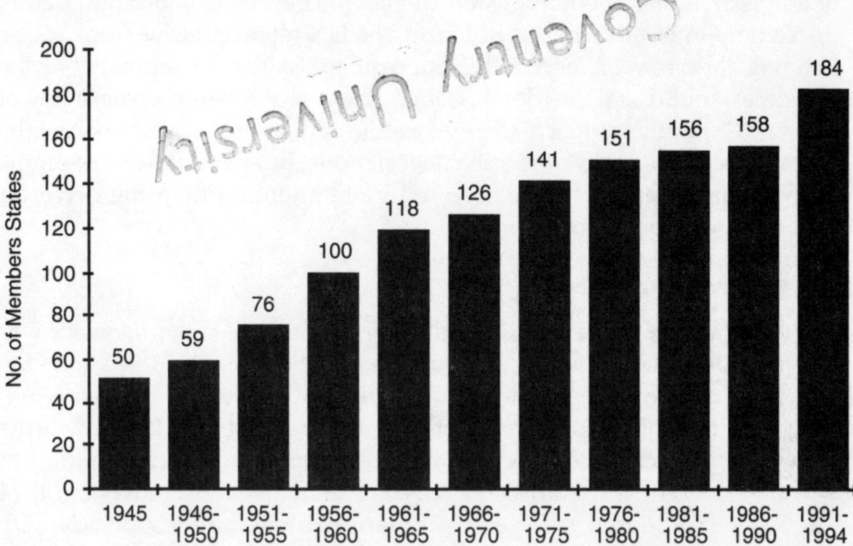

FIGURE 2.3 Growth in UN Membership (1945–1994). *Sources:* Compiled form Robert E. Riggs and Jack C. Plano, *The United Nations: International Organization of World Politics,* 2d ed. (Belmont, Calif.: Wadsworth, 1994), p. 45.

ward independence of all remaining colonial territories. By 1965 the only major territories remaining under colonial rule were the Portuguese colonies (Angola, Mozambique, Guinea-Bissau), South West Africa (now Namibia), and Southern Rhodesia (now Zimbabwe). During this time the UN provided an important forum for the **collective legitimation** of a change in international norms and the organization of the international system.

The consequences of expanding the number of independent states in the international system were manifold. Old issues became defined in new ways, as the Group of 77 commanded a majority of votes on a broad range of issues. For example, on the many issues connected with the Middle East the G-77 tilted toward the Arab states and the Palestinian cause, with support from the Soviet Union, while the United States and its allies steadfastly supported Israel. On the issue of apartheid in South Africa the G-77 sought to isolate the white minority regime through economic and military sanctions, while the United States, Great Britain, and France resisted the G-77's efforts to get the Security Council to take enforcement action beyond an arms embargo imposed after South Africa's bloody suppression of riots in Soweto in 1976.

During the 1960s new issues proliferated on the UN's agenda, many at the urging of the G-77. For example, the 1967 UN resolution proposing new international negotiations on the law of the sea was brought before the General Assembly by Arvid Pardo, the UN representative from Malta. Echoing the view of the newly independent states, he argued that the resources found on the deep seabed were the "common heritage of mankind," not the property of any specific nation. From this initiative the UN sponsored the Law of the Sea negotiations. But of all the issues on the agenda from the G-77, none received more attention than the drive for economic and social development.

The North-South Split

By the late 1960s the agenda of the UN and its subsidiary agencies was heavily tilted toward issues of economic development and relations between the developed countries of the industrial North and the less developed countries of the South. The ideological leaning of the G-77 toward a heavy government role in economic development and redistribution of wealth shaped the programs and activities of many IGOs. Indeed, in 1974 these states proposed the **New International Economic Order** (NIEO), marshaling support in the UN General Assembly for the Charter of Economic Rights and Duties of States.

The developing countries argued that the existing international economic order was structured to their disadvantage by **weighted voting systems** in the World Bank and International Monetary Fund (IMF) and by adverse **terms of trade.** The proposed norms and principles were reiterated in numerous meetings and resolutions. The NIEO dominated and polarized debate in a number of forums during the 1970s. The stalemate in these discussions at times made agreement on both economic and security issues impossible to achieve. Chapter 5 explores the UN's handling of development issues and the NIEO. During the Cold War the impasse on security issues within the Security Council and the stalemate within the General Assembly over the New International Economic Order led to several persistent institutional problems.

PERSISTENT ORGANIZATIONAL PROBLEMS

Three types of institutional difficulties arose during the post–World War II era: politicization, administration, and financing. Each of these problems developed from the proliferation of issues undertaken by the organization. The newly independent members of the UN had interests that were thrust onto the agenda of the General Assembly, and with bloc voting they had the numerical majority to present their agenda forcefully. But the capacity of the system to respond effectively was continually challenged.

Politicization

Throughout the UN's history member states have linked issues, some logically according to subject matter and others illogically according to political purposes. This process of **politicization** has focused on three areas: the intrusion of extraneous politics into the work of the organization, the double standard with respect to national sovereignty, and the exercise of selective morality.

During the 1950s and early 1960s the Soviet Union accused the United States of politicizing the organization, introducing an East-West dimension to every problem. In the late 1960s and 1970s the United States complained that extraneous issues were being introduced into the specialized agencies' work that had little relationship to their basic tasks. These issues most frequently concerned apartheid in South Africa, Palestinian rights, and the state of Israel.

The Israeli issue represented the greatest concern for the United States. Beginning in 1974–1975 there was a series of actions in UN bodies questioning Israel's right to exist. Israel was excluded from both the UN Economic Commission for West Asia and the Asian group within UNESCO. The campaign reached its nadir in November 1975 when the General Assembly adopted Resolution 3379, which equated Zionism with racism. Through the late 1970s and 1980s General Assembly resolutions singled out Israel for promoting policies of "hegemonism" and "racism" and "for committing war crimes." As Israel was condemned, the Palestine Liberation Organization's (PLO) position was strengthened. The PLO was given the unique status of permanent observer in all conferences held within the UN framework, and its chair, Yasir Arafat, was permitted to address the General Assembly. For the U.S. government such actions represented interference in a member state's right to participate and an effort to legitimize a nonstate member—both clearly contrary to the UN mandate.[11]

Double standards also hampered General Assembly activity. From the U.S. perspective Third World states persistently maintained the inviolability of their sovereignty while simultaneously trying to limit other states' sovereignty in areas essentially within states' domestic jurisdiction. And during the 1970s these same states introduced agenda items in UN agencies that criticized white racism, Zionism, and neocolonialism while selectively ignoring black racism, sexism in Muslim countries, and violations of human rights in Eastern Europe and the Soviet Union. These tensions over Israel and double standards at times boiled into hostility between the General Assembly and the United States, undermining the effectiveness of the organ and the UN's legitimacy.

Administration

UN effectiveness was also plagued by administrative problems. As the UN bureaucracy expanded to deal with the proliferation of issues, charges of political bias and administrative inefficiency surfaced. Once again the United States led much of the charge.

During the 1950s and early 1960s Soviet Secretariat personnel, because they were not permanent employees of the UN but were seconded from the Soviet government, were charged with maintaining too close a relationship with the Soviet government, contrary to the ideal of the neutral civil service. During the 1970s the charge was that heads of particular specialized agencies, UNESCO's Amadon-Mahtar M'Bow, FAO's Edouard Saouma, and WHO's Halfdan Mahler, were militant spokespersons for the Third World. These accusations squarely challenged the notion that the UN's international civil servants were truly unbiased and neutral, further undermining the organization's legitimacy.

Accusations of political bias were often coupled with charges of mismanagement and ineffective administration. On this issue the United States was not alone. Indeed, as early as 1970 and later in 1978 UN studies themselves pointed to the dearth of coordination within UN economic development programs, making them costly and ineffective. Such criticisms were reiterated with increasing vigor in the 1980s as programs were approved with little consideration of financing and program evaluation was weak to nonexistent. The United Nations own Joint Inspection Union published reports on UN personnel problems, including inadequacy of staff qualifications, excessive remuneration, and rapid increase of staff costs. A study by the United Nations Association of the United States of America (UNA/USA) lamented, "Yet there is no center at the center of the U.N. system and therefore no means for putting to work the system's rich potential for interdisciplinary analysis to identify the globai issues on which national interests converge and where high levels of cooperation are necessary and feasible."[12] Given this persistent attack on administrative inefficiency in UN agencies, it is no surprise that administrative reform holds such a key place in the post–Cold War UN, as is discussed in Chapter 6.

Finances

States have often expressed their unhappiness with the UN by failing to fund its programs and operations, thereby creating periodic financial crises.[13] The regular budget has always consisted of contributions from member states assessed on the basis of ability to pay. The formulas are reevaluated every three years. In 1946 the U.S. share was 40 percent; the Soviet share, 6 percent; and the minimum contribution, 0.04 percent.

Those figures have changed over time, with the U.S. share being reduced to 25 percent, the Soviet Union's increasing to 13 percent, and the minimum dropping to 0.01 percent. The regular budget is not, however, the sole source of UN financing. The UN raises money from its sales operations and from voluntary contributions from member states for the specialized agencies and specific programs. There is also a separate assessment for peacekeeping.

In the early 1960s the first of the budget crises arose over funding for UN peacekeeping operations in the Congo, with the Soviet Union, other communist countries, and France refusing to pay because, in their view, the action was illegal. The second budget crisis arose in the 1980s as a result of U.S. withholding of contributions. The budget crisis reflected unhappiness with specific policies and politicization, discontent with the one state–one vote format in the General Assembly, dissatisfaction with UN administration and management, and domestic pressures within the United States to lower its share and increase that of Japan and Germany. Between 1985 and 1993 Japan's share increased slightly from 11.82 percent to 12.45 percent and Germany's from 8.26 percent to 8.93 percent, while the Soviet/Russian figure declined from 11.98 percent to 6.71 percent, reflecting Russia's reduced size and increased economic difficulties.

What the financial picture of the UN generally shows is not the inability of states to pay their assessments but their unwillingness to do so. The absence of any significant independent source of funding makes the UN dependent on its member states' commitment to provide the financial resources for operations and activities.

CONCLUSION

Among the persistent issues for international organizations, including the UN, in the post–Cold War era are those of structure and participation. Although the broad outlines of structure for most IGOs were well established by the time the UN was created, questions persist about how best to organize for the support of different activities. And particularly as the UN system has grown in both number of structures and programs, how best can these be coordinated to ensure both efficient use of personnel and resources and effective programs that address the global community's needs? With the growth in numbers of member states, issues of participation in limited-member bodies such as ECOSOC and the Security Council are also inevitable. The voting procedures in the latter as well as in the World Bank and International Monetary Fund are likewise controversial since they do not grant equality to all states. But the issues of participation are not limited to states. Increasingly, they involve the role of nongovernmental organizations. And, finally, with growing demands for

UN activity, the scope of its powers is an issue, as is the role of the secretary-general.

Differing interests and value systems contribute to the post–Cold War controversies over these issues. The major industrialized countries tend to be interested in promoting order in the international system. The developing countries tend to be concerned even more with promoting justice, that is, greater economic and political equality through redistribution of resources. NGOs increasingly promote the concerns of peoples over those of states.

Although IGOs like the UN have been created largely to promote and protect the interests of states, they have also facilitated their own emergence as actors in the international system as well as enhanced the opportunities for participation and influence by small states, coalitions of states, and NGOs. The post–Cold War era has afforded new opportunities for the various actors in the UN system, as we see in Chapter 3.

THREE

□ □ □

Actors in the UN System

The United Nations was formed by states, it depends on states for its sustenance, and it is actually or potentially directed by states on the supposition that its existence and operation may be useful to states. The UN could therefore be said to be a **league of states** designed to protect the integrity of existing states and the state system.

Although the UN Charter accords special status to five states with respect to matters of peace and security—namely, through permanent membership on the Security Council—middle powers and small states have historically played important roles. Thus, it is important to consider the roles of states such as Canada, Australia, Brazil, India, Egypt, the Netherlands, Singapore, and Tanzania. A major debate of the post–Cold War era concerns the future roles of Germany and Japan.

International organizations, the UN foremost among them, also provide a stage or forum for states to form regional blocs and coalitions, as noted in Chapter 2. These actors have become important to the functioning of the UN. Nongovernmental organizations, accorded observer status by ECOSOC, also have become increasingly important actors in the UN system.

Furthermore, as the UN and other international organizations have evolved, they have also assumed the role of actors in their own right. The members of the Secretariat, particularly the secretary-general, have acquired influence and legitimacy that enable them to act without the explicit direction of the governing bodies and a majority of member states. Our discussion of actors in the UN system, then, must consider not only various member states but also these coalitions and blocs, NGOs, and the secretary-generalship itself.

UN AS A LEAGUE OF STATES

As a league of states, the UN is both an instrument of the member states and a source of influence on member states' policies and policymaking processes. States may use the UN to gain a collective stamp of approval on specific actions, points of view, principles, and norms; they may seek to create new rules, enforce existing ones, and settle disputes. The UN and many of its agencies gather and analyze information, improving the quality of information that governments have available. The very fact that the UN brings representatives of states together regularly affords opportunities for them to gather information on other governments' attitudes and policies to the benefit of their own decisionmaking. This continuing interaction also enhances the value of maintaining a good reputation. The UN's own decisionmaking processes encourage states to form coalitions and to link issues together so as to enhance bargaining power. And the UN system provides a variety of valuable programs and activities for addressing global problems ranging from development assistance, disease eradication, and aid to refugees to peacekeeping, election monitoring, and human rights promotion.

The UN is not only an instrument of its member states. It also exercises influence and imposes constraints on its members' policies and the processes by which those policies are formed. Year in and year out the meetings of the UN General Assembly and all other bodies set international and hence national agendas and force governments to take positions on issues from the Middle East to environmental degradation, Cyprus and chemical weapons to Cuba's human rights record and the status of women. These meetings and ongoing data gathering on states' economies, trade, balance of payments, population, and so on also subject states' behavior to international surveillance. To coordinate participation in various UN bodies dealing with related issues, or even to ensure effective participation, many governments have developed specialized decisionmaking and implementation processes, such as interagency committees, bureaus, and offices. UN-approved norms and principles, whether on human rights, the law of the sea, or ozone depletion, as well as UN rules force states to realign their policies if they wish to maintain a reputation for law-abiding behavior or enjoy the benefits of reciprocity from other states. Particularly in democratic, pluralist societies, norms and rules created by the UN may be used by domestic interest groups to press for changes in national policies.

For the UN to function as a key instrument for creating and sustaining patterns of international cooperation, it must in some ways and to some extent influence even the largest, most powerful states in the system. It must be valued by them as a means to get other states to change their behavior, to redefine their interests, and to accept certain constraints. But that means reciprocity. The UN must also be seen as an influence and constraint on a state's own behavior. How much a state must reciprocate depends on its power in a given situation.

Role of the United States

The United Nations and its allied organizations were an important part of the international system structure that the United States helped shape as the dominant political, economic, and military power emerging from World War II. Although U.S. support was not automatically assured, government and public commitment was very strong. As Ruth B. Russell reported in 1968, "On the whole, Washington has found the standards of the Charter in line with the United States' interests, and was for long in the happy position of having a majority of members on its side in both of the major organs and on most of the major issues."[1]

Thus, from 1945 onward the United States generally supported the UN and its agencies broadly as instruments of its national policies. The United States utilized the UN and its specialized agencies to create the broad outlines of institutions and rules compatible with U.S. interests. The creation of the UN and other organizations also served domestic political purposes. Among those was the creation of a web of international entanglements and domestic-support constituencies that made it difficult for future administrations to return to more isolationist policies.

More specifically, during the post–World War II period the United States used the UN and its specialized agencies for collective legitimation of its own actions, particularly in crisis situations such as Korea in 1950, and for delegitimating others' actions that it opposed, such as the British, French, and Israeli occupation of Suez in 1956. The UN was particularly useful for this purpose during the height of the Cold War and the process of decolonization. Iran's seizure of U.S. hostages in 1979 and Iraq's invasion of Kuwait in 1990 demonstrated that the United States had not forgotten the value of the UN for collective legitimation, that is, garnering votes in support of a particular policy. Nor had the United States lost entirely the ability to mobilize votes, although changing majorities in the UN system after 1960, with the influx of newly independent states in Africa, Asia, and Oceania, made it more difficult for the United States to muster support for its own actions. Indeed, the Third World's own success in using the UN for coalition building made it a "hostile place" for the United States throughout the 1970s and early 1980s.

The United States has tended to place a high value on the rule-enforcement and dispute-settlement activities of specialized agencies such as the International Monetary Fund, International Atomic Energy Agency (IAEA), and General Agreement on Tariffs and Trade. In the security area the lack of consensus on basic norms has generally reduced the value of the UN for dispute settlement. The United States has also placed a high value on UN peacekeeping. The resurgence of interest in peacekeeping since 1987 (discussed in Chapter 4) has led to a proliferation of operations with expanded missions that by 1993 began to strain the capacity of the UN. This, coupled with questions about the effectiveness and risks of peace enforcement operations in, for example, Somalia, Haiti, and Bosnia, has raised public and congressional doubts in the United States.

The United States has generally had high regard for certain other UN operational activities, including World Bank lending, IAEA safeguards on nuclear materials, and World Health Organization (WHO) disease eradication programs. The UN's information-gathering and analytical activities provide information about the behavior of other states and hence increase U.S. ability to predict their behavior.

Our own study of the United States and multilateral institutions affirmed the continuing utility of many UN institutions as instruments of U.S. policies and as a means for maintaining a number of regimes.[2] The usefulness of many specialized, technical agencies has remained constant over time, although the United States withdrew from the International Labor Organization (ILO) in 1978 and from UNESCO in 1983; the United States has had difficulties with politicization and bureaucratic inefficiency in both as well as in FAO. In the case of the major economic institutions (the World Bank, IMF, and GATT), changes in international economic relations in the 1970s resulted in periods of decreased utility. Both the World Bank and IMF gained renewed importance in the 1980s, however, with the international debt crisis, structural adjustment, and new norms for multilateral development assistance.

The perceived utility of the UN and its specialized agencies for the United States has been strongly shaped by the ability of U.S. diplomats to influence procedures and outcomes. The membership increases that accompanied the decolonization process made it more difficult for the United States to use the UN as an instrument of its policies, for international organizations not only enlarge the possibilities of multilateral diplomacy but also add to the constraints under which member states operate.

In short, the creation of the UN system both enhanced U.S. influence and also contributed to its decline. The United States found that it could not always control outcomes within the UN and its agencies. They could serve as vehicles for other states' interests. After 1960 changing majorities in the UN General Assembly reflected interests of the LDCs that were different from those of the United States. As shown in Figure 3.1, the frequency with which the United States voted with the majority of states in the General Assembly steadily dropped. Third World demands for the NIEO (discussed in Chapter 5) and politicization of debates on a broad range of issues frequently put the United States on the defensive. Its support for the UN was tested by programs and activities regarded as detrimental to U.S. interests. The long decline in U.S. voting with UN majorities was reversed in the early 1990s.

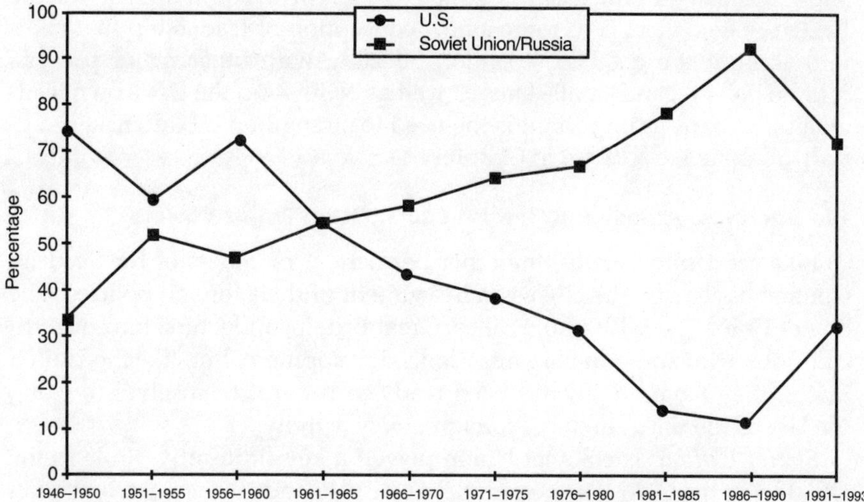

FIGURE 3.1 U.S. and Soviet Union/Russia Percentage Agreement with the Majority, UN General Assembly Roll-Call Votes, Regular Plenary Sessions, 1946–1993. *Source*: Inter-University, Consortium for Political Research, Ann Arbor, Michigan, for years 1946–1985; United Nations, *Index to Proceedings of the General Assembly*, 41–49 part I, (1987–1993) ST/LIB/SER. B/A.

Despite erosion in U.S. power relative to what it was in the early post–World War II years, in the 1990s the U.S. role in the UN system has been and is likely to be much greater than that of any other member state. As the sole global power, the United States remains a major actor whose ability to shape actions and through them the behavior of others makes it a critical member (or nonmember). The United States is still the largest contributor of funds to the UN, despite persistent shortfalls in its assessed contributions since the mid–1980s because of congressional refusal to provide full funding. The United States has continued to sponsor a variety of multilateral program initiatives. Domestic political factors, however, will be critical to future U.S. support, including funding. Also critical to that support will be evidence of reforms within the UN to strengthen the organization's effectiveness (and ensure a strong U.S. say in UN budget decisions).

The dilemma for the United States is the need for leadership in a changing world and in the UN at a time of limited domestic support for such a role. The dissolution of the Soviet Union left the United States as the sole remaining superpower and with a fleeting sense of having "won" the Cold War. The realities of more diffuse power in the international system, further proliferation of states as well as other actors, and eroding sovereignty and increasing demands for global governance make it unlikely the United States can dominate on its own. The challenge for the United States, then, is to forge a new conception of leadership that takes into account the need for coalition building with other major powers, middle powers, and small states as well as NGOs and the UN's own leadership. Perhaps as important is the need to strengthen U.S. domestic support, an issue we address in Chapter 6.

Old Enemies, Allies, and New Partners: Other Major Powers

Like the United States, the other permanent members of the Security Council have used the UN as an instrument of their foreign policies. The Soviet Union (now Russia), France, Great Britain, and China have significant roles in shaping the organization's development, but, like the United States, they have not always been ready to commit themselves to using the UN as the major arena of foreign policy activity.

Soviet Union. The Soviet Union played a key (if negative) role in the UN during the Cold War period. Between 1945 and 1975 the Soviet Union used its veto 114 times to block the objectives of the West and to pursue its own. Three issues illustrate the complexity of the Soviet position.

First, more than one-half of the Soviet vetoes were on membership applications. For example, the Soviet Union vetoed the admission of Jordan, Portugal, and Ireland because it had no diplomatic relations with these countries; Italy and Austria because peace treaties had not yet been negotiated; and Japan because it served as a base for U.S. aggression. The West, under the leadership of the United States, opposed Soviet candidates for membership—Bulgaria, Hungary, Romania, and Albania—for reasons ranging from violations of human rights to their roles in regional conflicts. A package deal admitted sixteen states simultaneously in 1955, but the impasse over membership of the divided states of Korea, Vietnam, and Germany continued until the 1970s.

Second, the Soviet Union clashed with the United States over China's representation. The so-called Nationalist government on Taiwan (Republic of China) held the seat on the Security Council, and the People's Republic of China remained absent from the UN until 1971. The Soviets supported the latter and the United States the former. Both Chinese regimes rejected any two-state solution. Diminished support from U.S. allies and Third World control of a two-thirds majority in the General Assembly as well as the U.S. opening to China finally led to the seating of the PRC.

Third, during the 1970s and early 1980s the Soviets joined with the newly independent countries in support of several causes, such as self-determination for colonial peoples, opposition to apartheid in South Africa, legitimation of the PLO, and the NIEO agenda. As Figure 3.1 illustrates, this strategy enabled the USSR to vote with the majority in the

General Assembly a high percentage of the time. These various positions reflected Soviet national interests and interest in opposing causes that the United States strongly supported.

A dramatic change in the Soviet attitude toward the UN coincided with the 1987 publication in *Pravda* of an article by General Secretary Gorbachev expressing new Soviet interest in multilateral institutions, especially the UN, for promoting peace and security.[3] Gorbachev suggested more extensive use of UN military observers and peacekeeping troops, more use of UN mediation and good offices, a renewal of the Security Council mandate through periodic meetings and closed-door proceedings, use of the permanent members as guarantors of regional security, and resort to the International Court of Justice. The Soviet Union also announced that it would pay up financial arrears.

Thus, by the end of the 1980s the Soviet Union had adopted a facilitative attitude toward the UN, using the UN in Afghanistan to monitor and legitimize its own troop withdrawal, agreeing with UN action to end the Iran-Iraq War after years of opposition, and paving the way for the withdrawal of Soviet-backed Cuban troops in Angola. These changes were hastened by the speed and thoroughness of the Soviet Union's dismemberment, leaving its successor state and its new leader, Boris Yeltsin, to pull back further from international obligations.

Nowhere was the new attitude more evident than in the Gulf War of 1990–1991. The Soviet Union virtually abandoned its former ally Saddam Hussein and supported U.S.-UN actions in the Gulf, although it did not do so without expressed reservations. The official Soviet position accepted strong measures (UN sanctions against Iraq and later the UN blockade) if they were authorized by the Military Staff Committee, a largely defunct organ of the five permanent members' chiefs of staff. What the Soviets wanted was a "collective effort" carried out under UN approval. Their support of the U.S.-UN position was most problematic just before the start of the ground war. Their actions represented, in part, a desire to prevent bloodshed, an attempt to assert what little influence they had left, and an effort to limit damage to any future interests in the region.[4] Eventually they went along with the UN-authorized operation. The country's needs for U.S. economic and emergency aid to deal with its own internal problems and its desire for support in dealing with the crumbling empire overrode other considerations.

Russia, despite its seat on the council as the successor state to the Soviet Union, is no longer in a position to dictate policies. Nonetheless, Russia clearly seeks to continue being a player in world politics and the UN. In the former Yugoslavia as well as former Soviet republics, the Middle East, and elsewhere, Russia can exert influence. The dilemma for the United States is finding ways to work with Russia and other major powers through the UN.

France. Throughout the Cold War both France and Great Britain played secondary, yet key supporting roles on East-West issues in the UN Security Council. Both were placed in a defensive position by pressures in the 1950s to move their colonies to independence. Both faced U.S.-Soviet collusion during the Suez crisis of 1956. France, in particular, "resented being then pushed onto center stage over issues that she believed were beyond the authority of the General Assembly. France was stalled on a defensive position, characterized by a rigid legalism and a large number of abstentions. But she played the game."[5] In 1958 President Charles de Gaulle reiterated forcefully that France had no use for the UN. Only after the decolonization of black Africa was largely finished in 1963 and détente between the United States and the USSR had begun in the late 1960s did France once again begin to play a stronger role in the UN.

During the 1970s and 1980s France's role can best be described as mediator between the South's NIEO agenda and the North's reticence to comply. More than other developed countries, France was ready to accept state intervention in markets and make financial compensation for market failure. It supported regulation of commodity markets, unlike the United States, West Germany, or small European states. On other issues France's positions paralleled those of other developed countries—for example, voting with the United States and Great Britain against mandatory economic sanctions on South Africa. That position did not change until 1985, when France voted for voluntary sanctions against South Africa, while the United States and Great Britain abstained.

Britain. Britain has always had a prominent position in the UN, not only as a permanent member of the Security Council but also as a member of other restricted-member committees, notably the Geneva Group for review of budgets and programs. Britain is always voted to membership in ECOSOC and is a member of the Trusteeship Council, and a British national has always held a seat on ICJ. This privileged position also carries over to the specialized agencies, where Britain has occupied key leadership positions in the International Labor Organization and World Health Organization.[6]

There are several reasons that Britain holds such positions even though its financial contributions are only 5 percent of the assessed budget. First, British delegates and Secretariat members are skilled in drafting and are called on to exercise this skill at frequent intervals. Second, continued ties to Africa and Asia through the Commonwealth give the British established contacts with many of the UN's members. Third, Britain has been a leader, along with the United States, in promoting UN financial reform and accountability. Fourth, through special voluntary contributions Britain does pay a larger share of expenses than the 5 percent figure. Britain wants to keep this privileged position and has opposed efforts to restructure the Security Council.

On several major issues Britain has found itself in a delicate situation. With respect to South Africa, Britain consistently opposed the imposition of UN sanctions until the mid-1980s, a position that isolated it from many African states. Its defense of the Falkland Islands in 1982 was for many UN members a reminder of colonialism. During the Gulf War U.S. and British (and French) collaboration was close, "a continual, cumulative and intentionally visible process intended to give those not yet persuaded the impression of inexorable momentum."[7] Prime Minister Margaret Thatcher saw the Gulf as another Falklands and as an opportunity to repay critical U.S. help during that war.

France and Britain, although nowhere near the major powers they were at the close of World War II, continue in the post–Cold War era to exercise significant influence in world politics and in the UN. Both, for example, have had leading roles in efforts to deal with Bosnia, providing troops and commanders to the UN Protection Force in Yugoslavia (UNPROFOR). Both retain influence in the Third World, thanks to continuing ties with their former colonies, though these are steadily diminishing. Both are members of the nuclear club.

China. The People's Republic of China has become an increasingly important actor in the UN since the Cold War's end. From 1950 to 1971, however, the so-called China question—namely, the dispute over which regime should be represented and hold the permanent seat on the Security Council—was one of the major issues in the General Assembly. Only in the early 1990s did Taiwan begin to express interest in separate membership.

After taking a seat in 1971, the PRC generally played a low-key role, supporting G-77 positions on decolonization and economic issues and eschewing positions on security matters. That pattern changed in the waning years of the Cold War when China agreed to participate in the Cambodian settlement, thus paving the way for UN involvement, as described in Chapter 4.

During the Gulf War, however, China's position proved pivotal. It opposed using force to back sanctions against Iraq, believing great power involvement would make the situation worse. Yet China did not want to be "odd country out," so it chose to abstain on key votes. By agreeing not to obstruct the UN's efforts, China could claim both great power status and leadership in the developing world. (China abstained two times in 1991 and nine times in 1992; see Table 2.1.)

Since the end of the Cold War China has increasingly used the UN to promote its interests. In the General Assembly it seeks to dilute what it sees as excessive U.S. and Western influence. It has worked with Japan, yet opposes Japan's move for a permanent seat. Since Taiwan decided to seek admission to the UN, the PRC has made clear its determination to use its veto. China has fought efforts by the United States and others in the UN Commission on Human Rights to condemn its human rights record. It won a symbolic victory in being selected to host the 1995 UN conference on women.

Old Enemies, New Friends: Germany and Japan

One of the dilemmas for leadership in the post–Cold War era surrounds the roles for Germany and Japan. These were the defeated states of World War II, denied membership in the UN until 1956 (Japan) and 1973 (the Federal Republic of Germany and the German Democratic Republic, or West Germany and East Germany, respectively). As resurgent economic powers from the 1970s onward, both were reluctant to play active political roles, preferring to defer to U.S. leadership. Both had constitutional provisions that strictly limited the size, capabilities, and use of their military forces. Increasingly in the 1980s, however, their levels of financial contribution to the UN and their international economic weight suggested the possibility of greater independent influence. The Gulf War and increasing demands for UN peacekeeping highlighted the dilemmas for both Germany and Japan. They have followed similar strategies for increasing their influence.

Japan. During the early years of UN membership, Japan played a low-profile role, concentrating on a few selective issues, such as keeping the People's Republic of China out of the UN and supporting the UN as guarantor of the peace.[8] In the 1970s Japan's role in UN politics shifted markedly. Japan joined with the less developed countries in support of Arab causes, including upholding the right of self-determination for the Palestinian people and accepting the role of the Palestine Liberation Organization in the UN. These positions clearly reflected Japan's national interest, given its resource (particularly oil) vulnerability. The UN was just one of the forums where Japan supported the Middle East oil producers.

In the 1980s Japan undertook for the first time three key initiatives in the UN. First, Japan strongly supported efforts toward administrative and financial reform of the UN. By 1986 Japan's 10.84 percent assessment was second only to that of the United States. With an increasing share of contributions, Japan has fought, particularly in the International Development Association (IDA) and the World Bank, for a commensurate voting share.

Second, Japan supported strengthening the UN's peace and security capability in a 1980 proposal to reinforce the UN's fact-finding functions. The proposal called for strengthening the secretary-general's functions under Article 99 and limiting Security Council prerogatives. In formulating a whole series of resolutions, Japan worked closely with such states as Austria, India, Sweden, and Egypt, much to the chagrin of the permanent members of the Security Council.

Third, Japan became a major donor to the humanitarian activities of the UN: for example, becoming the largest donor to the UN High Commissioner for Refugees (UNHCR) in response to criticisms of its failure to accept Indochinese refugees. Japan also aided the UN's African famine relief effort and joined the Human Rights Commission in 1982.

Throughout this period Japan's representation in the UN Secretariat remained low, despite two assistant secretaries-general appointed in 1984. The picture changed dramatically in 1988 when Dr. Hiroshi Nakajima was elected director-general of WHO (he was reelected for another five-year term in 1993). Dr. Sadako Ogata was elected high commissioner for refugees in 1991 and reelected for a five-year term in 1993. (Dr. Ogata is also the first woman to serve in a top UN post.) For the first time major UN organizations were headed by Japanese nationals.

Despite these changes in Japanese participation in the UN, it was the Gulf War that brought the critical issue of Japanese direct participation in security issues to the fore.[9] Since Japan is not a permanent member of the Security Council, it did not participate in many of the deliberations. Japan did act swiftly, however, when sanctions were imposed, both freezing Kuwaiti assets and suspending oil imports from Iraq and Kuwait. The Gulf crisis also brought to Japan's domestic agenda a lively debate over the state's role in the international community. In September 1990 Prime Minister Toshiki Kaifu proposed a UN Peace Cooperation Corps, a plan for Japanese to participate in noncombat support capacities. That initiated a domestic debate on overseas deployment of Japanese Self-Defense Forces and the use of troops outside of Japanese territory. In the face of this debate Kaifu withdrew the cooperation bill. Once the war was underway in January 1991, and under pressure from the allies, the Japanese Diet (parliament) approved an additional $9 billion to help defray expenses. The domestic debate continued, however.

In June 1992, after repeated delays and heated debate, a bill passed the Japanese Diet stipulating that up to two thousand Japanese troops could be deployed in UN peacekeeping missions for limited tasks such as transport, medical care, construction, and restoration of communications. Participation in such tasks as monitoring cease-fires and removing land mines would require a separate vote of approval. Having taken this controversial step, the Japanese joined the UN operation in Cambodia (United Nations Transitional Authority in Cambodia, or UNTAC) with a proviso calling for their troops' return should the cease-fire fail or should any parties not support Japan's participation. (See Chapter 4 for discussion of the Cambodian conflict and UNTAC.) Despite the limitations, as one Japanese Foreign Ministry official put it, "The concept is in place."[10] And, indeed, even though the operation in Cambodia was a success, Japan learned valuable lessons. As Japanese writer Okazaki Hisahiko notes, "This work is not the picnic for which some seem to have mistaken it. The public made much ado about each and every facet of Japan's role in Cambodia, but from a global perspective this was a tempest in a teapot."[11] Nonetheless, this was an important step toward Japan's full contribution to the UN.

Germany. Germany was admitted to the UN as two partitioned states in 1973 after lengthy Cold War sparring over their status and diplomatic recognition. Until the late 1980s both German states were closely tied into their respective blocs and exercised little influence in the UN. West German financial contributions steadily rose, however, with its efforts to play an active and useful role in the UN system. Unification in 1990 raised for Germans and for others the possibility of a much more significant role in world politics. The Gulf War highlighted Germany's constitutional limitations for participating in any collective enforcement or peacekeeping operations. The fact that Germany, like Japan, was excluded from decisionmaking but expected to contribute significant monetary resources fueled German complaints. It also fueled international and domestic pressure for constitutional change and debate over Germany's role. Foreign Minister Klaus Kinkel noted, "As a reunited and sovereign country we must assume all the rights and obligations of a member of the United Nations to avoid any discrepancy between our verbal commitment to peace and human rights and our active involvement in their defense."[12]

The German Constitutional Court ruled in 1994 that German military forces may participate in UN peacekeeping operations (and those of other international organizations, such as NATO and the Western European Union, [WEU]). Even without that constitutional ruling, a German field hospital was deployed to Cambodia, and helicopters were being flown and maintained by German military personnel supporting UN arms inspection teams. Although the ruling requires approval by the Bundestag (German parliament) for all German armed military missions, it makes a larger German role in world politics possible and strengthens the multilateralism that is the cornerstone of German foreign policy.

Middle Powers

One group of states that has played and continues to play an important role in UN politics is the so-called middle powers. They were uniquely able to facilitate valuable UN activity during the Cold War era, when disputing parties were wary of great power involvement but less so of middle power mediation. These states act less out of their own interests than out of a belief in international responsibility.[13]

Both Western and non-Western middle powers can be characterized in terms of relative power or size in the international community. More important, they can be characterized in terms of the kinds of policies they pursue, including multilateralism, a commitment to compromise positions in disputes, and coalition building to secure reform in the international system. Among the middle powers are Canada, Australia, Norway, Sweden, Argentina, Brazil, India, and Nigeria.

During the Dumbarton Oaks conference in 1944 Prime Minister Mackenzie King of Canada called for a special position in the UN for Canada and others. His argument was that states ought to have a role commensurate with their contribution, that a division between the great powers and the rest was unworkable. Although the notion of special status for middle powers failed to become part of the Charter, the notion persisted.

When UN peacekeeping was developed in the 1950s, certain middle powers became frequent contributors of peacekeeping troops. Among them were Canada (to every UN peacekeeping operation), Australia, Finland, Sweden, India, Brazil, Chile, and Argentina as well as Iran, Nigeria, and the former Yugoslavia. Many of these same states played a substantial agenda-setting role on issues of disarmament. For example, in 1985 it was estimated that of the sixty-six disarmament resolutions proposed, 36 percent were proposed by middle states. One of these states, Mexico, sponsored 10 percent of the resolutions. These same states, especially Canada, also contributed to arms verification procedures.

Of the middle powers, Canada has played a vital role. Canadian political culture has influenced Canada's preferences in the UN "for pragmatic non-ideological compromise, a belief in pluralism and tolerance, and a commitment to the orderly mediation and resolution of conflicts."[14] In an assessment of Canada's role in UN peacekeeping during the Cold War, three Canadians pragmatically note:

> Canadian policy in the postwar world would try to maintain a careful balance between cooperation with the United States and independent action. This was especially true at the United Nations. And peacekeeping, while it often served US interests, to be sure, nonetheless had about it a powerful aura of independence and the implicit sense that it served higher interests than simply those of the United States, or even the West.[15]

In the post–Cold War era Canada's role in the UN is under scrutiny. The participation of more than one-quarter of Canadian troops in UN peacekeeping is costly and under fire in Canadian newspapers around that country. Indeed, Canada announced its intention to remove troops from the UN peacekeeping operation in Cyprus (United Nations Force in Cyprus, or UNFICYP) in December 1992 after twenty-nine years of participation, even though the conflict among Greece, Turkey, and the Greek and Turkish Cypriots has not been resolved.

Canada's position in the Gulf War stimulated this debate over its role in the UN. Canada wanted the United States to follow a step-by-step pro-

Finnish peacekeeping troops arrive in Namibia, April 1989. UN Photo 157214/M. Grant.

cedure and not act too fast. As Canadian representative Yves Fortier noted, "These are uncharted waters . . . there are no precedents, so why not play it as the framers of the Charter had envisioned it?"[16] Reluctantly supporting the military action, Canada nonetheless contended that the Security Council should approve the use of force. Thus "stuck" and committed, Canada played the role of "follower."

The essence of the middle powers' role lies in the very importance of secondary players in international politics, of followers as well as leaders.[17] And, indeed, fostering cooperation in the 1990s is likely to require leadership based not only on military capability and economic strength but also on diplomatic skill and policy initiatives.

There is renewed discussion of codifying middle power status in a reformed UN. Canada and others maintain that since they play a special role, they need expanded representation on the Security Council. In the post–Cold War era, when there is no effective counterweight to the United States, they do not want to find themselves "stuck" again.

Small States

For a large number of small member states, notably non-European, largely less developed countries, the UN has facilitated a number of foreign policy objectives. First, membership in the UN has served as a badge of international legitimacy. One of the first acts of new states is to apply for UN membership, a symbol of statehood. Second, small states in particular use the UN and the specialized agencies as the arena where they can carry on both bilateral and multilateral discussions, even on non-UN matters. With limited diplomatic and economic resources, the UN is a cost-efficient forum where multilateral ties are forged and bilateral talks are conducted on a range of issues. The fall General Assembly sessions are vehicles for conducting other business among representatives and visiting ministers. Third, small states, especially the small European and Latin American states, have used the UN to promote the expansion of international law in an effort to constrain the major powers and protect small power interests. Fourth, the UN enlarges the "voice" of small states and can offer opportunities to set the global agenda. For example, the 1967 speech to the General Assembly by Malta's UN ambassador, on behalf of the deep seabed as the "common heritage of mankind" and not of any specific nation, galvanized the General Assembly, creating a new norm to guide subsequent negotiations in the 1970s on the Law of the Sea. Fifth, small states have been able to use the UN as a forum to appeal to world public opinion on critical foreign policy issues. For example, Nicaragua used an appeal to the ICJ to condemn U.S. mining of its harbors and seek the world community's support on the high moral ground. Kuwait, because of the importance of its strategic resources, had even better success in mobilizing the international community's response to Iraq's invasion in 1990.

Participation in the UN has tended to force small states to specialize in particular issues. They do not have the diplomatic resources to deal with all issues in depth. Thus, they specialize or in some cases follow the lead of larger states within the Group of 77 or other coalitions.

Small state participation in the UN not only aids in achieving foreign policy objectives directly but also increases the number of avenues that can be taken. The UN presents opportunities for interest aggregation, facilitating the formation of coalitions among small states to enhance their influence. In the negotiations for the New International Economic Order the power of the G-77, forged by alliances among small and medium LDCs, got the issues on the agenda of all the UN-related development agencies, something that one small state could not have achieved alone. And with the proliferation of UN-related bodies, small states have the opportunity to find the body most favorable to their interests—a phenomenon known as "forum shopping."

Small states have been able to bargain with major powers in the UN for support of certain key issues in return for economic concessions. During the years of debate over admission of the PRC to the UN, the United States exchanged development funds for "no" votes from small developing countries. And in the Gulf War some small states that happened to be members of the Security Council at the time agreed to support U.S.-UN action in return for favors. Ethiopia extracted a promise from the United States to broker a peace between the government and rebels. Both Egypt and Malaysia received financial "rewards"—in the former case, a promise of debt forgiveness and in the latter case, hints of increased foreign aid. For Yemen, also on the Security Council at the time, opposition meant the withdrawal of U.S. aid and commitments. So small states have been able to capitalize on their votes by extracting concessions and promises. Yet the U.S. linkage of aid and UN votes in the 1970s and 1980s did not always serve small states' own interests.

For small developing states the most important impact of the UN is on the provision of economic resources, specifically development funds. As discussed in Chapter 5, small developing states apply to the World Bank and UN development agencies for project, technical assistance, and structural adjustment funds to augment their economic development plans. For example, Africa's share of total global assistance offered by the UN system increased from 40 percent in 1986 to 55 percent in 1989, from $1.2 billion to $1.6 billion. Some developing states have been particularly adept at receiving such economic development funds. For example, among the fifteen countries receiving the largest shares of UN Development Program (UNDP) expenditures during 1991 were Sudan, Bangladesh, Nepal, Myanmar, Afghanistan, Tanzania, Uganda, and Malawi. Since 1991 UNDP funds have been retargeted to the poorest forty-five states, mostly in Africa.

Small states are also the beneficiaries of funds from the specialized UN agencies. The World Health Organizations's goal of immunizing 80 percent of the world's children under one year of age against the various communicable diseases has dramatically decreased the infant mortality rate in developing countries. The same organization's AIDS prevention programs have instituted procedures for blood transfusions that have dramatically affected countries such as Uganda that have been severely affected by the epidemic. UNHCR has provided relief funds for 5 million African refugees affected by the severe droughts of 1985 and more than 1 million refugees in Central America. The UN Disaster Relief Organization's (UNDRO) emergency disaster funds have aided numerous countries experiencing natural disasters. And the UN Fund for Drug Abuse Control has aided Bolivia's efforts to stem illicit coca cultivation by donating funds for crop substitution programs. The examples are plentiful. Small developing countries are the direct major beneficiaries of most UN economic and development programs, which average about 80 percent of the total UN budget.

The end of the Cold War has resulted in a new explosion of small states with the dissolution of the Soviet Union and Yugoslavia, pushing the UN's membership from 150 to 185 since 1990. This proliferation diffuses power in the international system still further; it increases pressures for economic resources and demands for security and complicates coalition and consensus building for action.

COALITIONS, BLOCS, AND THE IMPORTANCE OF CONSENSUS

Early in the UN's history states from the same geographic region or with shared economic or political interests formed coalitions to shape common positions on particular issues and to control a bloc of votes. Several factors gave impetus to the development of such groups. First, the Charter itself specified that in electing the nonpermanent members of the Security Council the General Assembly give consideration to "equitable geographical distribution" but offered no guidance on how to do so or what the appropriate geographic groups should be. By informal agreement these came to correspond roughly to major regions of the world: Western Europe, Eastern Europe, Africa, Latin America, Asia, and the Middle East. Table 3.1 shows the regional groups.

Second, the UN General Assembly functions like a national parliament, with each state having one vote and decisions being made by a majority (either simple or two-thirds under specified circumstances). This means that a stable coalition of states comprising a majority of members, like a majority political party or coalition of parties in a parliament, can control most decisions. A key difference between the UN and a national parliament, however, is that a dominant coalition of states does not have to worry about elections turning out a significant number of its members. Foreign policies tend to be stable even with changes of government. Thus, coalitions within the UN have tended to persist for long periods.

Third, the Cold War divide in world politics inevitably led to the formation of two competing coalitions composed of states aligned with either the United States or the Soviet Union. In the latter case the Eastern European states could be counted on to vote consistently with the Soviet Union, thus forming a true bloc. Throughout the mid-1950s the Western European, Latin American, and British Commonwealth states also voted closely with the United States on any issue that involved Cold War competition and also often on human rights, social concerns, and internal UN administration. Colonial and economic questions, however, produced internal tensions and fragmentation in the U.S.-dominated coalition begin-

TABLE 3.1 UN Membership: Regional Groups, 1994

African States

Algeria, Angola, Benin, Botswana, Burkina Faso, Burundi, Cameroon, Cape Verde, Central African Republic, Chad, Comoros, Congo, Djibouti, Egypt, Equatorial Guinea, Eritrea, Ethiopia, Gabon, Gambia, Ghana, Guinea, Guinea-Bissau, Ivory Coast, Kenya, Lesotho, Liberia, Libya, Madagascar, Malawi, Mali, Mauritania, Mauritius, Morocco, Mozambique, Namibia, Niger, Nigeria, Rwanda, São Tomé and Principe, Senegal, Seychelles, Sierra Leone, Somalia, South Africa, Sudan, Swaziland, Togo, Tunisia, Uganda, Tanzania, Zaire, Zambia, Zimbabwe.

Asian and Pacific States

Afghanistan, Bahrain, Bangladesh, Bhutan, Brunei Darussalam, Cambodia, China, Cyprus, Democratic People's Republic of Korea, Fiji, India, Indonesia, Iran, Iraq, Japan, Jordan, Kuwait, Kyrgyzstan, Laos, Lebanon, Malaysia, Maldives, Marshall Islands, Micronesia, Mongolia, Myanmar, Nepal, Oman, Pakistan, Papua New Guinea, Philippines, Qatar, Republic of Korea, Saudi Arabia, Singapore, Solomon Islands, Sri Lanka, Syria, Tajikistan, Thailand, Turkey, Turkmenistan, United Arab Emirates, Uzbekistan, Vanuatu, Vietnam, Western Samoa, Yemen.

Eastern European States

Albania, Armenia, Azerbaijan, Belarus, Bosnia-Herzegovina, Bulgaria, Croatia, Czech Republic, Estonia, Georgia, Hungary, Kazakhstan, Kyrgyzstan, Latvia, Lithuania, Macedonia, Poland, Moldova, Romania, Russian Federation, Slovak Republic, Slovenia, Tajikistan, Turkmenistan, Ukraine, Uzbekistan, Yugoslavia.

Latin American States

Antigua and Barbuda, Argentina, Bahamas, Barbados, Belize, Bolivia, Brazil, Chile, Colombia, Costa Rica, Cuba, Dominica, Dominican Republic, Ecuador, El Salvador, Grenada, Guatemala, Guyana, Haiti, Honduras, Jamaica, Mexico, Nicaragua, Panama, Paraguay, Peru, St. Kitts and Nevis, St. Lucia, St. Vincent and the Grenadines, Suriname, Trinidad and Tobago, Uruguay, Venezuela.

Western European and Other States

Andorra, Australia, Austria, Belgium, Canada, Denmark, Finland, France, Germany, Greece, Iceland, Ireland, Italy, Liechtenstein, Luxembourg, Malta, Monaco, Netherlands, New Zealand, Norway, Portugal, San Marino, Spain, Sweden, Turkey, United Kingdom.

ning in the late 1940s. Nonetheless, it held a controlling position in UN voting until 1955 but by 1960 could not muster a simple majority because of the influx of African and Asian states. (See Figure 3.1.)

Even before the formation of the Group of 77 in 1964, its members constituted more than two-thirds of the UN's membership. Although their initial efforts to achieve common positions did not produce cohesion, by 1971 the G-77 had become the dominant coalition. It was often supported by the Eastern European states as the Soviet Union took advantage of opportunities to escape its minority position and accuse the West of being responsible for the problems of less developed countries. As scholars Donald J. Puchala and Roger A. Coate note:

> For more than a decade the G-77 could, and did, steer the United Nations in directions that it wanted to move, it could, and did, commit the United Nations to principles that it wanted to legitimize, and it could, and did, demand global actions conducive to its interests. The Group of 77 ultimately could not enforce compliance with its demands, but it could bring attention to them and impressively argue for their rectitude. There could be a North-South debate in the UN because there was also a "South" in the form of a solid bloc of Asian, African and Latin American countries standing together for development via global economic reform.[18]

Several other caucusing groups operate within the UN, with their level of activity and cohesion dependent on the issue. These include the African group, the Afro-Asian group, the Latin American group, the Nonaligned Movement, the Islamic Conference, the Scandinavian or Nordic group, the Western European group, and, more recently, the European Union.

Clearly, the Cold War's end eliminated the East-West divide in UN politics. The North-South divide remains, but the South (G-77) is far less cohesive now than in the heyday of the 1970s. "Practically speaking," Puchala and Coate note, "such third world solidarity no longer exists."[19] Bloc politics yielded little beyond symbolic victories for the G-77. More important, increasing differences in social and economic conditions among Asian, African, and Latin American countries make common policy positions difficult to forge. There are also widening differences in perceptions of regional needs. Such centrifugal tendencies are aggravated by the absence of strong and charismatic leaders to galvanize the South. The 1992 Rio Conference on the Environment and Development (UNCED) and Cartagena meeting of UNCTAD discussed in Chapter 5 dramatized conflicts of interest in the South.

The accelerating integration of the European Union has led its member states to act increasingly as a single unit in the United Nations. European Political Cooperation (EPC) is the vehicle for policy coordination among these states, with the aim of formulating common positions and voting as a bloc. There are several issues, however, on which EU members have found it difficult to take common positions: apartheid in South Africa, decolonization, the Middle East, disarmament, and budgetary issues.

The exact processes by which different groups formulate common positions vary. Consistent with the level of institutionalization in the EU generally, the EU has the most formalized process for continual consultation among the member states and for delegation of responsibility for enunciating common policies. This process is managed and aided by offices of the EU Commission in New York and Geneva. Other groups rely on processes of caucusing—formal and informal meetings of delegates to discuss positions and strategies. Inevitably, some states, especially small states with limited diplomatic resources, will behave like legislators in national parliaments following the leadership of "party"—a coalition such as the G-77 or a major power.

Although coalitions and blocs emerged in response to the UN's provisions for voting, more UN decisionmaking in recent years has been done by consensus, that is, without any formal vote. For example, a study of UN General Assembly voting in 1986 shows that of the 320 resolutions adopted, 52 percent were passed without a formal vote, and an additional 12 percent of those voted on received no negative votes.[20] In the post–Cold War era General Assemblies have continued to act by consensus. Seventy-one percent of the 367 resolutions in the 1990–1991 General Assembly session were passed without a vote, 75 percent in 1991–1992, and 73 percent in 1992–1993. Most of these resolutions are "routine," relating to matters recurring annually. Other consensus resolutions result from controversial decisions in which delegates avoid debate and explicit wording. In either case coalitions and blocs may be just as active in trying to forge consensus as in marshaling votes, but the outcome tends to be less divisive because states' positions are not readily apparent.

NGOS IN THE UN SYSTEM

Although the UN's members are states, the organization has long recognized the importance of nongovernmental organizations. The members of such organizations are not states but private groups and individuals. They are interest or pressure groups that operate across national borders in not-for-profit activities. Box 3.1 lists some representative NGOs.

Article 71 of the Charter authorized ECOSOC (but not the General Assembly) to grant consultative status to NGOs. Resolution 1296 formalized that arrangement into three categories. Category I NGOs include those with multifaceted goals and activities, reaching virtually all areas of ECOSOC's responsibilities. Forty-one NGOs enjoy Category I status. Category II NGOs, some 350 in number, are those that specialize in a particular area of economic and social activity—health, human rights. Category III NGOs are organizations that may have an occasional interest in UN activities. This consultative status permits NGOs to attend ECOSOC meetings, submit written statements, testify before ECOSOC meetings, and in limited cases propose items for the agenda. Most specialized UN agencies have similar provisions for limited NGO participation. One "exception" to the general pattern of NGO representation is the permanent observer status accorded the PLO and, prior to 1989, the South West Africa People's Organization (SWAPO). These liberation movements are recognized by many UN members. Within the UN they are recognized as "potential governments," having characteristics both of governments and NGOs.

BOX 3.1 Nongovernmental Organizations

NGO	*Type of Activities, Location*
World Wildlife Fund	Environmental protection, support of scientific research, funding of environmental projects; worldwide
Oxford Committee for Famine Relief	Rural development, disaster and famine relief; worldwide
Amnesty International	Human rights monitoring, publicizing of reports of violations; worldwide
Catholic Relief Services	Emergency relief, refugee assistance, famine relief; worldwide
Fundación Natura	Promotion of environmental education, facilitation of scientific research, scholarships, participation in debt-for-nature swaps; Latin America
Greenbelt Movement	Promotion of rural development and awareness of sustainable land use; assistance to farmers; East Africa
Campaign for Nuclear Disarmament	Peace movement revitalization (stimulated initially by opposition to nuclear testing, expanded as a broad-based populist movement); United Kingdom
Pacific Island Association	Coordination of activities of NGOs in the region and presention of a united position in UN-related bodies; Pacific Island region
Women of Greenham Common	Protest deployment of U.S. ground-launched cruise missiles; United Kingdom

In UN agencies with field programs and offices, such as UNDP, NGOs tend to cultivate relationships both at headquarters (whether New York, Geneva, Vienna, or Nairobi) and in the field. The number of NGOs has increased exponentially since the mid-1970s, as Figure 1.1 illustrates, but they are most numerous in the North and West because of the uneven spread of economic and technological development and of pluralist political systems. Numbering about forty-five hundred today, NGOs increased by an average of 5 percent per year from the end of World War II until the 1980s. Indeed, the diversity of NGOs "is nearly as great as the diversity of human interests, and the ranges in size and influence [are] . . . very great."[21]

NGOs perform a variety of functions and roles. They have become key sources of information and technical expertise on a wide variety of international issues from environmental to human rights, often obtaining grassroots information unavailable to governments. They act as advocates for specific policies and alternative channels of political participation to whatever exists in a given country. They mobilize mass publics. They play key operational roles distributing assistance in disaster relief and to refugees. They are critical to monitoring implementation of human rights norms or environmental regulations and to providing warnings of violations. Increasingly, they are developing regional and global networks through linkages among national-level groups.

The distinction between those NGOs with and those without ECOSOC consultative status has become largely academic as NGOs have found various means for influencing global policymaking and implementation. They lobby delegates when the General Assembly is in session. With the practice of holding UN-sponsored global conferences on specific issues such as the environment in 1972 and 1992 and women in 1975, 1980, 1985, and 1995, NGOs found powerful new outlets for their activity beyond lobbying at the General Assembly and ECOSOC. They have organized parallel conferences in the same city, providing an opportunity for both formal and informal interaction between NGO members and government delegates.

The process of NGO participation was particularly significant in connection with the 1992 UNCED in Rio, the 1994 Cairo Conference on Population and Development (ICPD), and the various UN conferences on women, as we explore in Chapter 5. In a certain sense growing NGO activity represents the "democratization" of international relations by promoting the involvement of ordinary people in addressing global issues.

Transnational corporations are a special type of NGO engaged in for-profit business transactions and operations across national borders. Since the 1970s TNCs have been increasingly recognized as significant international actors, controlling resources far greater than those of many states. Their activities can benefit or hurt both developed and developing countries and have raised a number of questions for UN agendas. How can TNC activities be regulated? How can TNCs be mobilized for economic development in collaboration with UN agencies and NGOs? How can less developed countries be assured that powerful TNCs will not interfere in their domestic affairs, challenge their sovereignty, and relegate them to permanent dependency? TNCs are also important actors in addressing trade and environmental issues.

UN AS AN ACTOR IN WORLD POLITICS

The emergence of the UN's secretary-general to greater international prominence has been a key to the emergence of the UN itself as an autonomous actor in world politics. Through the secretary-general's leadership "an international organization is transformed from being a forum of multilateral diplomacy into something which is more than the sum of its inputs . . . and make[s] more decisions on behalf of the whole community of nation-states."[22] Because of the secretary-general's mandate and position and his very availability, he and his representatives have a variety of formal and informal opportunities to play an intermediary role in disputes and negotiations and to exercise influence.

The establishment of permanent country missions in New York (and for many countries also in Geneva and Vienna) created what Secretary-General Dag Hammarskjöld called a standing diplomatic conference. They facilitate a variety of informal contacts, consultations, and diplomatic initiatives that make the UN headquarters a hub of activity. The fall General Assembly sessions bring heads of state and government as well as foreign ministers to New York, thereby creating further diplomatic opportunities. In addition, the secretary-general has a variety of opportunities to travel and hence to confer with high government officials.

Over more than fifty years a pattern of leadership has evolved that has taken advantage of opportunities for initiatives, applied flexible interpretations of Charter provisions, and sought mandates from UN policy organs as necessary. Six successive secretaries-general have contributed to developing their own roles and that of the institution (see Box 2.1). Their personalities and interpretation of the Charter, as well as world events have combined to increase the power, resources, and importance of the position. More than just a senior civil servant, the UN secretary-general has become an important international political figure "subject to the problems and possibilities of political leadership."[23]

Dag Hammarskjöld, the second secretary-general, played an important part in shaping the role and the UN during the critical period 1953–1961. Hammarskjöld articulated principles for UN involvement in peacekeeping. He demonstrated the secretary-general's efficacy as an agent for peaceful settlement of disputes, beginning with his successful 1954–1955 mediation of the release of eleven U.S. airmen under the UN command in Korea who had been imprisoned by the Communist Chinese. This accomplishment was particularly notable because the People's Republic of China was then excluded from the UN. Hammarskjöld also oversaw the initiation of UN peacekeeping operations with the creation of the United Nations Emergency Force (UNEF) at the time of the 1956 Suez crisis.

Secretary-General Dag Hammarskjöld inspects a UN force honor guard after arriving in the Congo on September 13, 1961. United Nations.

U Thant, the Burmese diplomat who followed Hammarskjöld, stated:

> The Secretary-General must always be prepared to take an initiative, no matter what the consequences to him or his office may be, if he sincerely believes that it might make the difference between peace and war. . . . The powers and possibilities of the Secretary-General must be husbanded so that they can be used to the best possible advantage in the common interests of all nations.[24]

Thant, his predecessors, and his successors shaped the secretary-general's position as a political role, drawing more on the spirit of the Charter than on its specific provisions. Article 97, for example, gave the secretary-general broad responsibility as the chief administrative officer of the organization. Article 99 authorized the secretary-general "to bring to the attention of the Security Council any matter which in his opinion may threaten the maintenance of international peace and security." This provided a broad basis for political judgment and for action in the secretary-general's own right.

Javier Pérez de Cuéllar, the fifth secretary-general, presided over the UN's transformation from the brink of irrelevance in the 1980s to an active instrument for resolving conflicts and promoting international peace.

Secretary-General Javier Pérez de Cuéllar holds a press conference on September 20, 1982. UN Photo 151263/Y. Nagata.

In his persistent, patient, low-key approach to Israel's 1982 invasion of Lebanon, the Falklands/Malvinas War, the Iran-Iraq War, and the ongoing problems in Cyprus, Namibia, Afghanistan, and elsewhere, he epitomized the ideal intermediary. Pérez de Cuéllar described the secretary-general as "a world citizen because all world problems are *his* problems, the Charter is his home and his ideology, and its principles are his moral creed." He also noted that Article 99 "contains the three elements of right, responsibility, and discretion ... [that over the years have led] the Secretary-General himself to help to moderate conflicts or negotiate solutions."[25]

A key resource for UN secretaries-general is the power of persuasion. In the words of U Thant, "The Secretary-General has to work by persuasion, argumentation, negotiation, and a persistent search for consensus."[26] He also commands the personnel resources within the organization, including members of the Secretariat, and has the ability to convene the heads of principal policy bodies, such as the Security Council and General Assembly, and senior delegates. Perhaps more important, however, is the "force" of majorities behind resolutions as well as the norms and principles enshrined in the Charter. A "covering" resolution from a policy organ may lend greater legitimacy to his initiatives, though it may not ensure any greater degree of success. It can also be a constraint. The support of members, especially the five permanent members of the Security Council, can strengthen the efforts of the secretary-general or his representatives. He can also call on member states to assist him by intervening with the parties.

Autonomy is key to the secretary-general's influence. For example, Pérez de Cuéllar refrained from comment when Iraq invaded Kuwait in August 1990 and the Security Council initiated action against Iraq. Likewise, he did not associate himself with the General Assembly's regular criticisms of South Africa. Thus, when the opportunity to resolve situations begins to develop, the secretary-general can demonstrate that he is "uninstructed by the political organ and can be employed as neutral intermediary between the position of the state and that of the UN organ."[27]

Secretary-General Boutros Boutros-Ghali has the benefit of enhanced information-gathering and analytical capability in his office. This enables him to have information on emerging problems independent of what governments provide and to pursue his activist's agenda. As one commentator describes:

> The 71-year-old Egyptian diplomat and academic has banished the old notion that the leader of the United Nations should be the polite child of international affairs—seen but not heard. He saw an opening for the UN in the post–Cold War disarray and plunged: prodding the United States to send thousands of American soldiers to rescue Somalis from famine; urging the United Nations into new terrain in Cambodia, Bosnia and Haiti; and, more recently, making a rare journey to North Korea to help solve an impasse over the nuclear program of the isolated Communist nation.[28]

Other reforms, too, have enhanced the secretary-general's capability to manage a greater number and variety of peacekeeping and peacemaking operations.

In short, the UN secretary-general is well placed to serve as a neutral communications channel and intermediary for the global community. Although he represents the institution, he can act independently of the policy organs even when resolutions have condemned a party to a dispute, maintaining lines of communication and representing the institution's commitment to peaceful settlement and alleviation of human suffering.

The end of Cold War tensions and renewed support for the UN have contributed to a renewed interest in the role of the secretary-general as

Secretary-General Boutros Boutros-Ghali walks on the runway at Sarajevo's airport in late 1992 with Lieutenant General Satish Nambiar, the force commander of UNPROFOR in Croatia and Bosnia-Herzegovina. UN Photo 182520/A. Morvan.

broker, mediator, and world figure and underscored the importance of the international context to that role. The configuration of power, the patterns of cleavage among states, and the support or acquiescence, especially of major states, are all critical, particularly for the secretary-general's relationship with the Security Council, now much more important than the General Assembly. With new patterns and actors changing the old state-centric, sovereignty-bound system, however, there is increasing emphasis on multilateral approaches to global problemsolving that places new demands on the UN's secretary-general as an actor and political leader.

CONCLUSION

States remain key actors in the UN system, although their sovereignty may be eroding and their centrality diminished by the proliferation of NGOs. Over time states have used the United Nations for different foreign policy purposes and have been, in turn, affected by the organization's actions. In the post–Cold War era, when there are proliferating demands for UN action on both security and economic issues, the commitment of states is vital. One key is the willingness of the United States to provide leadership and funding as well as build coalitions involving other states in both UN decisionmaking and decision enforcing. Domestic politics, including presidential leadership, congressional support, and public acquiescence, will be determining. But the willingness of other economically privileged states to contribute to the financial burden and of middle powers to furnish their own unique capabilities will also be critical. Likewise, the ability and willingness of small states to support global initiatives and to marshal the capacity to fulfill commitments are part of the picture. The proliferation of NGOs and the emergence of the secretary-general as an independent actor both complicate and enrich the cast of characters on the UN's stage.

FOUR

□ □ □

Maintaining International Peace and Security: Peacekeeping, Peacemaking, and Collective Security

The award of the 1988 Nobel Peace Prize to UN peacekeepers and the launching of twenty new operations between 1988 and 1994 have given United Nations peacekeeping high visibility in this post–Cold War era. Recognizing the UN's importance for future conflict management, the Security Council has stepped up efforts to increase the capacity of the UN to maintain international peace and security.

In this chapter we elaborate on a typology of peacekeeping activities. We examine how UN peacekeeping has developed and evolved over three time periods: during the Cold War from 1945 to the mid-1980s, during the transition period 1986–1989, and during the post-Cold War period. We examine the experience with collective security and enforcement during the 1991 Gulf War and consider what precedents that may have set for the future. We also look at new challenges, with brief case studies of Somalia, Cambodia, and Yugoslavia. Finally, we analyze the future ability of the UN to maintain peace and security in light of organizational constraints and changes in the international political system as well as the willingness of member states to bear the higher monetary costs and human casualties associated with new approaches.[1]

The issues raised by the increased demand for UN efforts to maintain peace and security link closely to all three dilemmas: the dilemma of state sovereignty versus its erosion, demands for global governance versus the capacity and will of both the UN and member states to fulfill commitments, and the need for leadership versus disintegrating trends in international relations. Not only has the post–Cold War period not ushered in a new era of peace, but it is also marked by new threats to security. A number of the situations the UN is being called on to address in the 1990s are results of the fragmentation trend.

UN CHARTER AND MAINTENANCE OF INTERNATIONAL PEACE AND SECURITY

The founders of the United Nations who gathered at San Francisco in 1945 recognized that the organization they were establishing was not going to abolish war for all time. Yet they believed it was "the best mechanism for maintaining international peace and security the statesmen assembled there could devise for the moment, and people generally would have been quite happy if the new instrument only helped in the prevention or regulation of war or in the settlement of disputes for a decade or two."[2] Indeed, maintaining peace and security was and has been the most important function of the organization. But how the UN undertook this task has changed over time in ways never envisaged by the founders, and somewhat ironically, the provisions of the Charter itself, which lay largely unused during the forty years of the Cold War, have seen far more use since 1989 than at any previous time. Indeed, it was in response to the inability of the UN to act as envisioned by the Charter that peacekeeping was developed.

The United Nations Charter in Article 2 (Sections 3, 4, 5) obligates all members to settle disputes by peaceful means, to refrain from the threat or use of force, and to cooperate with UN-sponsored actions. The Security Council has primary responsibility for maintenance of international peace and security (Article 24) and the authority to identify aggressors (Articles 39, 40) and decide what enforcement measures should be taken (Articles 41, 42, 48, 49). The latter include actions taken under Chapter VII of the Charter to respond to threats or breaches of peace; such actions can comprise economic sanctions, interruption of communications, military action, and a call on members to make military forces available, subject to special agreements (Articles 43, 44, 45). More generally, under Article 34 "the Security Council may investigate any dispute, or any situation which might lead to international friction or give rise to a dispute, in order to determine whether the continuance of the dispute or situation is likely to endanger the maintenance of international peace and security."

Because the Cold War made agreement among the permanent members of the Security Council on how to handle threats to international peace and security so rare, the Security Council has actually used its enforcement powers in only seven cases, five of them since 1990. The seven include sanctions against Southern Rhodesia (now Zimbabwe) in 1966, an arms embargo against South Africa in 1977, the 1990 economic sanctions and subsequent military action against Iraq, an arms embargo against Yugoslavia in 1991, and an air and arms embargo against Libya in 1992. In 1993 the council imposed oil and arms embargoes on both Angola—specifically on the non-government-controlled territory and the rebel group UNITA (National Union for the Total Independence of Angola) and on Haiti. Sanctions against the latter have been progressively tightened. For the most part the Security Council has relied on the Charter's peaceful settlement mechanisms in responding to the many situations placed on its agenda over the years. The Charter provisions for earmarked military forces and for the Military Staff Committee have never been operationalized, but during the Gulf War and with the increased demands for peacekeeping forces they have drawn renewed attention.

Other UN organs also have responsibilities related to peace and security. The secretary-general is authorized to bring to the Security Council's attention any and all matters that threaten international peace and security (Article 99). Frequently the secretary-general may be called on (or seek) to play a formal or informal intermediary role between parties to a dispute. Article 7 grants broad responsibility for securing and upholding the principles and objectives of the organization; combined with Article 99, it has been used as a legal basis for developing the political role of the secretaries-general.

On the basis of the General Assembly's right to consider any matter within the purview of the Charter (Article 10), the "Uniting for Peace Resolution" during the Korean War in 1950 established a precedent that enabled the General Assembly to act when the Security Council was deadlocked by great power veto. The General Assembly also has the right to make inquiries and studies that might trigger further united action (Articles 13, 14) and to be kept informed (Articles 10, 11, 12).

As noted in Chapter 2, the designers of the UN had assumed great power unity. Thus, the sanctioning of UN forces to counter the North Korean invasion of South Korea in 1950 was made possible only by the temporary absence of the Soviet Union. The Korean case came close to a collective security action, as did the UN enforcement actions against Iraq. In 1950 the UN provided a framework to legitimate U.S. efforts to defend the Republic of Korea and mobilize other states' assistance, with a U.S. general designated as the UN commander but taking orders directly from Washington. During the 1990–1991 Gulf War the UN provided a similar framework for the U.S.-led multinational coalition, for economic sanctions, for a peacekeeping force after the war, and for efforts to eliminate Iraq's nuclear, biological, and chemical weapon capabilities.

Peacekeeping was a creative response to the breakdown of great power unity and the spread of East-West tensions to regional conflicts, as we discussed in Chapter 2. Likewise, in the late 1950s Secretary-

General Dag Hammarskjöld instituted **preventive diplomacy** as a means for the UN to help settle conflicts before violence breaks out and without great power involvement. It includes fact-finding and preventive deployment of troops along a border to discourage hostilities. The innovative Uniting for Peace Resolution and the development of peacekeeping demonstrate that the United Nations has not been a static organization with respect to its role in promoting and maintaining international peace and security.

The post–Cold War era has seen a revival of interest in collective security, as well as various types of enforcement actions. **Peacemaking** represents yet another set of roles and challenges for the UN in this period; it involves efforts to bring parties to agreement and is often complemented by **peace building,** which comprises postconflict activities to strengthen and preserve peace, such as the organization of free elections, assistance with civil administration, the training of police, development aid, and the monitoring of human rights. (See Box 4.1 for a summary of UN peace and security approaches.) First, however, we explore the evolution of UN peacekeeping activities.

EVOLUTION OF PEACEKEEPING

Typology of Activities

Peacekeeping has taken a number of different forms in the varied circumstances in which it has been applied. Since there is no provision for peacekeeping in the Charter, a set of customs, principles, and practices defying neat definition have emerged from experience. These were drawn together when the second UN Emergency Force (UNEF II) was created after the 1973 Arab–Israeli (Yom Kippur) War and have provided basic guidelines for all subsequent operations. Thus, the UN refers to peacekeeping as "an operation involving military personnel, but without enforcement powers, undertaken by the United Nations to help maintain or restore international peace and security in areas of conflict."[3] The key distinctions between peacekeeping and enforcement have to do with the mandate, training, deployment, and equipment of the military units involved.

Inasmuch as the permanent UN military forces envisioned by the Charter were never created, peacekeeping operations have relied on ad hoc military (civilian or police) units drawn almost exclusively from the armed forces of nonpermanent members of the Security Council (often small, neutral, and nonaligned members). This pattern was particularly important during the Cold War era, when peacekeeping often was used

BOX 4.1 UN Approaches to Preventing and Managing Conflict

Collective security Theory and practice whereby all states thwart an aggressor state by joining together against it, first by preventing the outbreak of force and then by meeting aggression with force.

Enforcement measures Direct actions taken to ensure compliance with UN resolutions, such as economic sanctions, banning of air flights and communications, and use of armed force.

Peacekeeping Use of multilateral forces to achieve several different objectives: observation of cease-fire lines and cease fires, separation of forces, promotion of law and order, offering of humanitarian aid.

Preventive diplomacy Practice of engaging in actions before the outbreak of conflict, the monitoring of hot spots before conflict erupts, the use of technology for surveillance.

Peacemaking Efforts to bring parties to an agreement that settles a conflict.

Peace building Postconflict activities to strengthen and preserve peace, such as development aid, civilian administration, and human rights monitoring.

to prevent the escalation of regional conflicts by keeping the superpowers or, in the case of postcolonial problems, former colonial powers at bay. The size of peacekeeping forces has varied widely, depending on the scope of the operation and mandate. Small observer groups have numbered less than one hundred; major operations in the Congo in the early 1960s and in Cambodia and Yugoslavia in 1992–1993 required more than ten thousand troops. Table 4.1 indicates the size, among other characteristics, of many UN peacekeeping operations. Countries that have contributed contingents to one or more operations range from Canada, India, Sweden, Norway, Fiji, Ghana, Brazil, and Argentina to Bangladesh, Senegal, Togo, and Nepal. Many recent, nontraditional peacekeeping operations have used civilians and police as well as military personnel to perform a variety of tasks.

Former Undersecretary-General for Political Affairs Sir Brian Urquhart, widely regarded as the "father of peacekeeping," summarizes the political requirements for peacekeeping as follows:

1. The consent of the parties involved in the conflict to the operation's establishment, mandate, composition, and appointed commanding officer
2. The continuing and strong support of the operation by the Security Council
3. A clear and practicable mandate
4. The nonuse of force, except as the last resort in self-defense, which includes resistance to attempts by forceful means to prevent the peacekeepers from discharging their duties
5. The willingness of troop-contributing countries to provide adequate numbers of capable military personnel and to accept the degree of risk that the mandate and the situation demand
6. The willingness of the member states, especially the permanent members of the Security Council, to make available the necessary financial and logistical support[4]

The advantages of peacekeeping over collective security as envisioned in the UN Charter are numerous. Because peacekeeping requires the approval of the parties to the conflict, there is at least a nominal commitment to cooperate with the mandate of the forces. Troops are volunteered by member countries, so the commitment by most members is relatively small. No aggressor need be identified, so no one party to the conflict is singled out for blame. The precise form of peacekeeping, however, has varied and is becoming increasingly so because operations are tailored to the requirements of individual conflicts and situations. To date, UN forces have been deployed to deal with interstate wars over territory, intrastate civil conflicts, conflicts over ethnic or social differences, territories/peoples demanding self-determination, the independence of new states, and outright invasions. Peacekeeping activities can be grouped in five categories: observation, separation of forces, law and order, use of limited force, and enforcement (technically beyond the scope of peacekeeping). Humanitarian intervention, designed to ensure the safety and well-being of civilian populations, has emerged as a combination of several of these activities.[5]

Observation encompasses a variety of traditional peacekeeping activities:

1. Investigation of conflicts (e.g., the UN Commission of Investigation established in 1946 to examine the extent of involvement by the great powers in the Greek civil war)
2. Armistice supervision (e.g., the UN Truce Supervision Organization [UNTSO] established in 1948 to supervise the truce between the Israeli and Arab armies)

TABLE 4.1 A Guide to UN Peacekeeping Operations, 1948–1995

Operation	*Title*	*Location*	*Duration*	*Maximum Strength*
UNTSO	UN Truce Supervision Organization	Egypt, Israel, Jordan, Syria, Lebanon	June 1948–present	572 military observers
UNMOGIP	UN Military Observer Group in India and Pakistan	India, Pakistan	Jan. 1949–present	102 military observers
UNEF I	First UN Emergency Force	Suez Canal, Sinai Peninsula	Nov. 1956–June 1967	3,378 troops
ONUC	UN Operation in the Congo	Congo	June 1960–June 1964	19,828 troops
UNFICYP	UN Force in Cyprus	Cyprus	March 1964–present	6,411 military observers
UNEF II	Second UN Emergency Force	Suez Canal, Sinai Peninsula	Oct. 1973–July 1979	6,973 troops
UNDOF	UN Disengagement Observer Force	Syrian Golan Heights	June 1974–present	1,450 military observers
UNIFIL	UN Interim Force in Lebanon	Southern Lebanon	March 1978–present	7,000 military observers
UNGOMAP	UN Good Offices Missions in Afghanistan and Pakistan	Afghanistan, Pakistan	May 1988–March 1990	50 military observers
UNIMOG	UN Iran-Iraq Military Observer Group	Iran, Iraq	Aug. 1988–Feb. 1991	399 military observers
UNAVEM I	First UN Angola Verification Mission	Angola	Jan. 1989–June 1991	70 military observers
UNTAG	UN Transition Assistance Group	Namibia, Angola	Apr. 1989–March 1990	4,493 troops, 1,500 civilian police, and 2,000 civilian election observers

(continues)

TABLE 4.1 (continued)

Operation	*Title*	*Location*	*Duration*	*Maximum Strength*
UNOVEN	UN Observer Mission to Verify the Electoral Process in Nicaragua	Nicaragua	Aug. 1989–Feb. 1990	120 civilian election observers
ONUCA	UN Observer Group in Central America	Costa Rica, El Salvador, Guatemala, Honduras, Nicaragua	Nov. 1989–July 1992	1,098 military observers
UNIKOM	UN Iraq-Kuwait Observer Mission	Iraq, Kuwait	Apr. 1991–present	1,440 military observers and troops
UNAVEM II	Second UN Angola Verification Mission	Angola	June 1991–Nov. 1992	350 military observers and 90 police observers
ONUSAL	UN Observer Mission in El Salvador	El Salvador	July 1991–present	135 civilian and military staff
MINURSO	UN Mission for the Referendum in Western Sahara	Western Sahara	Sept. 1991–present	375 military liaison officers and civilian staff
UNAMIC	UN Advance Mission in Cambodia	Cambodia	Oct. 1991–present	380 military liaison officers and civilian staff
UNPROFOR	UN Protection Force (in the former Yugoslavia)	Former Yugoslavia: Croatia, Bosnia-Herzegovina, Macedonia	March 1992–present	30,500 troops and civilian personnel
UNTAC	UN Transition Authority in Cambodia	Cambodia	March 1992–Dec. 1993	15,900 troops, 3,600 police monitors, and 2,400 civilian administrators

(continues)

TABLE 4.1 (continued)

Operation	*Title*	*Location*	*Duration*	*Maximum Strength*
UNOSOM I, II	UN Operation in Somalia	Somalia	Aug. 1992–March 1995	28,000 troops and 2,800 civilian staff
ONUMOZ	UN Operation in Mozambique	Mozambique	Dec. 1992–present	7,000 military and civilian personnel
UNOMUR	UN Observer Mission Uganda-Rwanda	Uganda-Rwanda border	June 1993–present	81 military observers and 24 civilian staff
UNOMIG	UN Observer Mission in Georgia	Georgia	Aug. 1993–present	88 military observers
UNOMIL	UN Observer Mission in Liberia	Liberia	Sept. 1993–present	374 military observers
UNMIH	UN Mission in Haiti	Haiti	Sept. 1993–present	1,267 military and civilian observers
UNAMIR	UN Assistance Mission for Rwanda	Rwanda	Oct. 1993–present	2,548 troops with 5,000 additional authorized

SOURCE: United Nations

3. Maintenance of a cease-fire (such as military observers sent under the UN Commission for India and Pakistan to verify the position of troops and monitor activities prohibited under the terms of the cease-fire)
4. Cessation of fighting (the UN Iran-Iraq Military Observer Group [UNIMOG] established in 1988 to monitor cessation of fighting and withdrawal of forces)
5. Verification of troop withdrawal (e.g., the UN Good Offices Mission in Afghanistan [UNGOMAP] established in 1988 to oversee the withdrawal of Soviet troops from that country)
6. Observation of elections as occurred in Namibia, Nicaragua, Haiti, Cambodia, El Salvador, and South Africa

7. Verification of arms control and disarmament agreements (e.g., the 1989 Central American Esquipulas II agreement)
8. Human rights observation (e.g., the 1991 UN 1991 Observer Mission in El Salvador [ONUSAL])
9. Reconnaissance (e.g., preliminary missions to Cambodia and Central America)

Obviously, the range of UN activities covered under the category of observation is diverse. It is also "the least controversial range on the escalating spectrum of peacekeeping activities."[6]

Separation of forces involves interposing referees in a buffer zone between conflicting parties. It has been most extensively used in the Middle East, with the UN Emergency Force (UNEF II) between Israel and Egypt in the 1970s, the UN Disengagement Observer Force (UNDOF) between Israel and Syria from 1973 to the present, and the long-suffering UN Interim Force in (Southern) Lebanon (UNIFIL) being prominent examples. (See Figure 4.1 for an illustration of how peacekeepers are deployed to separate forces.)

The third category of UN operations involves situations requiring moral authority and sometimes defensive actions to preserve *law and order,* often within a society. The United Nations Operation in the Congo (ONUC) established in 1960, is a telling example of peacekeeping being used to restore law and order in a civil war. More recently in Cambodia peacekeepers took on law and order tasks, likewise, in Cambodia UN forces (UNTAC) undertook the complex tasks of civil administration and police as well as observation, election supervision, and rehabilitation.

The principle that UN peacekeepers use military force only as a last resort and in self-defense was a response to the difficulties encountered in the Congo in 1961 when the Security Council authorized ONUC to use force to prevent civil war and to remove foreign mercenaries in that country. The UN became embroiled in the civil war, incurring the wrath of the African states and the Soviet Union. *Use of force*—even limited force—is fraught with political and legal controversy: How much is limited force? Are such forces really used defensively? As two observers note, however, "the end of the Cold War provides an opportunity to reevaluate many of the assumptions and standard practices governing international cooperation, including the use of force. The collegiality that has characterized deliberations by the Security Council since 1987 means eroding respect for shibboleths . . . [and] as peacekeeping was a development of the restrictive Cold War atmosphere, it is likely to evolve significantly as great power tensions recede."[7]

Finally, *enforcement action,* although technically beyond the scope of peacekeeping, involves direct military action to ensure compliance with

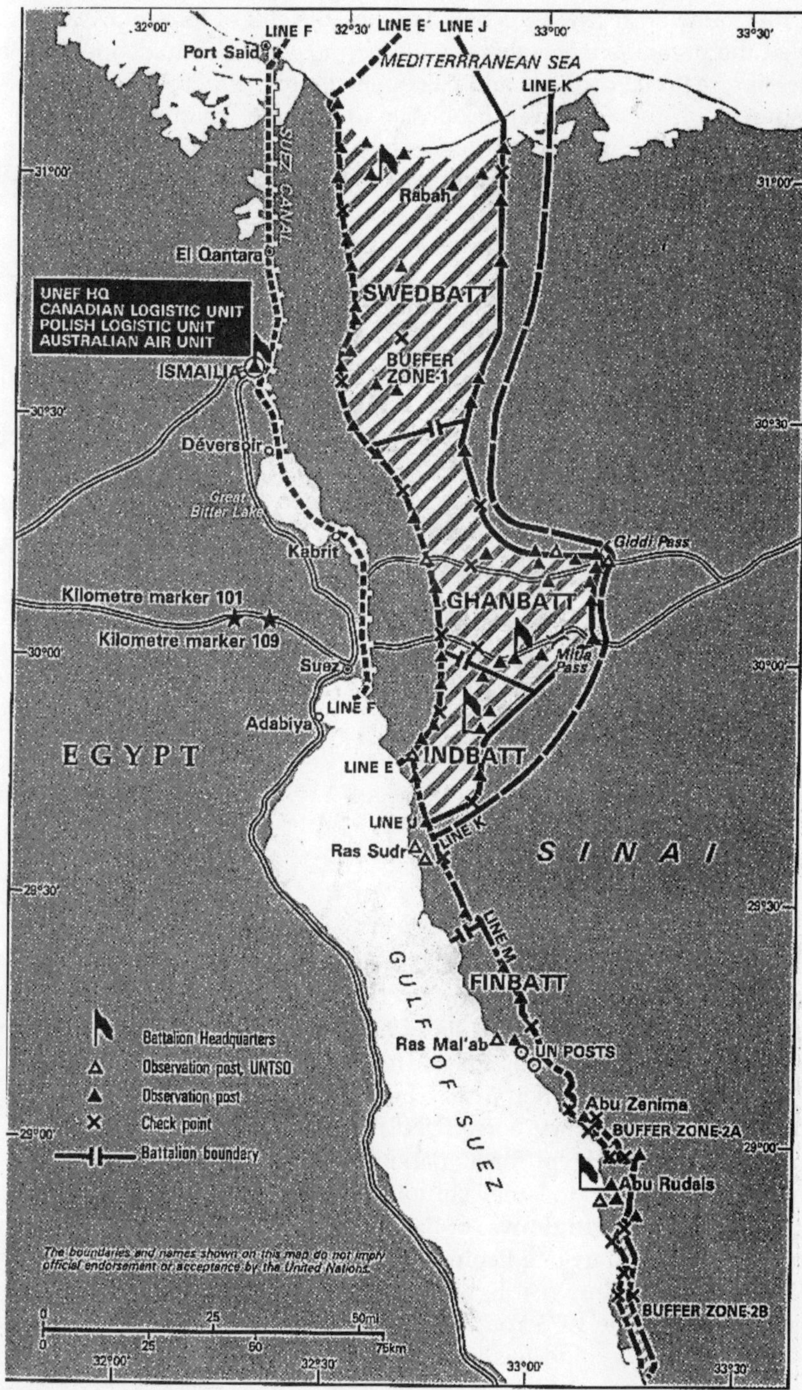

FIGURE 4.1 How Peacekeepers Are Deployed: UNEF II Deployment, July 1979. *Source*: United Nations, *The Blue Helmets: A Review of United Peace-Keeping*, 2d ed. (New York: UNDPI, 1990), Map 3329.3 Rev. 1 (June 1990).

Security Council directives. As noted earlier, the end of the Cold War has enabled the permanent members of the Security Council to cooperate in addressing regional conflicts and has opened a new era in UN activities, beginning with the Gulf War. Proposals to create a standing UN peace force anticipate the use of such forces for both traditional peacekeeping functions and enforcement. And, it is anticipated that the latter will become a more prominent feature of world politics.

A new use of UN peacekeepers, *humanitarian aid* and *intervention,* is based on the notion that suffering people have an enforceable right to basic needs. The provision of food and medical supplies and a secure environment necessary for their delivery is a fundamental human right that may be guaranteed by UN peacekeepers. Such peacekeeping may keep supply lines open, guard distribution centers, and guarantee law and order, as in the case of Somalia, or provide safe havens, as in the case of the Iraqi Kurds in 1991.

Many of the tasks UN peacekeepers have been called on to undertake were never specified in the Charter or envisaged by the founders. However, the broadening of UN functions in maintaining international peace and security shown in this typology of peacekeeping activities was a necessary institutional innovation if the UN was to play any role in this key aspect of world politics. Although this typology provides a useful overview of different UN activities subsumed under peacekeeping, in actuality most UN missions include at least several of the previously described functions. We turn now to examine briefly the evolution of peacekeeping during the Cold War era and the transition period from 1986 to 1989 as background to developments in the post–Cold War era that began in 1990.

Cold War, 1945–1985

UN peacekeeping forces were used most extensively during the Cold War era in the Middle East and during conflicts arising out of the decolonization process when the interests of neither the United States nor the Soviet Union were directly at stake. The Suez crisis of 1956 marked the first major example of their use. The General Assembly created the United Nations Emergency Force (UNEF I)following the British, French, and Israeli attack on Egypt for its nationalization of the Suez Canal and threat to close the canal to Israeli shipping. UNEF I separated the combatants; supervised the withdrawal of British, French, and Israeli forces; and thereafter patrolled the Sinai Peninsula and Gaza Strip.

UNEF I was withdrawn at Egypt's request just before the Six-Day War in 1967. Following the 1973 Yom Kippur War, UNEF II was established to monitor the cease-fire and facilitate the disengagement of Egyptian and

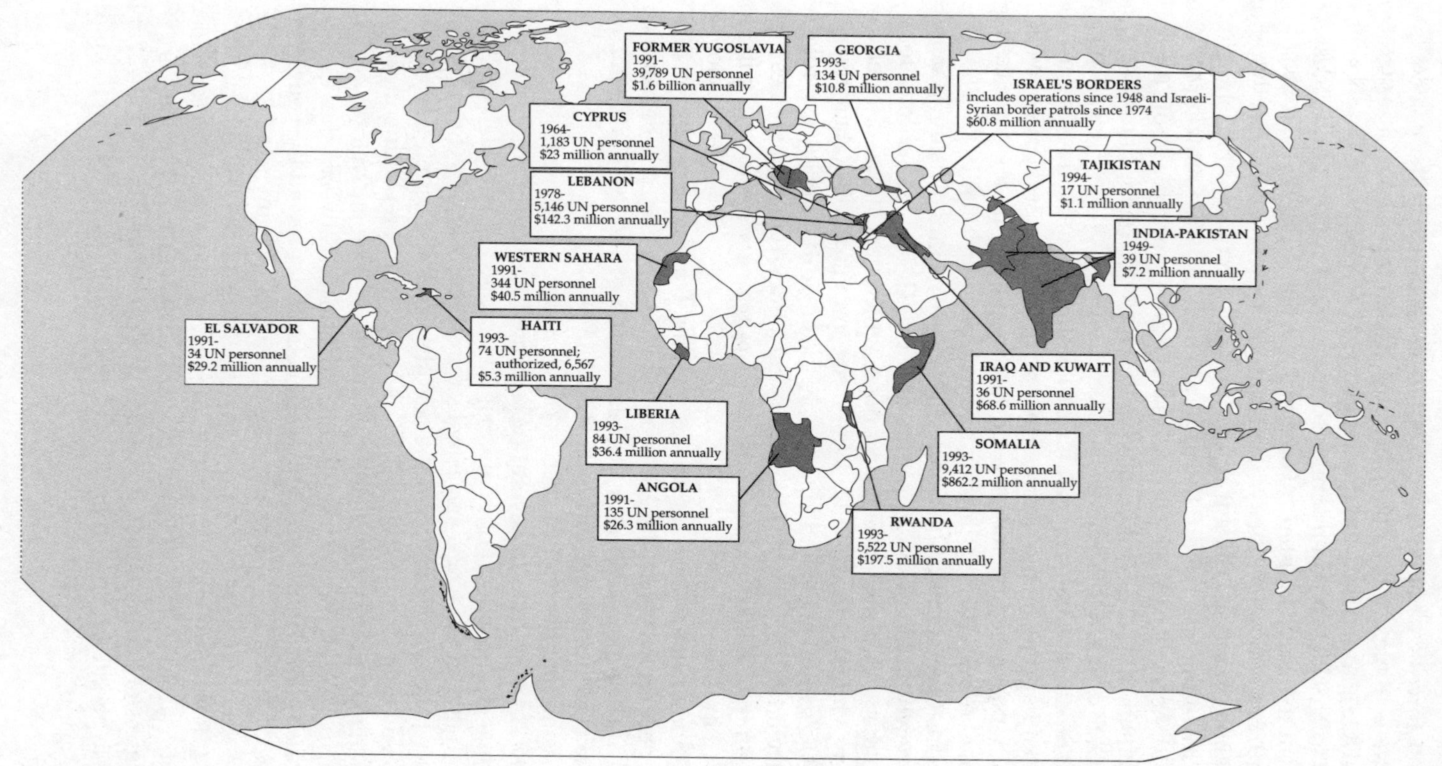

FIGURE 4.2 UN Peacekeeping Around the World (as of January 1995). *Source:* Compiled from UN.

Israeli forces by supervising a buffer zone between the combatants. A separate force, the United Nations Disengagement Observer Force (UNDOF), supervised the disengagement of Syrian and Israeli forces on the Golan Heights and a similar buffer zone. A fourth Middle East force, the United Nations Interim Force in Lebanon (UNIFIL), was established in 1978 to monitor the withdrawal of Israeli forces from southern Lebanon and assist the government of Lebanon in reestablishing its authority in the area. UNEF II was terminated in 1979 following the Camp David Accords, whose provisions have been monitored by a non-UN Multinational Force and Observers that includes one U.S. battalion. Both UNDOF and UNIFIL remain in place despite UNIFIL's inability to prevent repeated Israeli raids and the vulnerability of its members to attack and kidnapping by the various warring groups in southern Lebanon.

UN peacekeeping forces were also deployed in the former Belgian Congo (now Zaire) following its independence in 1960. The United Nations Operation in the Congo (ONUC) was initially designed to help the newly independent government establish law and order and to ensure the withdrawal of Belgian troops, which had returned to the Congo when violence broke out. When the province of Katanga seceded, ONUC's mission expanded to restore the territorial integrity of the Congo and avert full-scale war. The controversial operation, which led the UN to the brink of bankruptcy because of disputes over payment for the force, ended in 1964.

Another operation, the United Nations Force in Cyprus (UNFICYP), has been in existence since 1964 to provide a buffer zone between Greek and Turkish populations on the island of Cyprus. UNFICYP remained in place even during the Turkish invasion in 1974.

Evaluating the relative success of peacekeeping in the Cold War period is not an easy task. In several cases armed hostilities were stopped, but permanent resolution of many disputes proved elusive. UNEF I averted war between the Arabs and Israelis for eleven years. UNEF II was one of many factors that facilitated the negotiation of the Israeli-Egyptian peace agreement at Camp David. ONUC succeeded in preventing the secession of Katanga province and, at a minimal level, helped restore order in the Congo. UNFICYP averted overt hostilities between the Greek and Turkish communities on Cyprus but could not prevent the coup d'état by Greek officers in 1974 or the subsequent Turkish invasion. UNDOF can take credit, at least in part, for the quietness of the Golan Heights since 1974. For those whose definition of success is the peaceful settlement of conflicts, only UNEF II would be deemed successful. If success is defined in terms of ending armed hostilities and preventing their renewal at least for a period of time, then all the operations except UNIFIL could be

UNIFIL observers in southern Lebanon in late 1990 staff an observation post. UN Photo 157853/John Isaac.

deemed successful. Secretary-General Boutros Boutros-Ghali characterizes these thirteen pre-1988 Cold War peacekeeping operations as follows:

> They were largely military in composition and their tasks were to monitor cease-fires, control buffer zones, investigate alleged arms flows, prevent a resumption of hostilities and so on. In other words, they were to maintain calm on the front lines and give time to the peace-makers to negotiate a settlement of the dispute which had led to conflict in the first place. Sometimes the peace-*makers* succeeded. More often they did not, which is why so many of the pre-1988 operations are still in the field.[8]

Many important issues of peace and security in the Cold War era, including the Vietnam conflict, never made it to the UN agenda. The innovation of peacekeeping, however, provided a valuable means for limiting superpower involvement in regional conflicts (with their consent) and coping with the threats to peace and security posed by the emergence of new states, border conflicts among those states, and intractable conflicts in the Middle East. The UN also developed a body of experience and practice in peacekeeping that has proven even more valuable in the transition period of the late 1980s and in the post–Cold War era.

Transition Period, 1986–1989

The most striking feature of UN efforts to deal with threats to international peace and security in the late 1980s was the cooperation among the five permanent members of the Security Council in supporting not only peacekeeping but also peacemaking in a series of long-standing regional conflicts. Never before in the forty years of the UN's existence had there been such consensus. With the acquiescence of the nonpermanent members and new collaboration between the Security Council and the secretary-general, UN peacekeepers chalked up a series of successes that led to the Nobel Peace Prize in 1988.

The single most important factor contributing to this development was the dramatic set of changes in Soviet foreign policy initiated by Mikhail Gorbachev. In early 1986 the Soviets began to pay close attention to the quiet efforts of Diego Cordovez, an assistant to Secretary-General Pérez de Cuéllar, to mediate the Afghan conflict and to find ways in which the UN could facilitate the withdrawal of Soviet forces. These small signals took on more significance with the 1987 publication in *Pravda* of an article by Gorbachev in which he noted, "We are arriving at the conclusion that wider use should be made of the institution of UN military observers and UN peace-keeping forces in disengaging the troops of warring sides, observing ceasefire and armistice agreements. . . . The Security Council permanent members could become guarantors of regional security."[9] To back up this verbal commitment, the Soviet Union announced that it would pay up financial arrears of $127 million, including assessments for UN peacekeeping forces it had long opposed. Thus, Gorbachev's speech and actions represented a new Soviet commitment to the United Nations.

A second important factor that contributed to changing Soviet and other permanent members' perceptions of the role the UN could play with respect to regional conflicts was the quiet diplomacy of Pérez de Cuéllar and his aides. During the first half of the 1980s the secretary-general and others patiently sustained discussions with Iran and Iraq over possible bases for ending their war and with the various parties in Afghanistan over terms for Soviet withdrawal.

The peacekeeping successes of the late 1980s also required a reversal in the attitude of the United States, which under the Reagan administration had become increasingly hostile to the UN and many of its specialized agencies.[10] In 1985 the U.S. Congress reduced U.S. contributions to the UN below the assessed amounts. The United States was not the only country that was delinquent in its contributions, but when one country contributes 25 percent of an organization's regular budget, failure to pay creates a financial crisis. By late 1987, however, there were signs that the Reagan administration's antagonism toward the UN was moderating. The alterations in Soviet attitude and reforms in the UN administrative and budgetary processes as well as evidence of UN successes in conflict management contributed to the changes.

The attitudes of the two superpowers, then, were critical ingredients in facilitating UN efforts to end the war between Iran and Iraq, the Soviet presence in Afghanistan, the long stalemate over Namibia, and conflict in Central America. Successes in each of these regional conflict arenas spurred unprecedented interest in the possibilities of UN peacekeeping. We highlight aspects of the operations in Afghanistan, Namibia, and Central America.

Afghanistan. In 1988 the quiet efforts by UN mediator Diego Cordovez to find a way to facilitate Soviet withdrawal from Afghanistan paid off. Under pressure to devote more resources to domestic economic needs, and with counterinsurgency operations against Afghan mujahideen threatening to prolong a costly presence indefinitely, Gorbachev agreed to withdraw Soviet troops from Afghanistan. Fifty UN observers under the United Nations Good Offices Mission in Afghanistan and Pakistan (UNGOMAP) monitored and verified the withdrawal of more than 100,000 Soviet troops, with a schedule for withdrawal and a map of routes furnished by the Soviets, outposts at major border crossings and airports, and regular meetings with Afghan and Soviet military representatives. These innovations would have been impossible during the height of the Cold War. Yet they illustrated the utility of a small number of UN soldiers observing the agreed departure of combat troops—"a face-saving device" that would prove to be a helpful component in other negotiated settlements, such as Angola in 1988. Unfortunately Soviet withdrawal did not end the conflict in Afghanistan, which continues in the mid-1990s largely unnoticed by the UN and world community.

Angola and Namibia. Also in August 1988 an agreement on the withdrawal of Cuban and South African forces in Angola opened the way to the implementation of UN Security Council Resolution 435, which had been approved ten years earlier in September 1978 to provide a framework for Namibia's independence. In the 1970s the independence of Namibia, a former German colony administered by South Africa since the end of World War I, was the subject of intense efforts by five major Western powers acting outside of but in close cooperation with the UN to bring South Africa, the main liberation group in Namibia, SWAPO (South West Africa People's Organization), and the so-called Front Line states in southern Africa to an agreement. The Western powers' ad hoc efforts led to the agreement embodied in the Security Council resolution but were unsuccessful in getting South Africa to undertake the next steps—implementation. Lack of progress was blamed on the Soviet-backed Cuban presence in Angola, which supported the Angolan government in the ongoing civil war in that country. The South Africans perceived that presence as a direct threat to their security and, after the Reagan administration took office, they gained support from the United States in that view. In 1981 Assistant Secretary of State for African Affairs Chester A. Crocker linked a Namibian settlement to removal of Soviet and Cuban troops.

In February 1988 Cuba and Angola finally agreed to a withdrawal of Cuban troops as part of a regional peace settlement; in June the United States and Soviet Union jointly announced a target date for the withdrawal of foreign forces from Angola and for Namibian independence. By December the agreement was in place, and the UN was moving to mount the two peacekeeping operations required: the UN Angola Verification Mission (UNAVEM I) and the UN Transition Assistance Group (UNTAG). As in Afghanistan, a small number of UN military observers provided a valuable component to the agreement among Cuba, Angola, and South Africa. Between January 1989 and June 1991 seventy soldiers monitored the withdrawal of Cuban troops from Angola.

By contrast, UNTAG, deployed in April 1989, was not a traditional peacekeeping force. Its mandate included a diverse set of tasks, such as requiring military, police, and civilian personnel to create conditions for an electoral campaign in Namibia; securing the repeal of discriminatory and restrictive legislation, the release of political prisoners, and the return of exiles; conducting a free and fair election; monitoring the cease-fire and protecting against infiltration of the Namibian/Angolan border; monitoring the conduct of the local police and the departure from Namibia of the

Symbol of Namibian peacekeeping operation.

South African Defence Force; and monitoring the confinement to bases of SWAPO forces. For almost one year UNTAG, with personnel from 109 countries, played a vital role in creating conditions and supervising the process by which Namibia moved step by step from a cease-fire to independence. Because of the variety of tasks peacekeepers undertook in Namibia, UNTAG is frequently referred to as the first in the new (second) generation of peacekeeping operations.

Central America. The final peacekeeping operation of the transition period took place in Central America, where the United Nations Observer Group in Central America (ONUCA) played a key part in the peace process that ended protracted conflicts in that region. ONUCA was complemented by the UN Observer Mission to Verify the Electoral Process in Nicaragua (UNOVEN) and subsequently by the UN Observer Mission in El Salvador (ONUSAL). Although only ONUCA fits the criteria of a traditional peacekeeping operation, the three together played an important part in assisting the parties concerned in controlling and resolving the conflicts in the region, thus illustrating the complexity of peacekeeping and, most definitely in this case, of peacemaking.

UNOVEN consisted of civilian election observers who were deployed from August 1989 to February 1990 when the Nicaraguan elections took place under the scrutiny of the Organization of American States (OAS), nongovernmental organizations, and the UN. In November 1989 ONUCA deployed more than one thousand military observers to verify the implementation of the Esquipulas II Agreement. With two successive expansions of its mandate, ONUCA was charged with ensuring the cessation of aid to insurrectionist forces, the nonuse of the territory of one state for attacks on others, and the disarmament of demobilized forces. Its work covered the territory of five Central American states, although most was concentrated in Nicaragua and Honduras, and was completed in July 1992.

Overlapping ONUCA and initiated in the post–Cold War era to monitor agreements concluded between the government of El Salvador and the Frente Farabundo Martí para la Liberación Nacional (FMLN), ONUSAL marked a new step for UN peacekeepers of monitoring and verifying human rights violations and making recommendations for their future elimination. Military and police personnel as well as civilian staff investigated allegations of human rights violations and followed them up with competent state organs and with the FMLN. Their purpose was to establish the veracity of allegations and to monitor the actions taken to identify and punish perpetrators as well as to deter future violations. The peacekeepers also initiated human rights and information programs. The military and police divisions supervised the separation and redeployment of government and insurgent forces as well as the formation and training of a national civil police. Civilian monitors observed the March and April 1994 elections to ensure fairness.

Thus, the transition period of the late 1980s was marked by a change in the two superpowers' attitudes toward the UN and the possibilities of UN peacekeeping. The United Nations itself, with the cooperation between the secretary-general and Security Council, devised a number of innovative arrangements beyond the scope of traditional peacekeeping, including verification of troop withdrawals by a superpower and the conduct and monitoring of elections. These developments made it possible to manage a series of long-standing regional conflicts (although in the case of both Angola and Afghanistan, the conflicts continue despite the withdrawal of superpower involvement) and fueled the post–Cold War demand for peacekeeping and peacemaking. The 1988 Nobel Peace Prize was awarded to UN peacekeeping forces in recognition of their "decisive contribution toward the initiation of actual peace negotiations."

POST–COLD WAR ERA

Gulf War

The UN's first post–Cold War challenge came with Iraq's invasion and annexation of Kuwait in August 1990.[11] Iraq's aggression was well documented and almost universally condemned, even by the Soviet Union, despite its long-standing relationship with Iraq. Unity among four of the permanent members of the Security Council and China's abstention facilitated four types of UN activities. First, the Security Council imposed economic sanctions and in Resolution 678 (November 29, 1990) authorized member states "to use all necessary means" to restore the status quo ante. This legitimized the military action that began on January 16, 1991. Second, after Iraqi forces were ousted from Kuwait, the UN sent in a peacekeeping force, the UN Iraq-Kuwait Observer Mission (UNIKOM), to monitor the demilitarized zone between Iraq and Kuwait. Third, in response to Iraq's pressure on the Kurdish and Shiite populations within its borders, the UN undertook humanitarian intervention and provision of a safe haven for refugees. Fourth, IAEA and a special UN Disarmament Commission were charged with monitoring and dismantling Iraq's nuclear, chemical, and biological weapons programs. All of these activities continued in some way in 1994. They represent a variety of responses the UN has developed for dealing with a threat to international peace and security—albeit one that is unlikely to be duplicated in the foreseeable future.

Between August 2 and November 29, 1990, the Security Council approved twelve successive resolutions activating Chapter VII of the Charter in an effort to secure Iraqi withdrawal. These condemned the invasion, declared that it constituted a breach of international peace, demanded immediate and unconditional withdrawal, and authorized the imposition of mandatory measures. The resolutions imposed comprehensive, mandatory sanctions under Article 41; declared Iraq's annexation null and void; legalized enforcement of the embargo (e.g., stopping ships at sea) and expanded it to include air traffic; and demanded release of hostages. January 15, 1991, was set as the deadline for Iraq's compliance.

The military operation launched on January 16, 1991, was *not* a peacekeeping operation. Indeed, it did not qualify as a collective security action under Article 42 of the Charter either, though it has been portrayed as such by many people. The U.S.-led multinational coalition was rather a type of subcontract . . . acting on behalf of the organization.[12] Unlike the Korean situation in the early 1950s, UN flags and symbols were not used in the military action. Nor was the United States responsible to the authority of the UN through regular reporting and participation by UN personnel in decisionmaking. Between January 15 and March 2 the UN faded from the picture as U.S.-led bombing raids and ground action forced Iraqi withdrawal from Kuwait. With that goal secured, attention turned again to the Security Council to set the conditions for peace with a long series of resolutions.

In April 1991 the Security Council authorized the secretary-general to demarcate the boundary between Iraq and Kuwait and send an observer unit to monitor the cease-fire and a demilitarized zone. It demanded the unconditional destruction of chemical and biological weapons as well as ballistic missiles, formed a special commission to oversee this activity, and authorized the IAEA to inspect and destroy known and suspected nuclear facilities and materials. The resolution also made Iraq liable for environmental and other damages, created a fund for compensation (to be drawn partly from Iraq's petroleum revenues), and continued the economic sanctions with the exception of food and medicines. Thus, the resolutions addressed three broad categories of issues: the boundary between Iraq and Kuwait, the future of Iraq's military capabilities, and Iraqi liability for losses and damages to foreign governments, nationals, and corporations as well as the environment.

The unarmed UNIKOM force reports on violations of the demilitarized zone (including minor incursions by soldiers and overflights by military aircraft) and investigates complaints. What has distinguished UNIKOM from traditional peacekeeping operations is the absence of Iraqi consent, the normal prerequisite for such activities.

The effort to maintain peace in the region by destroying Iraq's chemical, biological, and nuclear weapons capabilities represents a further innovation in enforcement. Prior to the war IAEA had inspected Iraqi nuclear facilities but concluded that it was not involved in a covert weapons program. The postwar effort revealed the weaknesses of these earlier inspections and, indeed, of IAEA and the nonproliferation regime of which it is a central part. Despite these weaknesses, IAEA and the UN Special Commission for the Disarmament of Iraq (UNSCOM) took on the charge to inspect nondesignated sites and dismantle missile production and other facilities. This was the first time the Security Council undertook enforcement of IAEA safeguards.

In carrying out these tasks, IAEA inspection teams have encountered repeated problems, including detention and denial of access to documents and facilities. One showdown in July 1992 resulted in an eighteen-day "siege" of Iraq's Agricultural Ministry by UN officials waiting outside in parked vehicles. Despite the problems, the inspectors gathered extensive information on Iraq's nuclear program, evidence of the biological weapons program, and lists of foreign suppliers. What gives the entire

Members of the UNSCOM team from Japan and Switzerland verify the number of chemical weapons in an Iraqi storage site during an October–November 1991 visit. UN Photo 158681/H. Arvidsson.

effort "clout" is the requirement that no Iraqi petroleum may be exported or civilian goods imported until UNSCOM certifies the total dismantlement of the nuclear, biological, chemical, and ballistic missile programs. Nonetheless, Special Commission chairman Rolf Ekeus concedes that in all likelihood, once the sanctions are removed, Iraq's unconventional weapons programs will "sprout up again like mushrooms after the rain."[13]

The sight of thousands of Kurds fleeing Iraqi repression into Iran and Turkey and many more trapped in the open on mountains inside the Turkish-Iraqi border led to humanitarian intervention on behalf of the Kurds and another pathbreaking step for the UN. The Security Council condemned Iraqi repression as a threat to international peace and security—an unprecedented intervention in the domestic affairs of a sovereign member state—and authorized humanitarian NGOs to offer assistance. Thus, it linked humanitarian and security issues. However, the Kurdish problem was not just an internal Iraqi affair. According to UN estimates, 750,000 Iraqi Kurds crossed the border into Iran, 280,000 fled to Turkey, and another 300,000 were amassed on the mountainsides along the Turkish border.

The hide-and-seek of weapons inspection in Iraq. Matt/*The Telegraph plc,* London/Rothco.

Because of the objections to UN intervention, the United States and other Western allies (Great Britain, France, the Netherlands, Spain, Italy, and Germany) created refugee havens for the Kurds under Operation Provide Comfort. They also established "no-fly" zones to keep out Iraqi aircraft both in the north and later in the south, where Shiite refugees were located. Subsequently, a representative of the secretary-general and UNHCR took over the humanitarian tasks.

Though the U.S.-led military action in the Gulf was widely regarded as exemplifying a new, stronger, post–Cold War UN, that role, as distinct from the UNIKOM mission, came under critical scrutiny. Lacking a direct link to the UN, most UN members had no say in the operation. Germany and Japan, which were expected to contribute monetary resources for the collective action, were excluded from important decision making meetings (which fueled their interest in permanent membership on the Security Council). And developing states, although supporting the action, worried about precedents for UN interference in states' internal affairs and the diminution of national sovereignty when the UN-supported construction of refugee havens for the Kurds in northern Iraq under the justification of humanitarianism. The long-time Arab League representative at the UN, Clovis Maksoud, captured the concerns of many when he noted, "U.S. domination of the proceedings, the precipitous rush to war, the open-ended language of some of the resolutions adopted—these and other aspects of the U.N.'s response to the Gulf crisis raise serious questions about the ability of the organization to serve the interests of the world community and not merely or primarily those of its most powerful states."[14]

The Gulf War thus highlighted an important problem of the post–Cold War era: "The ambivalence of many states toward a stronger UN is now coupled with apprehension about a pax Americana, even a UN-centered one, without a Soviet counterweight."[15] Yet the Gulf War did leave a generally positive legacy for the UN in the minds of many people, especially Americans. Even more perhaps than the increased demands for UN peacekeeping, it illustrated what McGeorge Bundy, former U.S. national security adviser, described as "the astonishing role that has been played—and is still being played—by the U.N. Security Council. It is a role that no one can yet claim to understand fully; the principal participants are still learning as they go, and each new resolution has been more astonishing than the one before."[16]

Post–Gulf War Period

Since the conclusion of the Gulf War, the UN has launched fourteen new operations—in Angola, El Salvador, Western Sahara, Cambodia, Yugoslavia, Somalia, Mozambique, Georgia, Liberia, Rwanda, Haiti, and South Africa. (See Figure 4.2.) These post–Cold War efforts to respond to conflicts have required further innovations in traditional peacekeeping tasks—a second generation of operations that include military, political, social, humanitarian, and environmental dimensions. There is little doubt that the dramatic demand for and support of UN peacekeeping and peacemaking activities stem from the experiences of the transition period in the mid-1980s, the response to the Gulf crisis, the speed and thoroughness with which the Soviet Union was dismembered, the withdrawal of superpower support for many Third World states, and a set of persistent regional conflicts. Most are responses to problems within states rather than between them, problems arising from weak institutions, secessions, ethnic and tribal clashes, and civil wars.

More than ever before the UN is being called on to use force in ways never envisioned by the framers. One of the most dramatic changes in the post–Cold War era is the frequent use of the Chapter VII provisions for enforcement action as well as greater use of force in peacekeeping. But with these changes, one observer suggests, "the UN has entered a domain of military activity—a vaguely defined no-man's-land lying somewhere between traditional peacekeeping and enforcement—for which it lacks any guiding operational concept."[17]

Peacemaking or peace building represents a further set of innovations designed to create an environment in which peace can be sustained. The combination of military and civilian activities it encompasses includes protecting relief shipments and aid workers, aiding refugees, monitoring human rights, removing mines, disarming warring parties, undertaking administrative management, building institutions, restoring infrastructure and services such as basic utilities (water, electric power, transportation), and preparing for, conducting, and monitoring elections.

As democracy has spread around the world during the post–Cold War era, the UN has been in heavy demand to assist with elections in many countries. This involvement has not necessarily been linked to peacekeeping and peacemaking activity. Among the countries for which the UN has provided technical assistance with elections in their transitions from authoritarianism to democratic rule are Albania, El Salvador, Ethiopia, Guyana, Mali, Zambia, Malawi, and South Africa.

We focus on three major undertakings: Cambodia, Somalia, and the former Yugoslavia. In particular, the UN's experience in the former Yugoslavia and in Somalia exemplifies the problems associated with enforcement and humanitarian intervention. Cambodia illustrates well the second generation of peacekeeping and peace-building operations. Both, by their very size and complexity, have taxed the resources of the UN and the commitment of member states.

Cambodia. In October 1991 the Agreements on a Comprehensive Political Settlement of the Cambodia Conflict were signed in Paris.

An UNTAG election monitor verifies a ballot during Namibia's 1989 elections. UN Photo 157134/Milton Grant.

Cooperation between the United States and the Soviet Union provided the impetus for China and Vietnam to support a cease-fire in Cambodia, demobilization of the armies, repatriation of 350,000 refugees, and elections by mid-1993. The four Cambodian parties accepted the framework of the settlement and agreed to form the Supreme National Council as the authority in Cambodia during the transition period. Security Council Resolution 718 on October 31, 1991, requested the secretary-general to prepare a detailed plan of implementation.

The UN was given a central role in implementation, including responsibility for administering the country during an eighteen-month transition period. A small advance mission was to facilitate communication among the four Cambodian parties to maintain the cease-fire prior to deployment of UNTAC in March 1992. UNTAC exercised direct control over Cambodia's defense, foreign affairs, finance, public security, and information administrative structures to ensure a neutral political environment prior to general elections. It also monitored the police, promoted human rights, and organized the elections that turned authority back to Cambodians themselves. The military component of UNTAC was charged with a variety of tasks associated with supervising the cease-fire and disarming and demobilizing forces. UNTAC was also charged with the repatriation and resettlement of refugees in cooperation with UNHCR and with the rehabilitation of basic infrastructure and public utilities. Never before had so many UN peacekeepers been asked to undertake such diverse and complex tasks in a single operation. The seven distinct components of UNTAC's mandate engaged up to twenty-two thousand military and civilian personnel at the peak period. As Secretary-General Boutros Boutros-Ghali noted, "Nothing the UN has ever done can match this operation."[18]

The problems, however, were formidable, and as of mid-1994 the long-term outlook remained uncertain. The most critical problem all along had been the Khmer Rouge, the Maoist-inspired rebels under whose rule in the 1970s an estimated 1 million Cambodians perished. They refused to put their soldiers under UN supervision and to participate in the elections. UN personnel were attacked, and violence against Cambodians threatened to disrupt the elections. Without the cooperation of all four parties, it was difficult to envision how the election results could be respected as the basis of a new government. Nonetheless, in September 1993 the secretary-general declared UNTAC's role in Cambodia ended with the installation of a new constitution and government based on the will of the people expressed through the May 1993 elections. Peacekeepers were withdrawn in phases over the next three months, and a small contingent of military observers remained for monitoring the tenuous peace.

Elsewhere the UN found itself facing post–Cold War challenges of a very different kind, with no peace to keep and humanitarian concerns raising demands for intervention with no clear guidelines on how to proceed. The principles of consent, impartiality, and nonuse of force (or minimal use of force) that had served traditional peacekeeping operations so well seemed inappropriate. In neither the former Yugoslavia nor Somalia did the parties show much will to maintain a cease-fire or to settle their differences through negotiation. Both cases illustrate the problems of enforcement linked with peacemaking, of commitment and willingness to sustain casualties, and of ambivalence over mandates.

Somalia. In 1991 and 1992 civil order totally collapsed in the east African country of Somalia as warring clans seized control of parts of the country. Widespread death and famine accompanied the fighting, forcing hundreds of thousands of civilians to need emergency humanitarian assistance. Control of food was a vital political resource for the Somali warlords and a currency to pay the mercenary gangs that formed their militias. International relief was delayed for months because the Security Council assumed that it had to have the consent of the Somali warlords to

act. A small (five-hundred-troop) contingent of lightly armed Pakistani troops (the UN Mission in Somalia, or UNOSOM I) finally sent to Somalia in August 1992 with a mandate to protect relief workers and food deliveries proved totally inadequate. Meanwhile, in fall 1992 it was reported that an estimated one thousand Somalis were dying daily and that three-quarters of Somalia's children under the age of five had perished. International relief agencies were forced to hire their own security, thus subsidizing the clan militias and prolonging the fighting.

In November the secretary-general informed the Security Council that the situation "had deteriorated beyond the point at which it is susceptible to the peacekeeping treatment. . . . The Security Council now has no alternative but to decide to adopt more forceful measures."[19] On December 3 Security Council Resolution 794 authorized a large U.S.-led military-humanitarian intervention (Unified Task Force on Somalia, or UNITAF, also known to U.S. audiences as Operation Restore Hope) to secure ports and airfields, protect relief shipments and workers, and assist humanitarian relief efforts. Almost immediately disputes arose over UNITAF's mandate. The resolution itself referred only to establishing "a secure environment for humanitarian relief operations" and "a prompt transition to continued peacekeeping." The secretary-general clearly wanted the U.S.-

led force to undertake political-military tasks, imposing a cease-fire and disarming the factions. The Bush and Clinton administrations just as clearly expressed their objectives in humanitarian terms and were determined to commit U.S. forces only for a limited time.

As one observer notes, "There could be no such thing as a purely humanitarian intervention for Somalia. Even a narrowly conceived humanitarian mission was political in Somalia's context because it denied the clans the ability to manipulate food as a tool of political control."[20] Likewise, the peacekeepers could not limit their efforts to guarding food at airports, in convoys, and at distribution centers. Despite these problems, UNITAF was largely successful in achieving its humanitarian objectives, easing the famine, and freeing food supplies from the warlords' control. It also imposed a de facto cease-fire in areas of its deployment, which facilitated peacemaking efforts. Yet despite these accomplishments, the larger tasks of peacemaking in Somalia remained. With the dispute between the United States and the secretary-general over the mandate and duration of UNITAF (and especially the length of stay of the U.S. forces) having taken place in full public view, the warlords could easily conclude that time was on their side. "The factions signed ceasefire and disarmament agreements which they had no intention of keeping as long as they knew the bulk of U.S. forces would soon be withdrawn, and that such agreements might not be enforced."[21] And, indeed, 1993 brought far more difficulties for the UN efforts in Somalia as UNITAF was replaced by UNISOM II.

UNISOM II was a larger and more heavily armed force than peacekeeping contingents were. It was authorized to use force in disarming the factions, but that increased risk to the peacekeepers. Twenty-three Pakistani soldiers died when the contingent was attacked by the militia of Somali warlord General Mohamed Farah Aidid. In the summer of 1993 the UN gave up any pretense of impartiality when it targeted General Aidid for elimination. "The UN war on Aidid put UNOSOM in the worst of all possible worlds, which past peacekeepers had scrupulously avoided, . . . [and] made it one of the players in the conflict."[22] Rifts opened within UNISOM when the Italian force commander continued to negotiate with all factions, including Aidid, despite the UN secretary-general's insistence on not negotiating with those who killed peacekeepers. Conflicts over participation in operational planning and control also simmered, fueled by U.S. insistence on not placing U.S. troops under UN command.

The deaths of eighteen U.S. soldiers in Mogadishu in October 1993 and the resulting public outcry in the United States echoed public unease in other countries over the UN's role in Somalia. The Clinton administration was forced to rethink its commitment to UN peacekeeping, especially those operations that entailed casualties. Most immediately affected were UNOSOM, Bosnia, and Haiti. Within days, in fact, the United States halted the landing of U.S. troops and advisers in Haiti, where they were to help in the transition to a democratic government, because demonstrators in Port-au-Prince threatened to create "another Somalia."

UNOSOM remains a controversial and uncertain undertaking. As one scholar concludes, "That the U.S. wanted to keep the operation short, and was afraid to take any casualties, gave UNOSOM's enemies a source of leverage by targeting U.S. and other soldiers. Complex Chapter VII operations which require a great deal of staying power cannot be effective if troop-contributing countries, especially the world's sole remaining superpower, fly into a panic when uncooperative local factions play rough."[23] Humanitarian objectives must be linked to political ones—to peacemaking—to ensure that the conditions leading to hunger are not allowed to continue.

The Somali operation took place in what might best be described as a "failed" state, where the concept of sovereignty was virtually meaningless and where media images of famine propelled humanitarian intervention into a complex internal struggle. It highlighted institutional weaknesses within the UN and the importance of the secretary-general's leadership in steering the UN's path through situations in which impartiality is difficult to maintain.

We turn next to a situation that has posed even more problems than Somalia and raised even more questions about how best to deal with post–Cold War conflicts.

Yugoslavia. Yugoslavia was a field on which the Cold War competition between East and West was played out and where centuries-old fault lines of ethnic, religious, political, cultural, and historical differences were frozen and buried for half a century. The collapse of the Yugoslav Communist Party in 1990 unleashed conflicts whose ferocity has shocked those who imagined that Europe was immune from such horrors. The issues raised by the unraveling of Yugoslavia go to the heart of the nature of the international order and international law in the post–Cold War era, touching questions of self-determination, individual and group rights, and the exercise and limits of sovereignty. The UN has repeatedly debated whether to intervene, to what end, and with what means. European institutions, notably the European Union, the Conference on Security and Cooperation in Europe (CSCE), the Western European Union (WEU), and NATO, have all been involved in efforts to address the Yugoslav conflict. Peacekeeping efforts in Yugoslavia have confronted complex domestic realities, massive and systematic violations of human rights, demands for enforcement action verging on war making (e.g., bombing), and very little interest by the parties in making peace. The Yugoslav case illustrates why the key to successful peacekeeping in the past has been the readiness of the parties to cooperate.

The civil war in Yugoslavia was brought about by the Serbian leadership's attempts to maintain the country's unity in the face of strong separatist movements in Slovenia, Croatia, and Bosnia-Herzegovina. The former two republics declared their independence in June 1991, followed by Bosnia-Herzegovina and Macedonia in 1992. During 1991 the UN largely deferred to EU and CSCE members that sought to negotiate cease-fires among the warring ethnic groups. This effort was consistent with Chapter VII of the UN Charter, which stipulated that regional organizations make every effort to resolve local disputes before referring them to the Security Council. Although EU mediation was successful with respect to the independence of Slovenia, the Europeans could not agree on what their role should be with respect to the rest of Yugoslavia. Should diplomatic recognition be extended to the other self-proclaimed republics, such as Croatia? If so, when? Should sanctions be applied against Serbia? Should the Europeans supply forces to protect the newly created borders? Diplomatic efforts continued in spite of the EU's inability to agree on these questions. Cease-fire agreements were negotiated and broken in rapid succession as fighting among the various groups increased.

On September 25, 1991, the UN Security Council appointed former Secretary of State of the United States Cyrus Vance as the secretary-general's personal envoy to Yugoslavia to assist with negotiations. Vance was ultimately successful in securing agreement from all the Yugoslav parties on the establishment of a UN peacekeeping operation, and the UN Protection Force for Yugoslavia was authorized in February 1992.

UNPROFOR was approved for an initial period of twelve months, with military and civilian personnel to be stationed in regions where Serbs and Croats were living in close proximity. In March 1992 the UN dispatched more than fourteen thousand peacekeepers to Yugoslavia, mostly to Croatia, a decision criticized for allowing the Serbians to concentrate their efforts on Bosnia-Herzegovina and its capital, Sarajevo. In May 1992 the Security Council imposed economic sanctions against the Serbian-dominated government of Yugoslavia (reduced to the territory of Serbia and Montenegro), reflecting the widespread Western view that Serbia's leader, Slobodan Milošević, was largely to blame for the ethnic chaos. In June 1992, with public pressure building to provide humanitarian assistance to the people of Sarajevo, the Security Council authorized the sending of peacekeepers there to reopen the airport and secure a truce to facilitate humanitarian relief efforts. UNPROFOR's restrictive mandate, however, precluded UN forces from intervening to halt the "ethnic cleansing" by Serbian regular and irregular forces that forced thousands of people, especially Bosnia's Muslims, to flee their homes—a gross viola-

Reprinted by permission of Tribune Media Services.

tion of human rights reminiscent of World War II atrocities. The UN did approve investigations of human rights abuses and war crimes.

Other institutions also responded. Both WEU and NATO sent naval forces to the Adriatic Sea to monitor compliance with the economic sanctions. UNHCR became the lead agency for coordinating the relief efforts of UN agencies and the International Committee of the Red Cross.

With the humanitarian situation throughout Bosnia increasingly desperate, UNPROFOR contingents were deployed in August 1992 to help assure the delivery of humanitarian aid and to monitor compliance with a ban on military flights. Subsequently Bosnian Serb violations of the flight ban prompted debate over U.S. proposals to strengthen enforcement. In December 1992, in an effort at preventive diplomacy, UNPROFOR troops, including a contingent of 300 U.S. soldiers, were deployed to Macedonia to forestall the expansion of the conflicts to that province of the former Yugoslavia, now an independent state.

As Serb forces harassed and held up relief convoys, shelled the airport at Sarajevo, and steadily tightened their siege of several cities, UN forces repeatedly faced the question of whether to use force to carry out their humanitarian mission, although authorized to do so. The issue was not only fear of triggering problems elsewhere but also lack of capabilities and will to fight a conventional war in support of the humanitarian operations. Nonetheless, UNPROFOR units provided the aid organizations and relief agencies with information on changing front lines in the war; accompanied convoys of relief supplies, sometimes escorting them with armored personnel carriers; rescued aid workers; airlifted supplies into cities and towns under siege; repaired roads; discouraged looting and harassment; and built confidence among civilians. By October 1993 the relief flights into Sarajevo's airport protected by UNPROFOR troops outnumbered those in the Berlin airlift of 1947.

There has been no lack of proponents for more aggressive approaches to the Bosnian situation. Sometimes differences have arisen between different commanders of UNPROFOR contingents (e.g., British and French) and between NATO headquarters and the UN's special representative, Yasushi Akashi. Generally, however, governments have been unwilling to back up the rhetoric of Security Council resolutions with more military force. The situation demands both a tougher, clearer mandate to use force other than in self-defense and larger numbers of troops with heavier weapons and equipment. By continuing to operate under the principle of consent, the UN has accepted the Serbs' refusal to permit the stationing of UN troops in areas they control. Ethnic cleansing can be going on in one area and humanitarian personnel be at risk for their very lives, and UNPROFOR troops are nowhere near. Thus, as one observer concludes, "the Yugoslav experience demonstrated the limitations not only of humanitarian action but also of force and political will."[24]

As of mid-1994 the economic sanctions had been further tightened, NATO air strikes had been used, the International Tribunal for Crimes in the Former Yugoslavia had been established, and peace plans and ceasefires had been negotiated. Yet the fighting continued and all sides were still obstructing relief efforts and targeting UNPROFOR, UNHCR, and other international aid personnel. The Security Council has passed a record number of resolutions in its effort to deal with the conflict, trying to provide legitimacy for a range of military activities. In the process, however, its very credibility has been eroded.

It has become increasingly clear that traditional methods of mediation and peacekeeping will not be sufficient to either halt the fighting or ensure aid to civilians. Despite Security Council authorization, the reluctance of governments and their militaries (especially those of Europe and Canada, which largely made up UNPROFOR until Russian contingents were added in 1994) to use force more extensively demonstrates the limitations of the UN's enforcement role except in cases where traditional transborder aggression has occurred and where strong national interests are at stake, as in the Gulf War.

Initially, the UN avoided involvement in Yugoslavia because the consensus held that primary responsibility for helping solve the conflict resided with European institutions. Once it became clear that the European institutions, especially the EU and CSCE, were not up to the task, pressures from other nations, especially members of the Islamic Conference concerned about the failure to protect the Bosnian Muslims, forced the UN to become involved. As in the case of Somalia, it is clear that the Security Council is prepared to authorize the use of force to help deliver humanitarian relief but is much more reluctant to authorize measures to remove or reduce the source of the problem. And, as we have seen, UNPROFOR commanders have generally declined to use force even to guarantee delivery of humanitarian aid. In the absence of commitment from the conflicting parties to a settlement, there can be little basis for peacemaking.

As one observer notes, the international community has been torn between two conceptions of its role in the post–Cold War world.[25] One argues the need for an active role in civil and ethnic conflict on the grounds of the fundamental importance of human rights and the consequences of global interdependence. The other contends that without the superpower confrontation, conflicts such as that in the former Yugoslavia are tragic but pose little danger to global stability and are too deep-seated to be susceptible to international intervention. Government leaders and publics alike have been caught between these two conceptions: horrified by the brutality of conflict so close to the center of Europe and reluctant to commit the lives of their own sons and daughters to what might well be a new Balkan war.

Rocky Road from Peacekeeping to Enforcement

Thus far in the post–Cold War period the UN has been called on to provide more peacekeeping forces than in any previous four-year period. As of mid-1994 more than eighty thousand troops and civilians were wearing the blue helmets of UN peacekeepers. Each of the major post–Cold War peacekeeping operations has added to the diversity of tasks for which UN forces may be used and has raised complex issues.

Of the two new directions—enforcement and peacemaking—the enforcement activities have proven, not surprisingly, the most controversial and problematic. In Bosnia and Somalia there was no peace to be kept, and there was little interest in making peace. Since the displacement and cleansing of Muslims in Bosnia were deliberate objectives of the Serbs and domestic anarchy and hunger were part of the Somali warlords' strategies, UN peacekeepers, even if limited to humanitarian missions, were not seen as an impartial presence. They were participants operating without the consent of the parties.

What makes post–Cold War peacekeeping, and especially enforcement, different from traditional concepts of collective security are the scale and nature of the conflicts. Rather than interstate aggression across established boundaries, many conflicts have been civil wars with international dimensions. Collective security traditionally assumed that since any nation might be a potential aggressor, all nations would be expected to gang up on the aggressor. The world has never proved so simple. Defining aggression has itself proved an elusive task. The veto provisions of the Charter clearly acknowledged that the UN would not be able to act against the major powers. The predominant military capability of the two superpowers in any case precluded the possibility of a coalition of other states with sufficient military force to serve as a deterrent, let alone enforcer against either the United States or Soviet Union. Thus, Korea and the Gulf War have shown that collective security and enforcement are most likely to involve ad hoc coalitions of states. And they are most likely to include the major powers so that a force of appropriate size, equipment, and capability can be mustered. This reality is an uncomfortable one for many small and weak states in the UN because it magnifies the role of the major powers, especially of the United States, making the former feel vulnerable to the latter's interests and objectives.

The UN's record of peacekeeping successes has been tarnished, however, by the problems encountered in Somalia, Haiti, and Yugoslavia and the inability of the organization to respond to the massive killings of Rwandan civilians. It remains to be seen how durable the UN's peacemaking efforts in Cambodia will prove to be over time or how new roles, such as human rights monitoring and promotion, election assistance, and civil administration, will be applied in the future.

The heavy demand for UN peacekeeping has also dramatically increased the financial resources, personnel, equipment, and training required to support operations. Member states are far quicker to approve new peacekeeping operations than to meet their financial commitments. Proposals to strengthen the capacity of the UN to support peacekeeping have proliferated. We examine some of these as part of our concluding assessment of the past and future value of UN peacekeeping.

CONCLUSION

The UN's experience with peacekeeping has highlighted a number of lessons that represent key issues for the future. These issues relate directly to the dilemmas posed.

Consent of Parties: Challenges of Sovereignty

"For traditionalists, no requirement of peacekeeping is clearer than the consent of parties in conflict. . . . It is a political and operational imperative."[26] But opinions are changing on both the political and legal necessity of consent of the parties. The plight of Iraq's Kurds in spring 1991, Sarajevo's citizens besieged since 1992, and Somalia's starving thousands in 1992 highlighted justifications for humanitarian intervention without the consent of the parties. Strict adherence to a requirement for parties' consent will be impossible if the UN is to play any role in trying to manage or resolve conflicts involving insurgent ethnic groups and limited central government control, let alone "failed states."

What lends further support to moderating the adherence to the principle of consent is the changing views of sovereignty and of Charter Article 2(7)'s ban on UN interference in matters "essentially within the domestic jurisdiction" of states. Numerous precedents in the field of human rights, humanitarian relief, IMF and World Bank "conditionality," and the growing field of environmental law underscore the observation that "the time of absolute and exclusive sovereignty . . . has passed."[27] Indeed, sovereignty may be viewed more as belonging to people than to states or governments. Thus, the ways in which people respond to the dilemma of strict adherence to state sovereignty versus an acceptance of its erosion will have major implications for future uses of UN peacekeeping.

Support of Member States: Challenges of Commitment

The consensus among the permanent members of the Security Council that emerged in the late 1980s has been a critical variable in providing support for increased use of UN peacekeeping in very diverse circumstances. Such support is crucial both for an operation's success and for peacekeeping to be related to peacemaking. Yet we cannot assume consensus in the future. Following the December 1993 parliamentary elections in Russia, President Yeltsin adopted a more assertive tone toward the conflict in Bosnia, signaling Russia's desire not to be overlooked as a major power. Third World states' fears of a new pax Americana, or great power condominium, as a result of Security Council consensus have also not materialized as a real threat. The five permanent members no longer command, as they might have during the 1950s, the votes of the nonpermanent members. And as Somalia, Yugoslavia, and other situations have shown, "the breadth of values, interests, and perspectives represented at the UN tends to limit even the Council to expeditious and decisive intervention only in the exceptional cases, and then for ends considerably more limited than promoters of liberal values might prefer."[28]

Providing the necessary financial and logistical support for peacekeeping has long been a problem. Disputes over members' obligations led to a crisis for the organization in the early 1960s. Although the International Court of Justice in 1961 affirmed that peacekeeping expenses should be borne by all member states, in fact arrangements for financing vary. Observer missions are generally funded from assessed contributions. Peacekeeping operations have generally been funded through a modified version of the scale of assessments for the regular UN budget. Thus, the permanent members of the Security Council account for 57 percent of the peacekeeping budget. A few operations have been funded either by the parties themselves or voluntary contributions. But member states large and small are frequently in arrears. And as more peacekeeping operations are mounted, the financial strains increase. In 1987 the cost of peacekeeping was $233 million, in 1991 it doubled to $421 million, and in 1994 it was projected to reach $3.8 billion.

An additional dimension of the funding problem is the need for ready capital to enable the UN to respond immediately. A reserve fund has long since been exhausted. Only a small number of troop-contributing countries, such as Canada and the Nordic countries, can afford to sustain their troops in the field without reimbursement; for developing countries such as Fiji, India, and Ghana, lack of repayment constitutes a further burden on their own peoples. Under present conditions it is necessary to solicit funds when a new operation is launched, causing delays. Secretary-General Boutros-Ghali has proposed that a revolving capital fund be established to finance start-up costs, that member states pay immediately one-third of the estimated cost and pay other assessments on time, and that a reserve stock of commonly used equipment and supply items (such as field kitchens, water purification equipment, and tentage) be maintained. Without the commitment of funds necessary for more extensive UN peacekeeping operations, statements of support for the UN are moot.

The issue of personnel for peacekeeping is more than just a funding issue, however. Historically contingents have been drawn from middle and smaller powers, nonaligned and neutral countries being frequent contributors. As peacekeeping demands increase, however, more military units will be drawn from countries without UN peacekeeping experience. In his 1992 *An Agenda for Peace,* the secretary-general called for a standing UN police force to enable the organization to respond quickly to crises with trained contingents.[29] Operations with mandates to use force or in situations where there is no cease-fire in place also require heavier equipment and weapons than peacekeepers have traditionally needed. This will mean either drawing the contingents from countries that both have and will provide such equipment (which means largely Northern and Western countries) or getting troops and equipment from different sources.

After the experience in Somalia, the United States was notably reluctant to commit U.S. troops (and, by implication, to risk lives) for UN peacekeeping in Yugoslavia unless or until there was firm agreement on a peace settlement. In early 1994 the Clinton administration also adopted a narrow view on when the United States would support new operations as well as participate. The conditions include military aggression, natural disasters, attempts to subvert democracy, gross violations of human rights, as well as the involvement of U.S. interests, and a UN strategy for ending the intervention. These conditions were published in the Presidential Decision Directive known as PDD–25, which provides for U.S. forces to serve only under U.S. command (or under NATO command in the case of Yugoslavia). Key members of Congress have been skeptical about the introduction of any U.S. forces into the Yugoslav conflict unless or until there is firm agreement on a peace settlement. Efforts to pay up U.S. arrearages and maintain payments to the UN were frustrated by congressional budget cuts in fall 1993. Thus, the United States has retreated from providing leadership for UN peacekeeping, particularly when there is pressure for more interventionary action, such as in Somalia and Yugoslavia.

Operational Mandates and Organization: Challenges of UN Capacity

The operational mandates for peacekeeping operations provide guidelines for lawful action that UN-appointed commanders have to translate into practicable orders for the various military contingents and other personnel. Commanders prefer to have precise, clear mandates; diplomats, however, may prefer ambiguity, either because efforts to achieve clarity will lead to a breakdown in negotiations or because they wish to preserve leeway to influence future developments. For example, UN forces in Bosnia-Herzegovina have had a mandate to facilitate relief efforts, enforce a no-fly zone, and protect safe areas around Bosnian cities, but not to halt ethnic cleansing. They have been reluctant to use their mandate to confront the belligerents, preferring to use diplomacy to secure consent.

The issue of peacekeepers using force is thus particularly difficult. Most peacekeeping troops have been authorized to use force only in self-defense. In Nicaragua ONUCA was responsible for collecting and destroying weapons from the Nicaraguan resistance. Where future peacekeepers are expected to disarm local groups as in Somalia or Bosnia, they need clear mandates to use force if they are challenged, but they also need the political will to sustain casualties and to risk wider confrontation. And when force is authorized, rules of engagement are needed to ensure the use of force in a measured and restrained way.

The control and command of peacekeeping operations will be a critical issue as more UN peacekeepers are put in the field and responsibilities expand. To coordinate complex operations such as those in Namibia, Cambodia, or Central America and to provide a direct link to the secretary-general, his special representatives have been sent to the field. The Gulf War (and proposals from the former Soviet Union) revived interest in the moribund Military Staff Committee. The committee, composed of the chiefs of staff of the five permanent Security Council members, was designed under the UN Charter to be the key to managing UN enforcement actions. It was never activated. With or without its revival, the UN needs a structure to coordinate the military aspects of increased numbers of peacekeeping operations. The operations in Somalia and Yugoslavia have demonstrated the substantial problems of coordination when contingents drawn from more powerful countries do not answer only to UN command.

Other suggestions abound to strengthen the capacity of the UN to mount and support peacekeeping. These include the training of personnel, provision of logistical supports and appropriate armaments, and greater use of high technology for surveillance (such as remotely piloted vehicles and satellite monitoring). An added dimension of political support involves expanding the role of the secretary-general and increasing coordination between the Security Council and the secretary-general. The latter must be able to respond more quickly and flexibly to situations by assuming a more active role, identifying threats to peace, creating opportunities and an environment for negotiations, and ensuring that the United Nations does not become closely identified with one party. Secretary-General Boutros-Ghali has clearly taken an expansive definition of his responsibilities, noting in a 1993 address, "I am firmly committed to the concept of peace enforcement. It is essential if we are to strengthen international peace and security. But there is a new reality: member states are not ready for it. I must accept reality. I also must continue to give you my view."[30]

Future Uses

Many analysts of contemporary world politics predict increased violence within societies and between states as a result of the disintegration of the former Soviet Union and communist regimes in central Europe as well as a resurgence of ethnocentrism in many parts of the world. In the past the UN largely avoided dealing with issues of self-determination and secession beyond decolonization. It now faces new challenges.

The issue is not just whether there will be conflicts and situations where UN peacekeeping could be effective but also whether there will be political support to respond to such situations. Much as the end of the Cold War led to fears that international aid resources would be shifted from developing countries to Eastern Europe, there is a danger that conflicts in parts of Africa or elsewhere may be ignored. Yet by late 1993 the United States was not alone in recognizing that the United Nations cannot respond to every conflict in every corner of the globe. In the face of mounting violence throughout the world and mounting numbers of Security Council resolutions calling for action but failing to deliver, disillusion with the UN is likely to grow. Sir Brian Urquhart summed up the sentiments in late 1993 as follows: "After a brief post–Cold War honeymoon, the United Nations is once again suffering from the inability to enforce its decision in critical situations, this time without the excuse of the obstacles created by the Cold War."[31]

The United Nations will continue to be challenged as never before to respond to diverse threats to international peace and security. Meeting those challenges requires efforts to strengthen preventive diplomacy as well as the capacity of the organization to support increased numbers of peacekeeping operations performing complex tasks and to ensure the political support for peacemaking. It will require member states to reconcile the dilemmas of the post–Cold War world in making choices about where and how to utilize UN capabilities.

FIVE

□ □ □

Economic Development and Environmental Sustainability

The UN Charter commits the organization to promoting the economic and social advancement of all peoples and many of the goals of the modern welfare state, such as full employment and higher standards of living. Article 55, which addresses international economic and social cooperation, clearly links economic conditions and security in its beginning: "with a view to the creation of conditions of stability and well-being which are necessary for peaceful and friendly relations among nations." Yet the specific provisions for carrying out this mandate are quite limited, particularly when contrasted with the provisions for managing threats to international peace and security. The UN's powers include undertaking studies and preparing reports, making recommendations, preparing conventions, convening conferences, creating specialized agencies, and making recommendations for their coordination. The design clearly envisioned the specialized agencies playing primary roles in carrying out operational activities, with the UN relegated to a general coordinating role. Yet today the largest portion of the UN's budget (80 percent) goes to its economic functions and activities.

Over the fifty years since the UN's founding the attention to economic issues has steadily grown and with it the number of entities within the UN system devoted to economic development–related activities. As a result, one of the major issues facing the UN in the post–Cold War era is the rationalization and coordination of these organs and activities.

The changes that have taken place in this area and its importance were dramatized by both the 1992 UN Conference on the Environment and Development (UNCED) held in Rio de Janeiro (popularly known as the "Earth Summit") and the 1994 International Conference on Population and Development (ICPD) held in Cairo. The Earth Summit was the largest world gathering ever held, attended by representatives from 178 countries, including 100 heads of state, and representatives of 1,420 accredited NGOs. The parallel Global Forum was attended by 15,000 NGO representatives, women, and indigenous peoples. The range of topics on the agenda demonstrated the growing recognition not only of the connections between economic development and environmental issues but also of the links between these and many other concerns, including population.

Thus, the post–Cold War era is marked by new security concerns and demands for UN intervention and by the continuing challenges of promoting economic growth among all peoples and narrowing the gap between rich and poor. This era is also marked by the new challenge of safeguarding the environment, which is essential to life itself as well as human well-being. Hence, whereas the UN's founders were clearly influenced by traditional liberal ideas about the ability of science, technology, and human enterprise to achieve progress, the 1990s debates are marked by concerns over finite resources, limits to growth, the negative consequences of technology, and environmental sustainability. The dilemmas of sovereignty versus intervention, demands for global governance versus the capacity of both international and national government institutions, and leadership versus proliferation and fragmentation are no less sharp in the realm of economic and environmental issues. In many ways they are sharpened by the fact that these issues go to the heart of most governments' domestic policies.

In considering the challenges the UN faces in the 1990s with respect to issues of economic development and environmental sustainability, we look back first at the ideas that have shaped government policies on development. Then, we show how UN institutions evolved in response to the mandate to promote economic growth, the predominant thinking, and the challenges mounted by the less developed countries as their political strength increased in the 1960s and 1970s. Case studies of the debate over proposals for the New International Economic Order and the women-in-development (WID) agenda illustrate changing thinking as well as political and economic realities. Finally, we examine how environmental and development issues have been linked and the role of NGOs enhanced, using a case study of UNCED.

EVOLUTION OF DEVELOPMENT THINKING

Views about economic development are grounded in three contending schools of thought in political economy: economic liberalism, mercantilism (or statism), and Marxism and dependency.[1] These views differ on the basic nature of human beings, the relationship of individuals to society, the relationship between society and the state, the state and markets, and the organization of domestic and international society. They have shaped the debates on economic development within the UN system.

Economic Liberalism

Economic liberals, from Adam Smith to contemporary thinkers, share a set of assumptions about human beings and economic activities. Human beings, rational and acquisitive, will seek to improve their condition in the most expeditious manner possible; markets develop to ensure that individuals are able to carry out the necessary transactions to improve individual welfare. To maximize economic welfare and to stimulate individual (and therefore collective) economic growth, free markets epitomize economic efficiency. For markets to function as desired, economics and politics must be separated as much as possible. Even though government provides basic order in society, political institutions must permit the free flow of trade and economic intercourse that guarantees both equilibrium and inherent stability in the system. At the international level, if governments permit the free flow of commerce and if they do not interfere in the efficient allocation of resources provided by markets, then the increasing interdependence among domestic economies will lead to both aggregate economic development and greater cooperation. TNCs play a key role as engines of growth. As we explore further, the major international economic institutions established after World War II as part of the UN system were firmly embedded in the liberal economic tradition.

Mercantilism or Statism

Mercantilism, which is older than liberal economic thought, flourished between the fifteenth and eighteenth centuries in response to the creation of powerful states dedicated to the pursuit of economic power and wealth. Governments organized their then-limited capabilities to regulate all international economic transactions. A modern version of mercantilism emphasizes the role of the state and the subordination of all economic activities to the goal of state building, including its security and military power. Whereas liberals usually see power and wealth as a choice between "guns and butter," mercantilists, or statists, see them as complementary goals. Where liberals see the mutual benefits of international trade, mercantilists see such relations as basically conflictual and may stress national self-sufficiency rather than interdependence. The more benign contemporary forms of statism may be designed to protect a less developed country's economy from external political and economic forces.

Mercantilism, or **statism,** views competition and conflict as constants in international politics and economic instruments as important tools to achieve political outcomes. Success is measured by relative economic gain compared to other members of the international community. States desire an international division of labor favorable to their own national interest. Thus, as one political economist notes, "nations continually try to change the rules or regimes governing international economic relations in order to benefit themselves disproportionately with respect to other economic powers."[2]

Marxist and Dependency Perspective

Marxism and its various permutations from socialism to communism have clearly had worldwide influence since the mid-nineteenth century. Labor movements and political party competition in Europe and virtually everywhere except North America evidence the influence of Marxist ideas. It has inevitably influenced thinking about economic development.

Although interpretations of **Marxism** vary, economist Robert Heilbroner identifies four beliefs that unite the body of Marxist writing:

1. Society is broadly conflictual as well as dynamic.
2. The ensuing social conflict is caused largely by contradictions and struggles between groups over distribution of resources.
3. The capitalist system is inherently deterministic and expansionary. Capitalist economic systems must accumulate resources, eventually expanding to less developed regions in order to accumulate continual profits. Thus, the international system is basically conflictual.
4. There must be a more equitable distribution of resources both within societies and between societies in the international system.[3]

Because the former Soviet Union both embodied and championed one model of Marxist/socialist thinking on development, that model was the major competitor to liberal thought during the Cold War (as it was in the period between World Wars I and II). This model emphasized the importance of central planning and regulation of all economic activity by the state and of heavy industry at the expense of agriculture or consumer goods.

The Soviet Union and other communist countries refused to join the major international economic institutions of the UN system: the International Monetary Fund, the World Bank, and the General Agreement on Tariffs and Trade. It would in any case have been very difficult to integrate centrally planned economies into their market-based framework. The result of this refusal, however, was the effective division of the global economy and the coexistence of two fundamentally different approaches to the relationships between government and the organization of economic activity.

The anti-capitalism and anti-imperialism of Marxism (and of Soviet policies) had strong appeal among developing countries, as did the Soviet model of central planning and rapid industrialization. Indeed, it is sometimes hard to distinguish between Marxist and statist-oriented policies of some developing countries, except in the language used. Both clearly promoted a strong role for government in the process of economic development.

In the late 1950s a particular strand of thinking emerged in the writings of a number of Latin American economists that focused on the need for radical change in the distribution of international political and economic power if the disadvantaged position of developing countries was to be altered.[4] This strand, known as **dependency theory,** argued that the capitalist international system divides states into two groups: those on the periphery and those at the core. Those on the periphery are locked into a permanent state of dependency, irrespective of the domestic policies they pursue or the external assistance they receive. TNCs operating within the borders of peripheral states may exacerbate the dependency, making the companies a symbolic target for discontent. These views had strong appeal and came to undergird much of the thinking and the agenda of developing countries in the UN in the 1960s and 1970s. The New International Economic Order proposed and championed by the Group of 77 advocated major changes in the international economic system, including the institutions of the UN system.

The three schools of thought have shaped the policies of governments around the world toward economic development and international economic relations. As we have noted, two of these, liberalism and Marxism, were entwined with the East-West conflict during the Cold War period, resulting in the division of the international economic system. Elements of the third (mercantilism or statism) can be found in both state-sponsored capitalism and centrally planned socialist economies.

The UN Charter, however, and the major international economic institutions clearly reflected liberal economic thought. They reflected a vision of building institutions and programs to promote prosperity and peace through international cooperation and industrial change. Closely tied in was a set of ideas drawn from the U.S. New Deal and European social democracy about the importance of expanding government to deal with social and economic problems, that is, the welfare state. We turn, then, to examine those institutions and their evolution, the challenges mounted by developing countries as their numbers increased in the 1960s and

1970s, and the merger of environmental and development issues in the 1980s and 1990s.

THE BRETTON WOODS INSTITUTIONS

The convenors of the 1944 conference in Bretton Woods, New Hampshire, recognized that both reconstruction and economic development were necessary components of the post–World War II economic agenda. The conference laid the groundwork for what became known as the **Bretton Woods institutions:** the International Bank for Reconstruction and Development (IBRD, or World Bank), the International Monetary Fund (IMF), and the stillborn International Trade Organization, which was replaced by the GATT. These three are autonomous organizations within the UN system, reporting nominally to ECOSOC. Each is based on the notion that economic stability and development are best achieved when trade and financial flows occur with as few restrictions as possible. According to Norman Angell, the 1933 recipient of the Nobel Peace Prize, enhanced trade would be in the economic self-interest of all. National differences would vanish in the face of the world market; interdependence would flourish. It would lead to economic well-being and eventually world peace, with war becoming an anachronism.[5] Not all Bretton Woods participants believed this logic, but they did believe strongly in the vitality of liberal economic systems.

Reconstruction and Development: The World Bank

The World Bank was designed initially to facilitate reconstruction in post–World War II Europe. In fact, because the size of the task proved so great, the United States preferred to finance the bulk of reconstruction bilaterally through the European Recovery Program rather than multilaterally through the bank. During the 1950s the bank shifted from reconstruction to development. It generates capital funds from member state contributions and from international financial markets. Like all banks, its purpose is to loan these funds, with interest, to states proposing major economic development projects. Its lending is not designed to replace private capital but to facilitate its operation. Over the years a high portion of the funding has gone for construction of infrastructure: hydroelectric (dam) projects, basic transportation (bridges, highways), and agribusiness projects.[6]

To aid in meeting the needs of developing countries, the International Finance Corporation (IFC) and the International Development Association (IDA) were created in 1956 and 1960, respectively. IDA provides capital to the poorest countries, usually in the form of no-interest loans. Repayment schedules of fifty years allow the least developed countries more time to reach "takeoff," sustain growth, and hence develop economically. Such funds have to be continually "replenished" or added to by major donor countries. IFC provides loans to promote growth of private enterprises in developing countries. In 1988 the Multilateral Investment Guarantee Agency (MIGA) was added to the World Bank group. This agency's goal—to augment the flow of private equity capital to less developed countries—is met by insuring investments against losses. Such losses may include expropriation, government currency restrictions, and losses stemming from civil war or ethnic conflict.

The World Bank, like the other development organizations, the UN itself, and major donor governments, has changed its orientation over time, moving from an emphasis on major infrastructure projects in the 1950s and 1960s to basic human needs in the 1970s and to private sector participation in the 1980s. These changes in policy reflect the changes in thinking among the principal donors.

Stabilization in Monetary Relations: The International Monetary Fund

The task of the IMF was different: to stabilize exchange rates by providing short-term loans for member states confronted by "temporary" **balance-of-payments** difficulties. The IMF was not designed to be an aid agency, but its role in economic development is crucial insofar as stable currency values and currency convertibility are necessary to facilitate trade. Originally the fund established a system of fixed monetary exchange rates and currency convertibility to ensure liquidity of monetary flows. From the 1940s to the 1970s the United States guaranteed the stability of this system by fixing the value of the dollar against gold at $35 an ounce. However, in 1971 this system collapsed, with the United States announcing it would no longer guarantee a system of fixed exchange rates; the dollar was decoupled from the gold standard. So exchange rates were allowed to float.[7]

Since the early 1980s the IMF has played an increasingly key role in less developed countries plagued by persistent and high debts. Expanding its short-term loan function, the IMF provides longer-term loans and the "international stamp of approval" for other multilateral and bilateral lenders as well as private banks. In return for assistance, the IMF encourages **structural adjustment programs** and requires countries to institute certain policies. Box 5.1 outlines the characteristics of countries needing such programs, goals to be achieved, and policy areas typically pushed by the IMF. Note the range of different policies supported by the IMF and their compatibility with a liberal economic perspective. Once agreement is negotiated between the government and the IMF, the latter monitors the adjustment programs and determines whether performance criteria have been met. Currently virtually all forms of development and financial assistance, multilateral as well as bilateral, come with some of these conditions attached, which the donors believe will enhance the value of the aid.

With the institution of this **conditionality,** the distinction between the fund and the bank has been blurred. Both play key roles in structural adjustment lending. And both, but particularly the IMF, have been subjected to intense criticism from developing countries, especially in Latin America and Africa. Critics charge the institutions with providing too little aid, at too high interest rates, and only slightly below market rates. Vehement criticisms have arisen over the content and timing of the conditionality imposed. More fundamentally, many challenge the liberal economic bias, believing that the LDCs will never develop using liberal approaches.[8] Despite these criticisms, a consensus has emerged in the 1990s that economic success depends on a country's adoption of an IMF adjustment program. Likewise, debt rescheduling is dependent on conclusion of an agreement with the IMF.

As the tasks of the bank and the fund become less distinct, and as the level of direct involvement in national governments by these two institutions increases, they are faced with difficult problems. Consistency of policy advice and uniformity of policy dialogue toward any one country by these institutions may be increasingly difficult to maintain; inconsistent advice is clearly counterproductive. Hence, the bank and fund emphasize the importance of increased cooperation not only between themselves but also with the UN and the borrowing countries.

Promoting Trade: The GATT, UNCTAD, and Beyond

The third part of the liberal economic order was to be the International Trade Organization, proposed in 1948 but never established. In its place a multilateral treaty, the GATT, was negotiated; its members, the Contracting Parties, were initially the largest developed countries, excluding the Eastern bloc and the Soviet Union.

A number of important principles are enshrined in the original agreement:

1. Support of trade liberalization since trade is seen as the engine for economic development
2. Nondiscrimination in trade, or **most-favored-nation treatment,** by which states agree to give the same treatment to all other GATT members as they give to their best (most-favored) trading partner
3. Reciprocity
4. The exclusive use of tariffs as devices for protecting home markets

The original agreement also incorporated a number of procedures:

BOX 5.1 IMF Structural Adjustment Programs

Profile of a Country in Need of Structural Adjustment

Large balance-of-payments deficit
Large external debt
Overvalued currency
Large public spending and fiscal deficit

Typical Goals of Structural Adjustment Programs

Restructure and diversify the productive base of economy
Achieve balance of payments and fiscal equilibrium
Create a basis for noninflationary growth
Improve public sector efficiency
Stimulate growth potential of the private sector

Typical Structural Adjustment Policies

Economic Reforms

Limit money and credit growth
Devalue the currency
Reform the financial sector
Introduce revenue-generating measures
Introduce user fees
Introduce tax code reforms
Eliminate subsidies, especially for food
Introduce compensatory employment programs
Create affordable services for the poor

Trade Liberalization Reforms

Remove high tariffs and import quotas
Rehabilitate export infrastructure
Increase producers' prices

Government Reforms

Cut bloated government payroll
Eliminate redundant and inefficient agencies
Privatize public enterprises
Reform public administration and institutions

Private Sector Policies

Liberalize price controls
End government monopolies

1. Disputes between countries are to be resolved through consultation.
2. Negotiations are to be conducted among those sharing major interests in the issue (major suppliers and consumers of a product).
3. The agreement reached by the major interested parties should subsequently be multilateralized to all Contracting Parties.
4. Countries may use safeguards to deal with domestic and balance-of-payment problems and impose special or countervailing duties to offset the dumping of foreign goods at less than market value.[9]

These principles and procedures have been modified to respond to changing international pressures. Most important, beginning in the 1960s, under pressure from many developing countries norms of nondiscrimination and reciprocity were modified to permit preferential treatment for less developed countries. **Preferential access** to the markets of the developed world was seen as a necessary stimulus to economic development.

The heart of the GATT are periodic rounds—eight so far—of multilateral negotations designed to reduce trade barriers. The negotiations in the 1960s, specifically the Dillon Round (1960–1961) and Kennedy Round (1962–1968), were concerned primarily with adapting the GATT system to the European Community (EC). Although the EC's Common Agricultural Policy proved to be an intractable issue, the Kennedy Round led to tariff reductions covering eight times as much trade as was included in the Dillon Round. The Tokyo Round concluded in 1979 resulted in still deeper tariff cuts, better treatment for the less developed countries, and agreements leading to the elimination of subsidies and countervailing duties. In addition, other issues were discussed and agreement reached on government procurement, customs valuation, and technical barriers and standards. During this round the GATT's broad rules and principles became enshrined in detailed regulations. These enhanced the orderliness of the trading system, and international trading arrangements became fairer from the perspective of the LDCs, even though protectionism was not reduced.

The Uruguay Round concluded in December 1993 after seven years of negotiations. These were complicated by the larger number of participants, by the consequences of slowed economic growth in the 1980s and 1990s, by the complexity of many issues, and by increased support for protectionism, especially in the United States. Although not as encompassing as originally planned, the latest agreement covers two areas previously excluded from GATT rules: agriculture and textiles. Negotiators for the United States and EU agreed to lower tariffs on each other's goods by 50 percent on average. Agricultural tariffs for industrialized nations will decline between 36 percent and 24 percent in developing nations. Quotas on textiles and finished apparel were negotiated, and quotas on farm products were replaced by tariffs, which would gradually be reduced. The ability of governments to favor local industry over foreign competitors in their own purchasing is somewhat curtailed. The Uruguay Round attempted to expand rules governing insurance, banking, and other financial services, but negotiators were able to accomplish little in this sector. They did agree to a successor for the GATT, the World Trade Organization (WTO), a multilateral institution with wider powers than the GATT to oversee both trade in services and agriculture.

Controversy over the GATT is not new. In the early 1960s the newly independent developing countries criticized the GATT for dealing mostly with problems of trade among developed countries and for being a "rich man's club." They proposed an international conference on trade and development to focus particularly on commodity trade, so essential to development for developing countries. As a result, at the first UN Conference on Trade and Development in 1964 the less developed countries functioned as a bloc for the first time and challenged the liberal economic order, as we shall discuss.

Membership, Power, and Decisionmaking in the World Bank, IMF, and GATT

In all three Bretton Woods institutions the major developed countries have historically dominated decisionmaking processes. In the World Bank and the IMF a weighted voting system guarantees major donors voting power commensurate with their contributions and hence assures that bank and fund policies conform to the wishes of the developed countries. In addition, the bank and fund bureaucracies are predominantly made up of economists trained in Western countries in the same liberal economic tradition in which U.S. decisionmakers have been trained. The outcomes of GATT negotiations hinge on agreements among principal suppliers, which by tradition has meant the United States, the countries of the European Union, and Japan. The terms of these agreements are then multilateralized to other parties.

Because the socialist countries were not members of the Bretton Woods institutions for much of the Cold War, the bank, fund, and GATT were smaller than most other UN system institutions. Membership in the GATT was always smaller than that in the bank and fund because most developing countries did not want to subject themselves to the discipline of GATT rules. They also preferred to use UNCTAD for discussion of trade issues and promotion of changes in trading rules. Since 1980, however, membership in all three institutions has increased as the former socialist countries, and the LDCs have accepted the discipline and benefits of membership. With increasing membership, the bank and fund have faced new demands for resources, especially in the countries of Eastern Europe and the former Soviet Union. For the GATT growing membership complicates the task of concluding trade agreements and increases the potential for trade disputes.

OTHER UN DEVELOPMENT INSTITUTIONS

Regional Commissions

In 1947 two of what was to become a network of regional commissions were established: the Economic Commission for Europe and the Economic Commission for Asia and the Far East (renamed in the 1970s the Economic and Social Commission for Asia and the Pacific, following the formation of the Commission for Western Asia). Shortly thereafter in 1948 the Economic Commission for Latin America convened, and ten years later the Economic Commission for Africa met. These regional commissions were designed to stimulate regional approaches to development with studies and initiatives to promote regional projects, including the sponsorship of conferences with functional experts from countries in the region.

The UN's regional approach has met with varied success. The Latin American group played a key role during the 1950s in critiquing the liberal economic development model's applicability to dependent states. In particular, their dependency approach formed the theoretical basis for the New International Economic Order of the 1970s, especially in the area of commodity policy. The Economic Commission for Latin America (ECLA) also contributed to the establishment of the Central American Common Market and the Inter-American Development Bank. All the commissions have produced high-quality economic surveys of their respective regions as well as country plans used by national governments and other multilateral institutions. But disputes among members within the region—for example, Arab versus non-Arab states in the Commission for Western Asia and lack of resources and expertise in the African case—have hampered the work of the commissions.

Technical Assistance Institutions

The provision of technical assistance has been the other mainstay of the UN system, the argument being that the Bretton Woods institutions stimulate the development of infrastructure and the mobilization of capital, while the UN's own programs supply people skills and new technologies. The tasks of expanding economic growth in LDCs by providing training programs and expert advice emerged in a December 1948 mandate to develop technical assistance programs. It was institutionalized in the 1950 Expanded Programme of Technical Assistance (EPTA). The UN has awarded fellowships for advanced training, supplied equipment for training purposes, and provided experts. Generally such projects have been jointly funded by the UN and several specialized agencies, such as the World Health Organization; Food and Agriculture Organization; UN Educational, Scientific, and Cultural Organization; or one of the regional economic commissions.

The establishment of the UN Development Program (UNDP) in 1965 was an organizational attempt to rationalize the proliferation of structures and programs of technical assistance by merging EPTA and the Special Fund established in the late 1950s to channel voluntary contributions for larger capital projects. UNDP was to be the lead organization in the provision of technical assistance, staffed by resident representatives in the recipient countries. These experts, because their residency makes them better equipped to assess local needs and priorities, are intended to be the focal point of UN development activities. They coordinate technical assistance programs, function as "country representatives" for some of the specialized agencies, and link the United Nations and the recipient government. Although the positions have clearly grown in significance, the amount of funds at their disposal is dwarfed by the funds of the World Bank and key bilateral donors. Hence, their power to effectively coordinate country-based activities is limited by available resources and the autonomy of the specialized agencies.

Thus, the regional economic commissions and UNDP link ECOSOC and the General Assembly programmatically with the specialized agencies of the UN system. These relationships vary in nature, however, and have been the subject of much controversy, particularly as the number of agencies has proliferated and responsibilities expanded. Nonetheless, amid the diversity there has been a high degree of congruence among the UN actors in the articulation of systemwide economic development doctrines.

As we noted earlier, however, the developing countries mounted a challenge to the dominant liberal economic system and to the UN system beginning in the 1960s, when their numbers gave them a majority in the General Assembly and ECOSOC. Statism, Marxism, and dependency theory all influenced these countries' perspectives. They sought political power and new economic policies that would focus more attention on their needs.

CHALLENGING ECONOMIC LIBERALISM: THE NEW INTERNATIONAL ECONOMIC ORDER

The establishment of UNCTAD owed much to ECLA's work. Grounded in Marxist and dependency thinking, ECLA economists' analyses of the obstacles to development led the G-77 to seek significant

A participant in a UNDP-supported weaving project in Bali designed to increase women's income spins her thread. UN Photo 155524/John Isaac.

trade concessions from the developed countries. In its view, reciprocity in trade relations would serve only to perpetuate underdevelopment and dependency. An inherently unequal international liberal trading system could not be made more equal without major changes. Thus, the developing countries argued that they needed special concessions, including preferential access to developed country markets, to improve conditions for their trade. The G-77 succeeded in institutionalizing UNCTAD as a permanent organ of the General Assembly (not ECOSOC), with triennial meetings and a permanent secretariat, to provide a forum in which to pressure the developed states. Through that forum some of the major changes in thinking about economic development were articulated, particularly the demands for the New International Economic Order.[10]

Even before UNCTAD's creation, the developing countries won approval of the first in a series of development decades. The 1990s is the

Fourth Development Decade. In conjunction with these, various goals are set, such as the target for annual resource transfers (aid) from developed to developing states, initially 1 percent of the **gross national product** (GNP). Other goals have focused on average annual growth rates, increases in exports, domestic savings for investment, and agricultural production.

The 1970s were a particularly difficult period for North-South relations and the international economy. The 1973 oil crisis led to sharp increases in the prices of energy and food. In 1973 and 1974, impatient with slow progress toward development, the G-77 increased its pressure for a New International Economic Order and met strong opposition from the developed states. U.S. opposition was especially strong.

The UN General Assembly and UNCTAD provided the major forums for articulating most of these demands, with the September 1975 Seventh Special Session of the UN General Assembly being the peak point of confrontation between North and South. Support from the members of the Organization of Petroleum Exporting Countries (OPEC), which were admired for their own challenge to the major oil companies and the North, was critical. Let us examine the South's demands more closely.

Demands by the South

The G-77 sought changes in six major areas of international economic relations. Each demand was designed to alter the relationship between the developed and developing countries, giving an opportunity for the LDCs to break the ties of dependency and hence to spur economic development. First and most important, the South sought changes in international trade, including adjustment in the terms of trade, to stabilize the prices of such commodities as coffee, cocoa, bauxite, tin, and sugar and to link those prices with the price of capital goods and finished products (e.g., computers and automobiles) imported from the developed world. Changes in unfavorable terms of trade could be achieved through indexation, price regulation, commodity cartels, and multilateral commodity agreements as well as a common fund to support the prices of commodities.

Second, the Group of 77 demanded greater authority over foreign investment for member countries, specifically regulation of TNCs, which were regarded as exploitative. Third, the South pushed for better means of technology transfer. It needed to be cheaper and more appropriate for the local population. And since TNCs were reluctant to transfer technology, government arrangements were needed.

Fourth, the South, overburdened with debt and weighed down by repayment schedules, especially beginning in the 1980s, demanded comprehensive solutions that would restructure debt burdens, reduce interest rates, and cancel debt outright. Fifth, to propel development even further, the South demanded increased foreign aid and improved terms and conditions of aid. Grants and aid without conditions were preferred.

Sixth, advocates of the NIEO sought changes in international organizations, specifically the weighted voting structures of the World Bank and the International Monetary Fund and the developed country bias within the GATT. Advocates sought, in short, to alter basic power relationships in international economic affairs, to curtail dependency, and to speed economic growth.

NIEO Outcomes

On some issues the South partially achieved its goals, although often outside the UN system. In 1975 members of the European Community and a group of African, Caribbean, and Pacific (ACP) countries signed the Lomé Convention. ACP countries were given preferential access to European markets for both agricultural and manufacturing goods, and a commodity price stabilization system was instituted to meet emergency conditions.

In 1989 the agreement establishing the Common Fund for Commodities entered into effect with ratification by ninety states, including the members of the Organization of Economic Cooperation and Development (OECD—Western European countries, the United States, Canada, Japan, Australia, and New Zealand), less developed countries, and Eastern European countries, though without the United States. Headquartered in Amsterdam, the fund has three functions: (1) to finance an international buffer stock to stabilize commodity prices, (2) to support commodity diversification in LDCs to mitigate overreliance on a few primary commodities and expand the processing of commodities, and (3) to promote general cooperation in the area of commodities. Eighteen commodities are singled out for special treatment.

Similarly, controls on TNCs and transfer of technology were negotiated in a number of different arenas. The twenty-four-member OECD developed a voluntary code for TNCs in 1976. The UN established the Center on Transnational Corporations to disseminate information and publicize activities. The World Bank's Multilateral Investment Guarantee Agency, mentioned earlier, was established to create confidence between investors and LDCs. Although the more comprehensive UN draft Code on Transnational Corporations was never approved, the increased use of the International Convention on the Settlement of Investment Disputes (also a World Bank affiliate) represented another step toward meeting the South's demands.

During the late 1970s and 1980s debt restructuring based on implementation of domestic reforms became acceptable. Under the guidance of the IMF, negotiations were conducted on a country-by-country basis for debt restructuring. The kinds of conditions discussed earlier in this chapter were widely used. These debt negotiations did not occur within the UN structure, as the South would have preferred.

Likewise, demands for increasing the volume and types of foreign assistance fell far short of the targets. Official development aid has been below 0.40 percent of developed countries' GNP since the late 1970s. Only the Netherlands, Denmark, Norway, and Sweden have exceeded the revised target of 0.70 percent. The United States trails with approximately 0.18 percent of its GNP devoted to foreign economic assistance. Only Japan substantially increased its foreign aid allocation from $458 million in 1970 to $3.4 billion in 1980 and then to $11.1 billion in 1992 (0.32 percent of GNP), making it the largest single donor.

The North has shown little inclination to negotiate over power within established international organizations. Indeed, the failure of efforts to institutionalize the NIEO within the UN has led some G-77 members to temper their expectations, recognizing that a new order requires many changes that cannot be forced by a coalition of economically weak states, even when that group commands a majority of votes in the UN General Assembly. The failure to achieve the NIEO—an agenda item in UN agencies for almost two decades—led some countries to explore alternative development strategies. Other developing countries have embraced economic liberalism as the most effective strategy. As two scholars note:

> The Southern tone in North-South diplomacy has moderated. Some in the United States and in other Northern countries attribute the moderating of Southern diplomacy to the South's having learned that name calling is useless; they claim that Southern diplomats have matured. Southern delegates, however, explain that their current more restrained approach actually signifies the growing realization that the UNO [United Nations Organization] is a limited mechanism for dealing with many of their most immediate concerns. The South, some say, is turning to other forums for many diplomatic activities, and thus much Southern diplomatic activity is presently taking place outside the UN General Assembly. It is happening in ASEAN [Association of Southeast Asian Nations], in the OAU, in the debtor's group in Latin America, in the Arab League, and in other regional settings, as well as in other UN agencies.[11]

Developing countries challenged economic liberalism because of their conviction that the free market could not ensure equitable development for all peoples as enunciated in the UN Charter. Their demands for change in the Bretton Woods institutions as well as in developed countries' policies represented a challenge to existing power structures and existing rules in the name of equity and justice. They sought to assure that their dependency and peripheral position in the international economic system would not be permanent.

Another challenge to share in economic development arose from a major group in all societies: women. Some of the demands for considering the role of women in development have also sought to overturn the existing international economic order. All have advocated radical reform in that system. Hence, both the NIEO and WID agendas require new approaches to economic development. Both have incorporated Marxist thinking and been strongly influenced by dependency writers. We turn now to a case study of the women-in-development agenda to illustrate the UN system's response to this challenge.

FROM ECONOMIC LIBERALISM TO RADICAL REFORM: THE WOMEN-IN-DEVELOPMENT AGENDA

During the 1940s and the 1950s the liberal economic framework clearly dominated development discussions. How development issues affecting women were addressed within the UN system during that time permits us to trace the evolution from economic liberalism to demands for radical reform influenced by Marxist and dependency thinking. The founders of the UN envisaged that the UN would play a key role in enhancing the political status of women, a goal that was consistent with liberal thinking. The Commission on the Status of Women (CSW), one of the six functional commissions of ECOSOC, had primary responsibility for trying to ensure that women had the right to vote, hold office, and enjoy equal legal rights.

By the 1940s women's economic role was increasingly recognized, including the need to gather more statistics on economic and social issues relevant to women. The UN Population Commission's initial mandate, for example, was to compile and improve population statistics and estimates, including the size and structure of population changes and the interplay of demographic factors and economic-social factors. In 1949 the Social Commission convinced the secretary-general to compile data on the living conditions of selected social groups in less developed countries. This became the *Preliminary Report on the World Social Situation,* first published in 1952. When technical assistance programs began in 1948, women's activities were incorporated. At that time liberal economic theorists believed that women participated in and benefited from the development process but that their contributions were not adequately documented. UN agencies could fill the gap by gathering data on women's economic status.

On December 19, 1961, when the General Assembly approved Resolution 1710 to inaugurate the First Development Decade, the secretary-general was instructed to orchestrate an integrated approach to development. The goal was to raise the annual growth rate of developing countries from 3.5 to 5 percent, a target that could be reached only if donors expanded assistance programs. Women were among the groups singled out for development funds, even though the absence of data disaggregated by sex meant women could not unequivocally be identified as beneficiaries.

In the 1970s some women challenged the assumptions of economic liberalism. Esther Boserup, an academic, activist, and UN consultant, for example, refuted the assumption implicit in liberal economic theory that women's rights and status automatically improve as modernization progresses. Indeed, she found that as technology improves, men benefit and women become increasingly marginalized economically.[12] By 1975 and the UN-sponsored International Women's Year, the conventional wisdom held that the development community could not sit idly by and assume that economic development would inevitably benefit all groups, as liberal theory contends. Women needed special attention, just as the developing countries needed special concessions to alleviate their economic dependency. Women would have to be participants and active agents in development. An agenda needed to be designed both to reduce women's traditional activities and to expand new activities into economically productive roles in agriculture, small business, and industry.

During the 1980s the UN adopted a more radical agenda for women and development. The UN-sponsored Second World Conference on Women in 1980 in Copenhagen concluded, for example, that the world economic crisis contributed to the worsening status of women. Lack of progress on NIEO demands continued to adversely affect the socioeconomic status of women, it was argued. As a result, Third World women articulated new visions of development in NGOs both before and after the Copenhagen meeting. Then in the preparatory conference for the Third World Conference on Women in 1985 in Nairobi, they cited the need for structural societal transformation since international economic disparity was, and is, the most critical obstacle to the advancement of women. To these delegates fundamental change was necessary to shift from focusing on women's role in development to addressing the Marxist notion of restructuring the international capitalist order. This would be a difficult, if not impossible, task for the UN, given power realities.

The UN system has met some of the challenges posed by the advocates of the women-in-development agenda. In addition to the conferences on women held every five years, the UN in 1982 established the International Research and Training Institute for the Advancement of Women (INSTRAW). Funded by voluntary contributions, INSTRAW's goals are to provide training to integrate and mobilize women in the development process and to act as a catalyst in promoting the role of women. The

Voluntary Fund for the UN Decade for Women (UNIFEM) supports projects designed to promote women's participation in UNDP's own development activities.

One example of such a project is found in the Temporal region of Mexico. The UN approved a $150,000 grant, channeled through the Asociación de Mujeres Campesinas de la Huasteca, a local women's organization, for a rural development program that included the manufacture of a small water pump. Another more substantial grant from UNIFEM enabled local women to receive training on manufacturing equipment, and with additional aid by mid-1990, the plant was producing and marketing pumps. In northeast Thailand UNIFEM helped fund a local lender extending credit for small silk-weaving businesses, thus providing an economic alternative to women who otherwise might migrate and become part of the region's sex trade.

Since the 1975 UN meeting that opened the Decade for Women (1975–1985), NGOs have played key roles in the articulation of and response to the women-in-development agenda. They have worked both directly with UN agencies and independently to shape agendas. The UN Development Fund for Women increased its direct work with NGOs between 1978 and 1984, funding projects in which the UN agencies and NGOs worked together, such as in the foregoing examples. And one NGO, Development Alternatives with Women for a New Era (DAWN), prepared an independent report for the 1985 Nairobi women's conference that focused on women's marginalization as a result of capitalist exploitation in the global labor system.

The UN's response to the WID agenda has not satisfied many critics, however. Indeed, the World Bank did not respond until fifteen years after the Copenhagen conference. In 1989 it published its first country study devoted entirely to women: *Kenya: The Role of Women in Economic Development*. The bank's record has improved dramatically since then.

The debates over the NIEO and women in development illustrate how issues permeate the UN system and are shaped by that system. In both cases the UN, the specialized agencies, and autonomous organizations were forums for articulating evolving positions as well as for responding to initiatives from NGOs and donor governments. The activity these debates spawned has also carried over to other issues, such as the environment.

NORTH AND SOUTH AND THE ENVIRONMENT

The North-South conflict was not only linked to the issues of the NIEO and women's role in development but was also apparent on environmental issues. During the preparatory meetings for the 1972 UN Conference on the Human Environment (UNCHE) held in Stockholm, the North em-

Women work and observe at a UNDP-funded maize mill in Tres Palmas Village, Mexico. UNDP Photo/Ruth Massey.

phasized narrow scientific concerns, such as the preservation of species and their environment and transborder pollution. The South, however, feared that environmental regulation could hamper economic growth.

The Stockholm Conference began a process that has resulted in the piecemeal construction of a number of international environmental institutions, the steady expansion of the environmental agenda, and increasing acceptance by states of international monitoring of environmental standards. That process has steadily linked development and concern for the environment as the depletion of natural resources raises questions about the limits of economic growth.[13]

The chief product of Stockholm—the United Nations Environmental Program (UNEP)—became the champion of this new development ideology and the first UN agency based in a less developed country, Nairobi, Kenya. "A dwarf agency compared with the World Bank or FAO,"[14] UNEP has a staff of fewer than four hundred people, a fifty-eight-member-country governing council, five regional offices, and an environmental fund. Its mandate is to promote international cooperation in the field of the environment, provide guidance for the direction of enviromental programs in the UN system, and review implementation of these programs, including both national and international policies for development plans in LDCs.

UNEP has a key role in gathering and disseminating information through Earth Watch and its components. It provides technical assistance for developing international law and treaties, such as the Montreal Protocol on the Depletion of the Ozone Layer (1987) and the Basel Convention on Trade in Hazardous Wastes (1989). In addition, UNEP coordinates the antidesertification work of the UN agencies and the regional sea initiatives (the Mediterranean Sea cleanup being the largest) and oversees environmental protection in the International Tropical Timber Agreement. Yet UNEP remains handicapped by its limited power to impose regulation on specialized agencies or governments and by a small budget. Actors in UNEP include not only the Secretariat and other environmentally concerned organizations within the UN family (e.g., FAO and WHO), but also NGOs, the scientific community, and national governments.

However, the consensus forged at Stockholm on integrating the environment and development was later challenged by the LDCs. The South argued that the **basic human needs approach** adopted by the World Bank during the 1970s diverted attention from the need for changes in the international power structure. Environmentalists challenged the emphasis on economic growth in the face of diminishing global resources. Conservatives in the North argued that the basic needs approach diverted scarce resources away from economically productive activities by focusing on housing, water supply, health, and education. A new concept was required to link environment and development. From these debates emerged the concept of sustainability.

Sustainable Development

In 1980 the UN General Assembly adopted the World Conservation Strategy, advocating the new but poorly defined concept of **sustainable development.** For those of a liberal persuasion it meant sustained growth or sustained change. For others, particularly in the environmental movement, it originated in the context of renewable resources necessary to support present and future human life. For those adopting a more radical vision of economic development, sustainable development signaled a positive response to NIEO demands for equity, incorporating environmental concerns with the agenda of the 1970s.[15] This revived the NIEO debate with linkages among environmental change, justice, and equity issues. For all, sustainability implies that economic development should enhance the resource base and not prevent future generations from meeting their needs and aspirations.

In 1983 UNEP convinced the UN General Assembly to establish the World Commission on Environment and Development (WCED), headed by Prime Minister Gro Harlem Brundtland of Norway. Its task was to formulate a new development approach around the concept of sustainable development. This approach proved politically astute since it recognized the fact that dealing with environmental problems would be ineffectual if global poverty and economic inequalities were not addressed. The 1987 Brundtland Commission Report (*Our Common Future*), called for "development that meets the needs of the present without compromising the ability of future generations to meet their own needs."[16] It sought to balance ecological concern and sustainable economic development with a number of objectives. These are summarized in Box 5.2. The commission drew from studies on the unsustainability of the North's growth patterns and stressed the responsibility of Third World governments and transnational corporations for maintaining habitats and biological diversity for the sake of planetary well-being. It also stressed the responsibility of the North toward the South, reflecting the moral argument that had been articulated much earlier by Southern proponents of the NIEO and their Northern allies.

The Brundtland Commission Report underscored that the South cannot develop in the same way that Great Britain, the United States, Germany, and other industrialized nations did because humanity may not survive a similarly radical transformation in the environment. Furthermore, even if the North developed itself by exploiting the South, the South cannot follow the same path, given the dearth of global resources. Pragmatic self-interest, then, dictates that the North aid Third World development.

BOX 5.2 Objectives of Sustainable Development

- Reorient the Bretton Woods system to sustainable development
- Reschedule debts in LDCs when they lead to overexploitation of natural resources
- Create new sources of financing for the global commons—ocean fishing, Antarctica
- Include environmental conditions in international commodity agreements and structural adjustment programs
- Strengthen UNEP and regional institutions

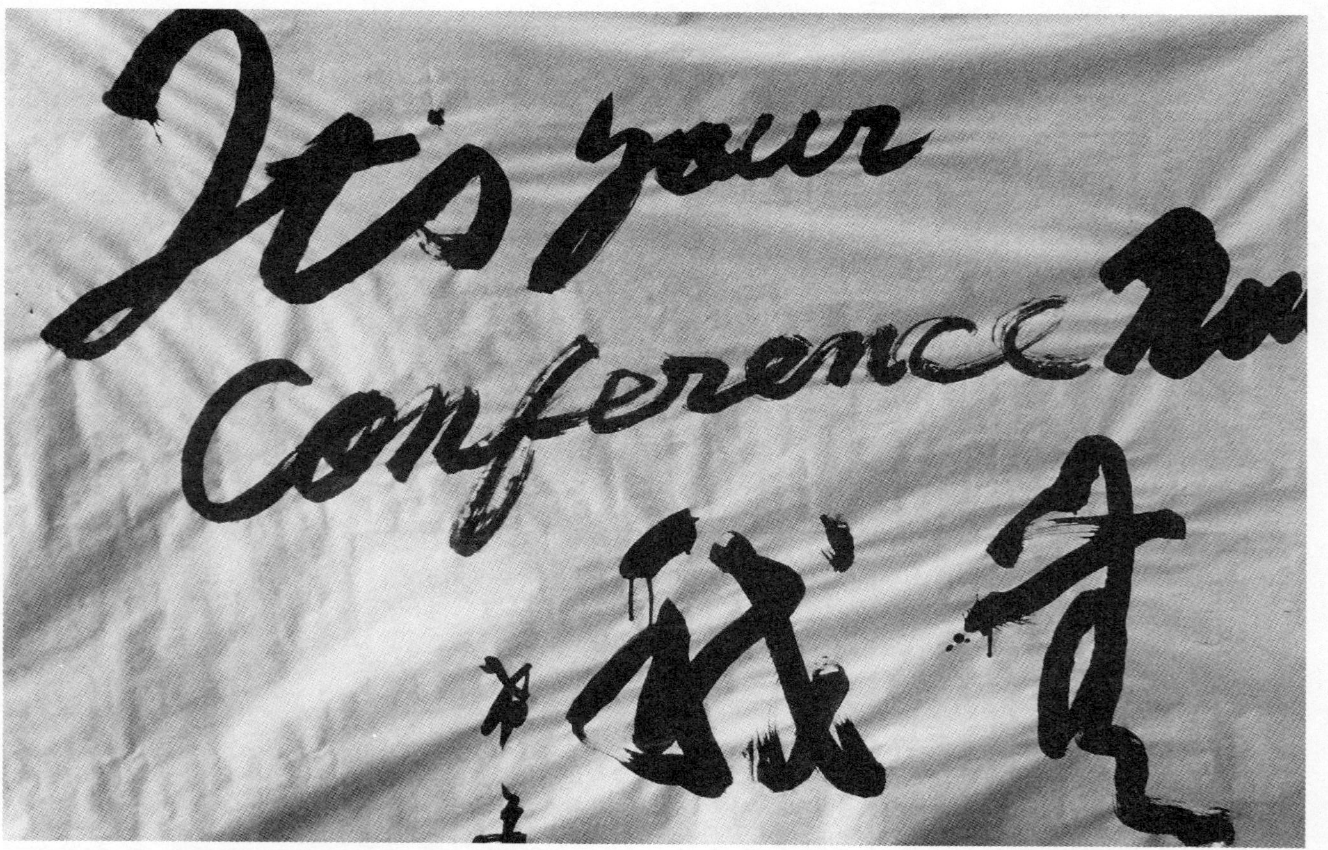

Banner at the UNCED—or Earth Summit—in Rio de Janeiro, 1992. UN Photo 180299/M. Tzovaras.

The Brundtland Commission's approach was adopted in 1987 by the Governing Council of UNEP, and subsequently by the World Bank, non-governmental groups (e.g., the World Wildlife Fund and World Conservation Union), and national development agencies in Canada, Sweden, and the United States. UNEP then developed a six-year environmental program that set priorities for the whole UN system for 1990–1995. The 1992 UNCED in Rio de Janeiro was the main follow-up of this agenda.

UNCED 1992 and Sustainable Development

Beginning in the 1970s the UN had sponsored a series of global conferences on various issues, including food supply, population, desertification, water, disarmament, women, and the environment. The function of these global gatherings was to educate and inspire people, NGOs, and governments to take action. UNCED was, however, the largest of these conferences both in the number of participants and in the scope of the agenda. As with other conferences, a series of preparatory meetings were used to articulate positions and hammer out basic issues. For example, at the second Preparatory Commission (PrepCom) meeting in Beijing in June 1991 the Secretariat's draft proposal represented an ecological bias; the G-77, acting as a group, reasserted the development-environment link. At PrepCom III, held in August 1991 in Geneva, discussions shifted from the proposed Earth Charter to the draft Rio Declaration on Environment and Development. At PrepCom IV, held in New York in March–April 1992, many of the principles advocated by the South found their way into the final draft document: state sovereignty, the obligation of all states to cooperate in eradicating poverty, priority to the needs of developing countries, the responsibility of the developed countries for global environmental problems, and the need for further financial assistance to the poorer nations.[17]

NGOs played key roles in both the preparatory process and the Rio conference. For the first time they were permitted to make statements from the floor during official working group and plenary meetings. They drafted documents, which were circulated on tables next to the document windows inside meeting rooms for easy access by government delegations. They were given access to working drafts of UN documents, often reviewing and passing on comments to key officials and delegates. They spoke up to support and refute specific phrasing.[18]

Although the environmental movement began in the North, by the 1980s it had spread in the South. UNCED provided even further impetus through opportunities for networking. The number of NGOs participating in Rio conference activities was greater than ever before. More than four hundred environmental organizations were accredited, including not only traditional, large, well-financed NGOs, such as the World Wildlife Fund; those working on specific issues, such as forests or oceans; and those with grassroots activities in developing countries, typically poorly financed, with few previous transnational linkages.

The persistence of the NGOs paid off. At Rio Section II (Chapter 4) of **Agenda 21** recognized the unique capabilities of NGOs and recommended that they participate at all levels from policy and decisionmaking to implementation. What began as a parallel informal process of participation within the UN system evolved into a more formal role. NGO participation at UNCED, in fact, provided the stimulus to review the whole question of NGOs' relationship with the UN. Many NGOs were admitted to UNCED even though they did not have consultative status at the UN. Some states and long-established NGOs argue that the proliferation of NGOs, many of which do not have international experience or logistical capacity, has undermined and delegitimized consultative status with ECOSOC. The newer NGOs, many of them small, grassroots NGOs from the South, see participation in the UN system as a significant breakthrough, one that makes the UN more representative of the "peoples of the world." For the 1995 Fourth World Conference on Women in Beijing, the issue of NGO participation has surfaced once again, as the Secretariat recommended that participation be limited to those having ECOSOC consultative status.

The final Rio declaration was a compromise between the North's environmental concerns and the South's interests in economic development. Unlike Stockholm, UNCED had placed side by side development issues and questions relating to the environment. This represented a major concession to the South. The South also succeeded in integrating broader issues of global economic reform into Agenda 21 (Chapters 2, 3, 4, 12). The South insisted that each program area (debt, structural adjustment, trade and commodities, poverty, and transnational corporations) incorporate "implementation methods to include financing and cost evaluations, scientific and technological means, and human resource development and capacity-building. . . . This procedural recommendation was fully implemented in the final document."[19]

Agenda 21 did not, however, accommodate all the objectives and demands of the South. The issues of reforming structural adjustment and the need to regulate transnational corporations' impact on the environment were not addressed. Commitments by the North for more financial assistance (Agenda 21, Chapter 33) were disappointing and have yet to be met. At PrepCom III the G-77 issued a draft resolution calling for additional financing entirely in the form of "compensatory" grants. It also

BOX 5.3 Main Outcomes of UNCED

Major Principles Adopted

Sovereign right of states to exploit their resources
Right of states to develop
Cooperation among states to eradicate poverty
Priority to the less developed countries
Responsibility of developed countries for global environmental problems
More financial assistance to poorer countries
Implementation of Agenda 21 based on principles of universality, democracy, cost-effectiveness, and accountability

Main Institutional Outcomes

Adoption of two treaties: the Convention on Climate Change and the Convention on Biological Diversity
Creation of the Commission on Sustainable Development
Establishment of UN General Assembly as supreme policymaking forum
Specification of UN secretary-general as high-level coordinator
Establishment of regional and subregional commissions to foster capacity building for achieving sustainable development
Agreement that states should produce national reports and action plans for sustainable development
Integration of nongovernmental organizations as partners in sustainable development efforts

Main Financial Outcomes

Developed countries commit to reach 0.7 percent of GNP to foreign assistance by year 2000
Agreement to strengthen the Global Environment Facility
Developed countries pledge new financial assistance to less developed countries at a rate of $607 billion per year to implement the conventions

Source: Adapted from Robert O. Matthews, "United Nations Reform in the 1990's," ACUNS Reports and Papers No. 5, 1993, pp. 15–38; and Peter S. Thatcher, "Evaluating the 1992 Earth Summit," *Security Dialogue* 23, no. 3 (1992):117–126.

called for mandatory contributions by the developed countries to ensure "predictability and an unconditional flow of funds," with the establishment of a "Green Fund" to administer these resources. The North was reluctant to come forward with new funds, preferring to reallocate existing funds more effectively. The North preferred to strengthen the World

Bank's existing Global Environmental Facility (GEF) rather than create a new institution. The compromise declaration announced that the developed countries would provide substantial additional resources on a grant or concessional basis. The flow would be "adequate and predictable." Progress would be monitored by the UN Commission on Sustainable Development (CSD). They also pledged new resources, to be provided through GEF, as part of the Framework Convention on Climate Change and the Convention on Biological Diversity.

Most participants opposed establishing new institutions, favoring enhanced coordination and cooperation. There was agreement about the creation of CSD as the body to oversee the implementation of the Rio decisions, review financial and technology transfers, and encourage high-level discussion, consensus, and decisionmaking. Thus far, CSD reports that progress has been limited and that funds remain a major constraint for effective implementation.

Box 5.3 summarizes the major outcomes of UNCED. As one observer argues, "Institutionalization of sustainable Third World development within the UN system may be the most important consequence of Rio for the less industrialized world."[20] Nonetheless, UNCED also symbolized the worldwide recognition of the magnitude and severity of the environmental threats. Accumulating scientific evidence, the pressure of a growing environmental movement, and changing public attitudes have increased states' and businesses' willingness to accept the monitoring of environmental standards. The breadth of UNCED's agenda symbolized the recognition that "everything connects"—trade, population growth, women's role, environmental degradation, species loss, expenditures on armaments, and promotion of economic development.

Although there were echoes of the NIEO demands at Rio and the North-South conflict is far from over, acceptance of the concept of environmentally sustainable development represents a new approach to issues of development. A new North-South consensus has begun to emerge, aided by the breakdown of the G-77 at the UNCTAD conference in Cartagena in 1992. Growing differences in developing countries' interests have eroded their solidarity. Latin American states have reestablished close ties with the United States. African governments still embrace much of the NIEO agenda, prompted perhaps by the deteriorating conditions throughout the continent. The rapidly growing Asian nations find little in common with other regions.

Whether the South is united or fragmented, whether conflict between North and South is sharp or muted, the UN, peoples, NGOs, and governments still search for the best strategies to achieve development. Secretary-General Boutros Boutros-Ghali published *An Agenda for*

Reprinted by permission of Harley Schwadron.

Development in May 1994 to counter the complaint that peacekeeping has been given priority over development issues. The document affirms the right to development and the connections among the economic, social, environmental, and political dimensions of development. It was not surprising, then, that the 1994 Cairo conference on population reaffirmed that "everything connects": population, environment, and sustainable development. There a broad consensus emerged that economic development is most effectively fostered by promoting women's rights. The final declaration of ICPD enshrined a new concept of population that gives women more control over their lives by promoting education for girls and a range of choices for family planning and health care. The conference declaration also promoted equality between the sexes. The ICPD placed women at the center of the development debate and sought to ensure that they are increasingly involved in development planning. This realization of the connections between the social status of women and development constitutes a major attitudinal shift within the UN system. Thus, the social status and political empowerment of women are now linked to poverty, violence, environment, sustainable development, and population control.

CONCLUSION

The challenges of promoting economic development and well-being for all peoples are no less great in the post–Cold War era than before. Indeed, many observers would argue that the gap between rich and poor has widened dramatically since the mid-1970s, making these challenges more urgent than ever. Both the demands on the UN to address development issues and the proliferation of institutions and programs have taxed the institutional capacity of the UN to respond and the willingness of states to commit the necessary resources. Thus, the dilemma of capacity and commitment is central to the debate over the role of the UN in dealing with development issues in the post–Cold War era.

Institutional Capacity Building

The capacity of the UN to respond to the broad economic agenda developed in fits and spurts, often in an ad hoc manner, despite the fact that ECOSOC was made one of the primary organs within the UN system. The emergence of the agenda of the newly independent countries, with their demands for the NIEO, challenged the capacity of the UN institutions. The specialized agencies took on new tasks; new groups were established, creating a largely unmanageable complex of organizations. The new demands cost money and challenged traditional power relationships. But the North proved unwilling to redistribute power or resources, which would undermine the liberal economic system.

In the post–Cold War system, as the Northern desire for environmentally sustainable programs is married to the Southern push for economic justice and equity, the institutional capacity question looms once more. Should the UN create more institutions to meet these new needs? Can the old institutions be reformed? Does the UN system have the capacity to effectively implement all the policies articulated?

The problems encountered by the women-in-development agenda within the UN will more than likely occur for the sustainable development push. For example, in 1988–1989 the UN reported that there were twenty separate UN programs and eleven specialized agencies sponsoring activities for the advancement of women; those agencies supported 594 and 913 projects, respectively. Because of the number of separate entities involved, it is difficult to obtain an accurate assessment of the effectiveness of UN programs for women. The sustainable development agenda is likely to encounter similar problems: a proliferation of agencies and programs whose effectiveness is difficult to determine.

Whether this institutional capacity should be reinvigorated at the global level, where it currently resides, or whether it should devolve to the regions—the intent of the regional economic commissions—remains a subject of controversy. The more programs are centralized, the more difficult the problems of cross-program and cross-institutional coordination become. The more decentralized they are, the greater is the likelihood of organizations working at cross-purposes and pursuing contradictory goals.

Institutional capacity is not only a question of establishing programs but also a question of implementation. Even though programs have been initiated, those associated with the UN have recognized that "legislative provisions are not always matched by adequate enforcement measures and machinery."[21] The rhetoric has not always been followed by action.

Delegates to both the 1985 Nairobi conference on women and the 1992 Rio conference were highly cognizant of the implementation debate. In the latter case conferees adopted "Forward-Looking Strategies for the Advancement of Women Towards the Year 2000," in which more than one-half of the resolutions called for action from governments and more than one-half of the total mandates related to development issues. Despite the implementation emphasis, the process "has been slow because of lack of financial and human resources, lack of national policy and lack of commitment by some governments to WID."[22] National governments themselves are primarily responsible, but the overall record is not encouraging. In the case of the Rio conference implementation has likewise been slow, although the major results of the conference may well have been the process of institutionalizing sustainability as the guiding norm and augmenting the capacity of the system to deal with sustainability issues.[23]

Demands for Participation

The debate over the UN's role in development issues also links to the dilemma over leadership versus participation. The need for one or more major states to play a leadership role is less acute for development than it is for peace and security issues. But clearly developing countries' demands for participation in the international economic system and NGO demands for participation in addressing the role of women, development, and environmental issues pose new challenges. These issues require broad-based participation by people and grassroots organizations in decisionmaking as well as implementation at the lowest possible levels for meaningful change (and development) to occur. Hence, there is a growing recognition of the importance of civil society and of more effective participation by NGOs in the institutions of the UN system.

Erosion of Sovereignty

Increasingly, efforts by UN-system institutions to address environment- and development-related issues confront the dilemma of respecting state sovereignty versus taking steps that amount to intervention in the domestic affairs of states. IMF and World Bank conditionality requires states to adjust their economic and fiscal policies in return for assistance. International environmental standards and regulations push governments, businesses, and citizens to change their behavior to avert further degradation. NGO monitoring increases the information about levels of pollution and dangers to human well-being. The World Bank and UNDP have mandated statements on environmental impact and the effects on women of proposed development projects.

The tendency for international activities regarding the environment and development to erode state sovereignty still further is likely to continue. Indeed, the cumulative effect of the various factors contributing to sovereignty's erosion may very well be a reinterpretation of sovereignty itself. Like any social construct or institution, sovereignty is subject to changing interpretations in spite of the tendency, especially by international relations scholars, to imbue it with fixed qualities and character.

Demands for participation by various groups will likewise continue, as will the issues of organizational effectiveness and efficiency. Many of these are at the heart of proposals for UN reform, which we examine in Chapter 6. Unlike the situation with issues of peace and security, however, the end of the Cold War did not significantly affect UN economic and social programs. If anything, they have received less attention as the UN's role in peace and security and especially the role of the Security Council have expanded. But the promotion of sustainable economic development, along with the maintenance of peace, remains a high priority for the UN and the international community. How to accomplish both more effectively and efficiently is the central question for the future of the UN.

SIX

□ □ □

The Future of the United Nations

The demands for global governance are many in the post–Cold War era. In the chapters on the UN's actions on peace/security and economic development/environmental sustainability issues, we can see the increasing demands the international community and individual states have made on the UN system. Demands have been made to gather more information on conflict situations; provide more and better trained peacekeepers and civilian personnel, including election monitors; institute emergency humanitarian relief; and make peace where it is absent. Demands have also been made to initiate new programs to address developmental dilemmas, to rationalize and coordinate the process of the proliferating development institutions, and to utilize more effectively the expanding network of nongovernmental organizations.

Yet confronted with such demands, the UN itself remains an institution hamstrung by Cold War structures, mired in largely unsystematic approaches to problems, and encumbered by a politically sensitive reform process. The UN Charter itself has been amended only on two occasions: in 1963 when the Security Council was increased from eleven to fifteen members and ECOSOC from eighteen to twenty-seven members and then again in 1971 when ECOSOC was expanded from twenty-seven to fifty-four members.

States, along with the UN itself, are a key source of the problem. As Michael V.D. Schulenberg, UNDP resident representative in Tehran notes, "It is beyond the capacity of the United Nations to reorganize itself. But governments do not allow the UN to organize itself rationally either."[1] Secretary-General Boutros-Ghali also recognizes this difficult task "of relating our aims to our means, of updating and reforming institutions set up at different times and with different imperatives."[2]

Who are the actors interested in UN reform? What changes can make the UN better equipped for the post–Cold War issues of peace and security, economic development, and environmental sustainability? What is the role of state leadership in guiding these reforms to meet increasing demands for global governance? How are these reforms likely to resolve the major dilemmas we have?

ACTORS INTERESTED IN UN REFORM

Over the years both governmental and nongovernmental actors have been concerned with UN reform. At the governmental level two groups have been prominent. The Group of 18 High-Level Intergovernmental Experts was established in 1985 by the General Assembly under Japanese impetus. This group was charged with making recommendations to streamline UN structure, with special attention to economic and social activities. Although given a deliberately limited mandate, the group produced seventy-one recommendations calling for critical changes in finance and budgeting.

In 1988 undersecretaries-general for development cooperation from Denmark, Finland, Iceland, Norway, and Sweden launched a three-year effort leading to proposals for UN reform. Focusing on problems of coordination and financing, the Nordic UN Project resulted in specific proposals for structural change.

Two nongovernmental initatives have also been instrumental in pushing the UN reform process. The United Nations Association of the United States of America (UNA/USA), representing 30,000 citizens organized in 165 chapters along with a 130-member council of organizations, sponsored a panel to study UN management and decisionmaking. The panel's recommendations, published as *A Successor Vision* in 1988, provide a comprehensive assessment of the UN and proposals for reform. The book, however, suffered from unfortunate timing, coming out just before the Cold War's end. In September 1992 the Ford Foundation, at the request of the secretary-general, established an independent advisory group, chaired by Shijuro Ogata of Japan and Paul Volcker of the United States. The group's recommendations have been key in rethinking reform of the UN's financial base.

From within the UN Secretariat there has been a concerted effort toward reforming the system, most notably from Secretary-General Boutros-Ghali. His pathbreaking *An Agenda for Peace* (1992) has provided the framework for much of the post–Cold War debate on reform to meet security needs. *An Agenda for Development* (1994), though less pathbreaking, has begun to shape debate on reform in the economic area.

CAPACITY OF THE UN IN PEACE AND SECURITY

The capacity of the UN to address peace and security issues depends on both the Security Council and the Office of the Secretary-General. We examine each briefly.

Security Council: Membership and Voting

The organ most responsible for intergovernmental security cooperation is the Security Council. Two issues—membership and voting—have continued to affect functioning of the organ. Security Council operations have been firmly rooted in post–World War II politics: the victors as permanent members, each with veto over substantive issues. The 1963 augmentation of membership from eleven to fifteen did not alter the status of the five permanent members. Yet since the mid-1960s UN membership has increased 60 percent, and power relationships have changed. France and Great Britain are no longer considered great powers by many, while Japan and Germany have gained power without commensurate status in the Security Council. Middle powers have challenged their systematic exclusion.

As states proliferate, should membership be expanded and diversified to accord more with democratic principles? What arrangements would satisfy the criteria of representativeness and efficiency? Should voting be modified to alter the antidemocratic bias of the veto power? Would legitimacy be enhanced by diversifying the geographic representation and altering the voting structure? These issues have been discussed since the early 1960s, when one proposal called for a forty-five-member Security Council with five maxipowers, fifteen major powers, eleven middle powers, eight minor powers, and six ministates! Since the end of the Cold War has ushered in an activist agenda for the council, these issues have gained increasing urgency.

Given the number of new members alone, as shown in Figure 2.3, the Security Council should be increased by nine members to a total of twenty-four. Some of the current inequities would also be alleviated by changing the composition of membership. Of the permanent members, China is the only Third World and Asian country. In terms of finances for UN peacekeeping, Germany and Japan both contribute more than China, Great Britain, or France; even Italy, Canada, and Sweden pay more than China. Yet none of these enjoys a permanent seat on the council. In terms of geographic representation, Europe is overrepresented at the expense of Latin America, Africa, and Asia. Thus, reforms have focused on keeping the Security Council relatively small for efficiency, changing the geographic composition to lessen European dominance, altering the voting system, and considering financial support as a basis for representation.[3] Table 6.1 outlines three proposals for altering the council's membership to change the criteria of geographic and economic representation and voting.

Deciding on a plan for Security Council reform will not be easy. The G-77, one of the principal groups advocating change, is divided. For example, Argentina, Bangladesh, and Malaysia oppose adding new permanent members; Turkey, Jamaica, Iran, and Egypt favor rotational representation to countries representing regions; Indonesia favors abolishing the veto; others such as Colombia, Iran, and Libya prefer limiting the exercise of the veto. Whatever structural reform is adopted, the council will

Members of the Security Council vote in August 1991. UN Photo 177953/M. Grant.

be pressured to broaden participation and to reverse the increasing tendency to conduct its business behind closed doors in informal consultations without formal records.

Office of the Secretary-General

The increasing demands for UN activity in peace and security came to a head in an extraordinary session of heads of state at the Security Council in January 1992. The secretary-general was charged with making suggestions on how to reform the system. Responding to that charge, Boutros Boutros-Ghali proposed *An Agenda for Peace,* a comprehensive plan to buttress traditional UN peacekeeping and to initiate new activities in the area of peacemaking.[4]

Preventive diplomacy measures were given primacy of place, including suggestions for UN intelligence capacities and monitoring of "hot spots" before actual conflict has broken out. These measures include the training of personnel, provision of logistical support, and greater use of high technology for surveillance, such as remote-piloted vehicles and satellite monitoring. Such proposals mean that the secretary-general could respond more quickly and flexibly to situations, identify threats to peace, create opportunities and an environment for negotiations, and ensure that the United Nations does not become so closely identified with one party that it is unable to act impartially.

TABLE 6.1 Proposals for Reform of the Security Council

Changes in Membership	*Changes in Voting*	*Advantages*
Increase number of permanent members by up to 5; likely candidates, Germany, Japan, Italy, India, Nigeria, Brazil	Veto for new permanent members	Gives equivalent power to new members; adds economic and geographic representation
Increase number of seats to 19 members by reserving 4 seats for regional powers: Egypt or Nigeria for Africa; Brazil or Argentina for the Americas; India or Japan for Asia, and Germany or Italy for Europe	No veto for new permanent members	No change in number of states with veto; power still with original permanent members; addition of geographic and economic representation
Make all members nonpermanent, elected by General Assembly for two years, requiring 2/3 majority	All equal votes, elimination of veto	Radical reform; meet needs for geographic representation and for democratic governance

Musical chairs: Who gets the Security Council seat? By Beata Szpura for the *Interdependent*, publication of the United Nations Association of the USA. Reprinted with permission.

In a significant departure from past practices, peacemaking proposals which involve strengthening the capacity of the Office of the Secretary-General to utilize force, were given pride of place in *An Agenda.* One idea would give increased power to the secretary-general to utilize pre-planned enforcement measures, including the authority to dispatch an unarmed rapid deployment force after a crisis has broken out, therefore alleviating the long lag time before international enforcement measures are instituted. A revival of the Military Staff Committee would also strengthen the secretary-general's hand and permit quicker, more authoritative responses. Enhanced training for UN activities would make these forces better equipped to deal with logistical problems and communications difficulties. *An Agenda* also envisages regional organizations as significant players. As Jan Eliasson, former undersecretary-general for humanitarian affairs, states, "Our new and innovative tools, from preventive diplomacy to peace-building, can only be effective if there is full collaboration with regional organizations and the support and participation of all those committed to peace and development."[5]

Although these changes in the area of peace and security are pathbreaking, augmenting the capacity of the secretary-general's office to carry out different peacekeeping and peace-enforcing activities, they do not resolve the overall system-level problems. The secretary-general neither is in the position nor has the power to coordinate systemwide activities effectively. He does not have the outright authority to convene meetings of either UN or specialized agencies, although the office is nominally responsible for the galaxy of specialized organizations and agencies, programs, and special bodies, some at New York headquarters and others around the world. Equally important, the secretary-general, even with a more streamlined Secretariat, still has the daunting task of improving intergovernmental support for programs.

CAPACITY OF THE UN FOR PROMOTING SUSTAINABLE DEVELOPMENT

Coordinating the UN system responses in the economic development area has proven a monumental task. ECOSOC has never been able to perform its coordinating function. The number of specialized agencies dealing with economic and social issues has exploded, as have their budgets. These agencies have been individually funded and instructed to act autonomously by design. Yet without a consolidated budget and set of controls, ECOSOC's coordinating function has been undermined since the outset. Furthermore, if World Bank funding is excluded, the rest of the UN system has never had the largest share of development finances. Not surprisingly, states have tended to send low-level representatives to ECOSOC, further undermining its work. The result is that ECOSOC has been systematically bypassed or its work duplicated in the General Assembly. For example, in two important development initiatives—the Third Development Decade in the 1980s and the UN Program of Action for Africa in 1992—the General Assembly bypassed ECOSOC, contending that it represented the elite rather than the interests of the Third World. This programmatic slighting has undermined consultative procedures. These problems have become urgent with the sustainable development agenda since by its very nature the issues at stake are interdisciplinary and require coordinated action.

The coordination problem is not new. As early as 1969 the Jackson Report warned that "the machine as a whole has become unmanageable. . . . It is becoming slower and more unwieldly like some prehistoric monster."[6] The regional commissions could not solve the problem. In 1978 a director-general for development and international economic cooperation was appointed but given few resources.

The problem of multiple agencies engaged in various tasks with lack of coordination plagued efforts to deal with the Gulf and Yugoslav crises. In both cases different agencies were given various tasks. A lead agency was eventually appointed, but its capacity and ability to coordinate such activities was limited.

During the Gulf crisis several agencies were mobilized to deal with the Kurdish problem—UNHCR was given camp management responsibilities, the UN Children's Fund (UNICEF) handled water and sanitation, and WHO handled the health sector. In practice these responsibilities overlapped, and UNHCR eventually became the "lead" agency, but conflicting procedures and approaches inhibited the coordinated response. As one observer illustrates,

> UNDRO [UN Diaster Relief Organization], WFP [World Food Program], and UNHCR representatives in Syria agreed among themselves, that an increase in sugar rations from 10 to 15 grams per person per day for a group of refugees in the desert was justified in the light of the bitter cold. They requested UNDRO headquarters for permission to proceed accordingly. UNDRO in Geneva deferred to WFP in Rome, which questioned the implications for sugar rations in other programs. Since an extra amount was involved beyond the WFP standard ration, WFP referred the matter to UNHCR in Geneva to underwrite any supplement. UNHCR ended by rejecting the request on the grounds that it lacked the necessary resources. After more than a month, the field request was denied.[7]

Similarly for other aspects of the Gulf crisis, the UN system was activated—ILO to provide employment and job retraining, UNEP to assess the impact of environmental damage on the Gulf, and the International Maritime Organization (IMO) to aid in oil slick cleanup. Yet as one observer notes, there was not a single UN but many, and this created confusion. "We never got the feeling that the entire system had a coordinated plan in which individual agencies played clear and specified roles."[8]

The result of this coordination crisis was a General Assembly resolution passed in December 1991 to strengthen coordination. In March 1992 the Department of Humanitarian Affairs was created, headed by an undersecretary-general. The department was allocated a $50 million emergency fund to respond more quickly to crisis situations. Creating a new agency did not solve the coordination problem, as the Yugoslavia crisis proved. The Department of Humanitarian Affairs lacked the authority to resolve interagency differences and showed a reluctance to take on a major role of aggressive fund-raising. More generally, "the United Nations did not respond as a system but rather as a series of separate and largely autonomous agencies. Each had its own institutional dynamics, formulated its own priorities, and moved according to a timetable of its own devising."[9]

Several groups have recommended reforms to improve the coordinating system. UNA/USA's *A Successor Vision* recommended that ECOSOC be expanded to include all UN members and that the Second and Third Committees then be abolished.[10] A small governing board of approximately twenty-five governments would monitor international problems outside the authority of the Security Council, build consensus on how to deal with such problems through ad hoc working groups, and convert agreements into actions to be undertaken by the UN and its member states. Third World states would presumably utilize ECOSOC as the forum of choice, especially if the General Assembly alternative was eliminated. In addition, debate within ECOSOC could become more focused through prioritizing the agenda, utilizing a timetable, and judiciously using reports. These proposals seek to enhance the legitimacy and effectiveness of ECOSOC as the main coordinating agency.

In 1991 the Nordic UN Project also offered proposals for reform of UN development activities. Given the absence of a systemwide policy on development issues, the Nordics proposed consolidating the governing councils of many UN development bodies into a single international development council under ECOSOC auspices. Such an approach would give ECOSOC budgetary control over UN field operations.[11]

Secretary-General Boutros-Ghali has also suggested ECOSOC reforms in *An Agenda for Peace* as part of his initiative to broaden the definition of security. ECOSOC would report to the Security Council on economic and social developments that might threaten international peace and security. He further suggested flexible intersessional meetings in order to react to crises in a more timely fashion. More generally, as Boutros-Ghali told ECOSOC in June 1993, "we have to rethink what we mean by social development and economic progress. And we have to recast our institutions in the light of our new thinking." That process, he said, "must start . . . in ECOSOC." The council "should be providing leadership on economic and social policy for the United Nations. It should also guide the overall management of operational activities."[12] ECOSOC must have the tools to become more efficient and more legitimate coordinators.

At the hub of the coordination effort is the Office of the Secretary-General. Yet forging a consensus is not easy, as the secretary-general must simultaneously meet the demands of two constituencies—member states and the UN system. States—the same units that elect the person to the office in the first place—must be satisfied. They do not want to be either upstaged or publicly opposed by the secretary-general.

The secretary-general also has to answer to the Secretariat and the personnel working in programs and specialized agencies across the UN system. Yet this group is unwieldly, lacking coherence. Sir Brian Urquhart, former UN undersecretary-general, notes, "Too many top-level officials, political appointments, rotten boroughs, and pointless programs had rendered the Secretariat fat and flabby over the years."[13]

Despite incremental changes, the organizational structure of the Secretariat remains top-heavy. One proposal suggests that four or at most five deputies report directly to the secretary-general: one responsible for peace and security; one for economic, social, and environmental problems; one for administration and management; one for relations with the public and nongovernmental organizations; and possibly one for humanitarian affairs and human rights. Programs would be consolidated under these functional categories, and a pyramidal structure would simplify decision-making authority.

Efforts to reform the structure of the UN Secretariat reflect a concern with enhancing organizational effectiveness and efficiency so that the UN can better meet demands for global governance. The institution's capacity to do so in the areas of peace and security as well as environment and development is also limited by member states' own commitment.

CAPACITY AND WILLINGNESS OF STATES TO COMMIT

Financial Problems

Although the financial problems of the UN are of long-standing origin, they are an important indicator of states' willingness to pay their assessed share of the costs of UN activities. **Arrearages** for peacekeeping, the shortfalls in members' payments of assessments, are particularly high. Between 1981 and 1987 these arrearages doubled from $178 million to $361 million. Between 1985 and 1988 U.S. arrearages for peacekeeping activities alone increased by $35 million a year.

In the mid-1980s the UN budget crisis came to a head. In 1985 the U.S. Congress passed three pieces of legislation designed to cut U.S. contributions. The Kassebaum Amendment proposed a reduction in the U.S. contribution to the UN budget from 25 percent to 20 percent unless a system of weighted voting for financial decisionmaking was passed. The Sundquist Amendment denied U.S. contributions to salaries of Soviet bloc UN staff members for ideological reasons. And the Gramm-Rudman Act (the Balanced Budget and Emergency Deficit Control Act) cut funds from federal government programs, including payments to the UN regular budget and forty-three other international organizations. These three measures led to a 50 percent reduction in U.S. contributions to the UN in 1986. Eighteen other contributors, including four of the five permanent members of the Security Council, likewise withheld payments for political reasons. For a variety of nonpolitical reasons, many other states were late in paying their bills, creating further budget problems for the UN. The consequences of late payments and arrearages include an inability to fund programs and to reimburse states for peacekeeping expenses (troops, transport, and equipment).

The decline during the 1980s in the value of the U.S. dollar, the currency of the UN, compounded the budgetary crisis. In 1986–1987 this decline resulted in a loss of $83 million for the United Nations. In 1987 the UN was reportedly within days of bankruptcy. The specialized agencies, such as ILO, WHO, and UNESCO, were similarly affected.

UN members responded to the crisis by establishing the Group of 18 mentioned previously. Along with its recommendation to cut back on UN staffing and simplify procedures to save money, the Group of 18 developed a compromise that gave the major donors increased power to review programs and establish priorities for use of financial resources: The twenty-one member Committee for Program and Coordination (CPC) would review budgetary expenditures and send them on to the Advisory Committee on Administration and Budgetary Questions, then to the Fifth (Financial) Committee, and finally to the General Assembly as a whole.

The key component to budgetary reform was that consensus voting at the CPC gave the United States and other major donors a virtual veto over budgetary questions. These would be "power steered" without technically altering the one state–one vote decision system. Once again UN members were able to make critical procedural changes without amending the Charter. For the larger donors this change led to a greater ability to influence key UN decisions and met a key condition of the U.S. Congress for resuming payment of U.S. contributions.

These changes did not, however, alleviate the general budgetary problems. Indeed, the problem of arrears has grown. Despite the reforms, the United States has yet to pay its arrearages in full, and in 1994 the total owed, including for peacekeeping, passed $1 billion. The new members as well as Russia have major economic problems that make UN payments difficult. Some states continue to withhold funds because of disagreements with policy. For example, the UN Fund for Population Activities (UNFPA) has lost $10 million a year because it supported coercive birth control programs in China. The shortfalls have been exacerbated by the practice of members to provide less funds for assessed contributions and more for voluntary contributions, where they have greater control over outlays. At the same time the need for additional funds has grown as the organization has taken on new responsibilities in the post–Cold War era. Peacekeeping expenditures grew from $233 million in 1987 to more than $3 billion in 1994 with the rise in the number and size of operations, such as those in Cambodia and the former Yugoslavia.

Boutros-Ghali's *An Agenda for Peace* called for a peacekeeping reserve fund of $50 million to match a new humanitarian revolving fund, but that sum is still small. Others have proposed putting up to 20 percent of the UN's annual peacekeeping bill into a revolving fund. Such a fund would be accumulated by making a one-time assessment or by collecting arrearages. Each of these proposals aims to provide the UN with the means for responding quickly to crisis situations. Currently the UN has to wait for members to volunteer troops and logistic support; the members in turn must wait for reimbursement of the costs for providing forces. In addition to seeking a reserve fund, *An Agenda for Peace* also proposed that members channel their peacekeeping assessments through defense departments or ministries rather than foreign affairs in the expectation that it would be politically easier to fund higher contributions, especially in the United States.

These suggestions were taken one step further by the distinguished group convened by Secretary-General Boutros-Ghali under the auspices of the Ford Foundation. The recommendations presented in early 1993 called for four changes. First, recognizing the cash flow problem, the group suggested that each member's annual assessment be paid in four equal installments, with penalities for late payments. Second, the Working Capital Fund should be increased from $100 million to $200 million or 20 percent of the regular budget. To capture both positive and negative changes in states' economies, and hence fluctuations in ability to pay, assessments should be based on a three-year rather than a ten-year average of gross domestic product for each member. Third, given the growth of voluntary contributions at the expense of regular assessments, the group recommended that in the development and humanitarian areas administrative costs be charged to the assessed budget *and* voluntary contributions for operational activities. It also recommended that states make multiyear commitments for voluntary contributions to facilitate long-term planning. Fourth, the group recommended a single peacekeeping budget rather than separate budgets for each operation. Such a single budget would give added flexibility to the secretary-general and the Security Council in overseeing such operations.[14]

The Nordic UN Project made a similar suggestion. Its emphasis was on a three-tier financing structure where assessments would pay for infrastructure, additional funds would come from negotiated multiyear pledges replenished periodically, and voluntary funds would be provided on an annual basis. The purpose of all proposals on UN financing is to provide stability and programmatic consistency in UN operations, based on a steady and predictable flow of resources for peacekeeping and the range of other activities.

By Frank Cotham. Reprinted with permission.

State Leadership

The most important group capable of reforming the UN and hence guaranteeing its future viability is states themselves. States must not only be committed to maintaining and reinvigorating the institution in the abstract but also provide resources and leadership for the myriad of tasks ahead. Increased demands for global governance necessitate a reformed UN and a renewal of commitment from specific states capable of providing leadership. The role of the United States will be determining, but as the former president of UNA/USA, Edward C. Luck, points out, the path will not be easy.

> In the end, however, the problem is not the system of collective security, or even its lack of resources. Rather it is the reluctance of the most influential member states—the United States first among them—to use it. Our thinking has still not adjusted to the realities of the post–Cold War world. If the member states see a U.N. that looks timid, weak, even anemic, it is in large part because they are looking at a reflection of their own policies. It is also because they are looking through myopic perspectives shaped by the history—not the potential—of internationalism.[15]

Will other states accept U.S. leadership in a post–Cold War era where there is no effective counterweight? Will the United States be willing to undertake these tasks and provide the financial resources that are at stake? The Gulf War crisis illustrates the "easy case" in terms of attribution of responsibility and commitment by the UN to "do" something. Confronted by the crisis posed by the Iraqi invasion of Kuwait and the threat to the world's oil supplies and galvanized by the changes in the Soviet Union, the United States willingly assumed a leadership role. "There was little doubt that the United States had its own agenda and interests independent of the United Nations. There was also little doubt that its interests and those of the principles of the United Nations overlapped such that serving one would serve the other."[16] In that case they were able to mobilize the financial resources of the Gulf states themselves as well as Germany and Japan to pay for the operation. But this may well have been a unique situation, as we discussed in Chapter 4.

In terms of peacekeeping and peacemaking the Clinton administration has been debating the limits of U.S. leadership and commitment as well as the UN's limits. It has made clear that the United States needs to know what its financial responsibilites are and be assured that others will participate. As the president said to the General Assembly in 1993, "The United Nations simply cannot become engaged in every one of the world's conflicts. If the American people are to say yes to U.N. peacekeeping, the United Nations must know when to say no."[17] The 1994 Presidential Decision Directive provides that U.S. forces can take part in both classic and relatively safe UN operations and in more dangerous peace-enforcement missions, even allowing U.S. troops to serve under foreign commanders, with certain conditions. The document suggests that the United States must be satisfied "there is a genuine threat to international peace and security, a major humanitarian disaster requiring urgent action, a legitimate democratic government is in danger, or there is a gross violation of human rights."[18]

Questions remain. Will the United States provide necessary financial and logistical support for expanded peacekeeping and peace-enforcement operations? Will the United States train troops for peacekeeping, as middle powers have done? Will the United States work with coalition partners more collaboratively than it did in the Gulf War and in Somalia? Will the United States let its troops serve under UN authority? Will the United States sustain the same level of commitment even when the going gets difficult? The danger exists that "acting as a world leader includes the danger of becoming the world's policeman."[19]

Whether the United States is willing to undertake leadership depends, in part, on domestic politics. Will domestic factors constrain the United States from playing a critical leadership role? Or will they support or enable the United States to do so? Presidential administrations make a difference. President Bill Clinton has made a difference, providing leadership at the 1993 Vienna human rights conference for accepting norms of economic and social rights as well as for upholding the principle of universal human rights norms and creating a high commissioner for human rights. The Clinton administration has been more supportive than either the Reagan or Bush administration for a broad range of other UN system activities: in the environment, in WHO's efforts to combat AIDS, in UNICEF's work with children, in population and UNFPA, and in arms control. However, the U.S. executive answers to Congress, which since the mid-1980s has been reluctant to fulfill U.S. obligations to UN budgets, a trend likely to continue with budget deficits, an unwieldy congressional budget process, unhappiness with rising UN costs, and the Republican majority elected in 1994. The continuing funding shortfall threatens to undermine the U.S. ability to exercise leadership. U.S. public opinion has historically been positive toward the UN, but that broad support is unlikely to counter Congress's negative attitudes. Since the end of the Cold War the public has become more ambivalent than the foreign policy elites about a leadership role for the United States in the UN.

Constraints of domestic politics—the Clinton administration's focus on domestic social and economic issues, a Congress constrained by the already huge budget deficits, and a public generally supportive of the UN but reluctant to support the use of U.S. troops in risky UN peace-enforcement operations such as Somalia, Haiti, or Bosnia—mean that the United States is unlikely to take a responsible UN leadership role without the strong support of other powers, providing people and financial resources. Other states must take the leadership mantle—namely, Germany and Japan as well as Russia. But each has powerful domestic constraints, economic in the latter case and political in the former. Leadership, however, requires not only the willingness to take initiatives, build coalitions, and provide financial support but also the willingness of others to be followers. And "followership" becomes all the more difficult to organize with the proliferation of states with diverse needs and with the increasing importance of nongovernmental actors. Yet from a political standpoint leadership in the UN has to include not just the United States but also other major industrialized countries if it is to ensure the power resources and financial wherewithal for action. Middle powers alone, like the G-77 in the 1970s and 1980s, cannot fully succeed in providing leadership. Yet as one academic asks, "Will other countries, especially those in the developing world—broadly speaking, the countries of the 'South'—accept the direction taken by the major industrialized countries as leading to norms that are 'fair and reasonable'?"[20]

ROLE OF NGOS IN UN REFORM

Leadership must also be exerted by transnational actors—particularly nongovernmental organizations, as representatives of civil society. As shown in Chapter 5, NGOs played a critical role in both the women-in-development and environmental sustainability agendas. Will NGOs gain a more formal role in the UN system as a result of the UNCED process? Will a greater variety of NGOs become represented? Will they be able to utilize and influence the UN system to greater effect than they have in the past? Will they be given more authority to enforce UN decisions and engage in more extensive implementation activities, as foreordained in Agenda 21?

If NGOs were given these tasks and responsibilities, they would be exercising leadership in a way not envisioned by the founders of the UN. In doing so, they would be accommodating the shift in sovereignty away from nation-states and toward the people, another trend neither imagined by the founders nor articulated during the Cold War era. All of the conditions are ripe for expanded NGO roles. NGOs reflect the growth in popular social movements, offering new channels of participation as states have diminished in importance. Many post–Cold War problems call for novel approaches, more apt to be found in NGOs than in states or state-centric organizations such as the United Nations. Giving NGOs a greater formal role in the UN system, like other reforms we have discussed, would require amending the Charter, a politically difficult and sensitive task.

CONCLUSION

The obstacles to amending the UN Charter are not procedural but political. The Charter's provisions on membership and representation in the Security Council and other bodies, on contributions, and on voting power were products of World War II–era political realities and of carefully worked out compromises. Furthermore, the major provisions of the Charter were drafted by Americans and a small number of representatives from other countries, who, in turn, worked on behalf of a total group of countries less than one-third the number of current UN members. Consensus and agreement were far easier to achieve under those circumstances than they would be today, when both the number of states and the diversity of interests and points of view are far greater. Charter amendment has thus always been regarded like the proverbial Pandora's box: Once opened, neither the agenda (i.e., the issues that would be discussed) nor the outcome could be controlled. In diplomacy there is a general aversion to convening meetings where neither the agenda nor the outcomes have been negotiated and are therefore known in advance.

What, then, are some of the concerns over Charter reform? Discussion of ways to increase the capacity of the Office of the Secretary-General and of the Secretariat invokes fears of centralizing powers in a single, powerful leader and diminishing states' control. Consideration of changing Security Council membership and altering the veto elicits fears of some current permanent members losing their status, either by having to resign from the council or more generally of diluting their power with the addition of new permanent members. Equally sensitive is the question of which states should gain permanent membership on the Security Council. There is also the anxiety of decentralizing power further from the few toward the many—from Europe and North America to Latin America, Asia, and Africa; from the wealthy to the poorer; from whites to people of color. And from the developing countries' perspective, increasing the role of the Security Council reduces their influence and "could well mean . . . the freedom [for the United States], through UN legitimacy, to impose its own values and world view on the vast majority of those member-states constituting the Third World."[21] As one expert on UN reform notes, "There are serious questions whether the Council represents the full range of values and aspirations of the world's peoples." If the UN is to be an effective instrument for global security, "the gap between the dominant industrialized states and those that consider themselves disenfranchised and marginalized will have to be bridged."[22]

Proposals to strengthen the mandate of ECOSOC to steer and coordinate the broadly conceived sustainable development efforts invoke concern for an overly centralized approach to development, long eschewed by groups from all political spectrums and anathema to proponents of sustainable development. Such proposals may reflect hopes for greater efficiency and coordination but will hardly address concerns over inadequate funding of UN economic and social programs, let alone over the management of international economic relations. The G-77 may have fragmented and the NIEO largely disappeared from UN agendas, but the political battle is not over. Proposals for budgetary reforms giving more power to those with economic resources elicit further charges of great power domination. And altering the reform process—making the procedure "easier"—means that the basic organizational compromises are challenged, leading to potential crises within the organization.

Whether the post–Cold War era will result in more fundamental changes is debatable. Peter Wilenski, a former Australian delegate to the UN, predicts that "radical reform of the United Nations is unlikely. Broad-ranging . . . recommendations come to nothing, incremental or step-by-step reform is more likely as the path ahead."[23] Others are more optimistic that the time is ripe for major changes.

The issues of UN reform, then, are not just debates over how to make an organization more efficient, effective, and representative. They are deeply political and philosophical questions of values and power. As one UN expert suggests, "In many respects, the struggles in the UN over the years were grounded in north-south differences as much, if not more than in east-west tensions."[24] The gulf between North and South remains, although for the moment at least the East-West divide has disappeared. The major industrialized countries, led by the United States, may well be able to gain support for a number of reforms in the UN, with or without amending the Charter. Nevertheless, the fault lines in debates over these reforms as well as over economic and social programs and peace and security activities are likely to be along the North-South axis. And underlying and shaping the debates will be the three dilemmas: sovereignty versus its erosion, demands for global governance versus the limited capacity of both states and the UN itself, and the need for leadership versus the proliferation of actors.

□ □ □

Appendix: Charter of the United Nations (Selected Selections)

Preamble to the Charter of the United Nations

WE THE PEOPLES OF THE UNITED NATIONS DETERMINED

to save succeeding generations from the scourge of war, which twice in our lifetime has brought untold sorrow to mankind,

and

to reaffirm faith in fundamental human rights, in the dignity and worth of the human person, in the equal rights of men and women and of nations large and small, and

to establish conditions under which justice and respect for the obligations arising from treaties and other sources of international law can be maintained, and

to promote social progress and better standards of life in larger freedom,

AND FOR THESE ENDS

to practice tolerance and live together in peace with one another as good neighbours, and to unite our strength to maintain international peace and security, and

to ensure, by the acceptance of principles and the institution of methods, that armed force shall not be used, save in the common interest, and

to employ international machinery for the promotion of the economic and social advancement of all peoples,

HAVE RESOLVED TO COMBINE OUR EFFORTS TO ACCOMPLISH THESE AIMS

Accordingly, our respective Governments, through representatives assembled in the city of San Francisco, who have exhibited their full powers found to be in good and due form, have agreed to the present Charter of the United Nations and do hereby establish an international organization to be known as the United Nations.

Chapter I

Purposes and Principles

Article 1

The Purposes of the United Nations are:

1. To maintain international peace and security, and to that end: to take effective collective measures for the prevention and removal of threats to the peace, and for the suppression of acts of aggression or other breaches of the peace, and to bring about by peaceful means, and in conformity with the principles of justice and international law, adjustment or settlement of international disputes or situations which might lead to a breach of the peace;

2. To develop friendly relations among nations based on respect for the principle of equal rights and self-determination of peoples, and to take other appropriate measures to strengthen universal peace;

3. To achieve international co-operation in solving international problems of an economic, social, cultural, or humanitarian character, and in promoting and encouraging respect for human rights and for fundamental freedoms for all without distinction as to race, sex, language, or religion; and

4. To be a centre for harmonizing the actions of nations in the attainment of these common ends.

Article 2

The Organization and its Members, in pursuit of the Purposes stated in Article 1, shall act in accordance with the following Principles.

1. The Organization is based on the principle of the sovereign equality of all its Members.

2. All Members, in order to ensure to all of them the rights and benefits resulting from membership, shall fulfill in good faith the obligations assumed by them in accordance with the present Charter.

3. All Members shall settle their international disputes by peaceful means in such a manner that international peace and security, and justice, are not endangered.

4. All Members shall refrain in their international relations from the threat or use of force against the territorial integrity or political independence of any state, or in any other manner inconsistent with the Purposes of the United Nations.

5. All Members shall give the United Nations every assistance in any action it takes in accordance with the present Charter, and shall refrain from giving assistance to any state against which the United Nations is taking preventive or enforcement action.

6. The Organization shall ensure that states which are not Members of the United Nations act in accordance with these Principles so far as may be necessary for the maintenance of international peace and security.

7. Nothing contained in the present Charter shall authorize the United Nations to intervene in matters which are essentially within the domestic jurisdiction of any state or shall require the Members to submit such matters to settlement under the present Charter; but this principle shall not prejudice the application of enforcement measures under Chapter VII.

Chapter II

Membership

Article 3

The original Members of the United Nations shall be the states which, having participated in the United Nations Conference on International Organization at San Francisco, or having previously signed the Declaration by United Nations of 1 January 1942, signed the present Charter and ratify it in accordance with Article 110.

Article 4

1. Membership in the United Nations is open to all other peace-loving states which accept the obligations contained in the present Charter and, in the judgment of the Organization, are able and willing to carry out these obligations.

2. The admission of any such state to membership in the United Nations will be effected by a decision of the General Assembly upon the recommendation of the Security Council.

Article 5

A Member of the United Nations against which preventive or enforcement action has been taken by the Security Council may be suspended from the exercise of the rights and privileges of membership by the General Assembly upon the recommendation of the Security Council. The exercise of these rights and privileges may be restored by the Security Council.

Article 6

A Member of the United Nations which has persistently violated the Principles contained in the present Charter may be expelled from the Organization by the General Assembly upon the recommendation of the Security Council.

Chapter III

Organs

Article 7

1. There are established as the principal organs of the United Nations: a General Assembly, a Security Council, an Economic and Social Council, a Trusteeship Council, an International Court of Justice, and a Secretariat.

2. Such subsidiary organs as may be found necessary may be established in accordance with the present Charter.

Article 8

The United Nations shall place no restrictions on the eligibility of men and women to participate in any capacity and under conditions of equality in its principal and subsidiary organs.

Chapter IV

The General Assembly

COMPOSITION

Article 9

1. The General Assembly shall consist of all the Members of the United Nations.

2. Each Member shall have not more than five representatives in the General Assembly.

FUNCTIONS AND POWERS

Article 10

The General Assembly may discuss any questions or any matters within the score of the present Charter or relating to the powers and functions of any organs provided for in the present Charter, and except as provided in Article 12, may make recommendations to the Members of the United Nations or to the Security Council or to both on any such questions or matters.

Article 11

1. The General Assembly may consider the general principles of co-operation in the maintenance of international peace and security, including the principles governing disarmament and the regulation of armaments and may make recommendations with regard to such principles to the Members or to the Security Council or to both.

2. The General Assembly may discuss any questions relating to the maintenance of international peace and security brought before it by any Member of the United Nations, or by the Security Council, or by a state which is not a Member of the United Nations in accordance with Article 35, paragraph 2, and, except as provided in Article 12, may make recommendations with regard to any such questions to the state or states concerned or to the Security Council or to both. Any such question on which action is necessary shall be referred to the Security Council by the General Assembly either before or after discussion.

3. The General Assembly may call the attention of the Security Council to situations which are likely to endanger international peace and security.

4. The powers of the General Assembly set forth in this Article shall not limit the general scope of Article 10.

Article 12

1. While the Security Council is exercising in respect of any situation the functions assigned to it in the present Charter the General Assembly shall not make any recommendation with regard to that dispute or situation unless the Security Council so requests.

2. The Secretary-General, with the consent of the Security Council, shall notify the General Assembly at each session of any matters relative to the maintenance of international peace and security which are being dealt with by the Security Council and shall similarly notify the General Assembly, or the Members of the United Nations if the General Assembly is not in session, immediately the Security Council ceases to deal with such matters.

Article 13

1. The General Assembly shall initiate studies and make recommendations for the purpose of:

a. promoting international co-operation in the political field and encouraging the progressive development of international law and its codification;

b. promoting international co-operation in the economic, social, cultural, educational, and health fields, and assisting in the realization of human rights and fundamental freedoms for all without distinctions as to race, sex, language, or religion.

2. The further responsibilities, functions and powers of the General Assembly with respect to matters mentioned in paragraph 1 (b) above are set forth in Chapters IX and X.

Article 14

Subject to the provisions of Article 12, the General Assembly may recommend measures for the peaceful adjustment of any situations, regardless of origin, which it deems likely to impair the general welfare or friendly relations among nations, including situations resulting from a violation of the provisions of the present Charter setting forth the Purposes and Principles of the United Nations.

Article 15

1. The General Assembly shall receive and consider annual and special reports from the Security Council; these reports shall include an account of the measures that the Security Council has decided upon or taken to maintain international peace and security.

2. The General Assembly shall receive and consider reports from the other organs of the United Nations.

Article 16

The General Assembly shall perform such functions with respect to the international trusteeship system as are assigned to it under Chapters XII and XIII, including the approval of the trusteeship agreements for areas not designated as strategic.

Article 17

1. The General Assembly shall consider and approve the budget of the Organization.

2. The expenses of the Organization shall be borne by the Members as apportioned by the General Assembly.

3. The General Assembly shall consider and approve any financial and budgetary arrangements with specialized agencies referred to in Article 57 and shall examine the administrative budgets of such specialized agencies with a view to making recommendations to the agencies concerned.

VOTING

Article 18

1. Each member of the General Assembly shall have one vote.

2. Decisions of the General Assembly on important questions shall be made by a two-thirds majority of the members present and voting. These questions shall include: recommendations with respect to the maintenance of international peace and security, the election of the non-permanent members of the Security Council, the election of the members of the Economic and Social Council, the election of members of the Trusteeship Council in accordance with paragraph 1 (c) of Article 86, the admission of new Members to the United Nations, the suspension of the rights and privileges of membership, the expulsion of Members, questions relating to the operation of the trusteeship system, and budgetary questions.

3. Decisions on other questions, including the determination of additional categories of questions to be decided by a two-thirds majority, shall be made by a majority of the members present and voting.

Article 19

A Member of the United Nations which is in arrears in the payment of its financial contributions to the Organization shall have no vote in the General Assembly if the amount of its arrears equals or exceeds the amount of the contributions due from it for the preceding two full years. The General Assembly may, nevertheless, permit such a Member to vote if it is satisfied that the failure to pay is due to conditions beyond the control of the Member.

PROCEDURE

Article 20

The General Assembly shall meet in regular annual sessions and in such special session as occasion may require. Special sessions shall be convoked by the

Secretary-General at the request of the Security Council or of a majority of the Members of the United Nations.

Article 21

The General Assembly shall adopt its own rules of procedure. It shall elect its President for each session.

Article 22

The General Assembly may establish such subsidiary organs as it deems necessary for the performance of its functions.

Chapter V

The Security Council

COMPOSITION

Article 23

1. The Security Council shall consist of fifteen Members of the United Nations. The Republic of China, France, the Union of Soviet Socialist Republics, the United Kingdom of Great Britain and Northern Ireland, and the United States of America shall be permanent members of the Security Council. The General Assembly shall elect ten other Members of the United Nations to be non-permanent members of the Security Council, due regard being specially paid, in the first instance to the contribution of Members of the United Nations to the maintenance of international peace and security and to the other purposes of the Organization, and also to equitable geographical distribution.

2. The non-permanent members of the Security Council shall be elected for a term of two years. In the first election of the non-permanent members after the increase of the membership of the Security Council from eleven to fifteen, two of the four additional members shall be chosen for a term of one year. A retiring member shall not be eligible for immediate re-election.

3. Each member of the Security Council shall have one representative.

FUNCTIONS AND POWERS

Article 24

1. In order to ensure prompt and effective action by the United Nations, its Members confer on the Security Council primary responsibility for the maintenance of international peace and security, and agree that in carrying out its duties under this responsibility the Security Council acts on their behalf.

2. In discharging these duties the Security Council shall act in accordance with the Purposes and Principles of the United Nations. The specific powers granted to the Security Council for the discharge of these duties are laid down in Chapters VI, VII, VIII, and XII.

3. The Security Council shall submit annual and, when necessary, special reports to the General Assembly for its consideration.

Article 25

The Members of the United Nations agree to accept and carry out the decisions of the Security Council in accordance with the present Charter.

Article 26

In order to promote the establishment and maintenance of international peace and security with the least diversion for armaments of the world's human and economic resources, the Security Council shall be responsible for formulating, with the assistance of the Military Staff Committee referred to in Article 47, plans to be submitted to the Members of the United Nations for the establishment of a system for the regulation of armaments.

VOTING

Article 27

1. Each member of the Security Council shall have one vote.

2. Decisions of the Security Council on procedural matters shall be made by an affirmative vote of nine members.

3. Decisions of the Security Council on all other matters shall be made by an affirmative vote of nine members including the concurring votes of the permanent members; provided that, in decisions under Chapter VI, and under paragraph 3 of Article 52, a party of a dispute shall abstain from voting.

PROCEDURE

Article 28

1. The Security Council shall be so organized as to be able to function continuously. Each members of the Security Council shall for this purpose be represented at all times at the seat of the Organization.

2. The Security Council shall hold periodic meetings at which each of its members may, if it so desires, be represented by a member of the government or by some other specially designated representative.

3. The Security Council may hold meetings at such places other than the seat of the Organization as in its judgment will best facilitate its work.

Article 29

The Security Council may establish such subsidiary organs as it deems necessary for the performance of its functions.

Article 30

The Security Council shall adopt its own rules of procedure, including the method of selecting its President.

Article 31

Any Member of the United Nations which is not a member of the Security Council may participate, without vote, in the discussion of any question brought before the Security Council whenever the latter considers that the interests of that Member are specially affected.

Article 32

Any Member of the United Nations which is not a member of the Security Council or any state which is not a Member of the United Nations, if it is a party to a dispute under consideration by the Security Council, shall be invited to participate, without vote, in the discussion relating to the dispute. The Security Council shall lay down such conditions as it deems just for the participation of a state which is not a Member of the United Nations.

Chapter VI

Pacific Settlements of Disputes

Article 33

1. The parties to any dispute, the continuance of which is likely to endanger the maintenance of international peace and security, shall, first of all, seek a solution by negotiation, enquiry, mediation, conciliation, arbitration, judicial settlement, resort to regional agencies or arrangements, or other peaceful means of their own choice.

2. The Security Council shall, when it deems necessary, call upon the parties to settle their dispute by such means.

Article 34

The Security Council may investigate any dispute, or any situation which might lead to international friction or give rise to a dispute, in order to determine whether the continuance of the dispute or situation is likely to endanger the maintenance of international peace and security.

Article 35

Any Member of the United Nations may bring any dispute, or any situation of the nature referred to in Article 34, to the attention of the Security Council or of the General Assembly.

2. A state which is not a Member of the United Nations may bring to the attention of the Security Council or of the General Assembly any dispute to which it is a party if it accepts in advance, for the purposes of the dispute, the obligations of pacific settlement provided in the present Charter.

3. The proceedings of the General Assembly in respect of matters brought to its attention under this Article will be subject to the provisions of Articles 11 and 12.

Article 36

1. The Security Council may, at any stage of a dispute of the nature referred to in Article 33 or of a situation of like nature, recommend appropriate procedures or methods of adjustment.

2. The Security Council should take into consideration any procedures for the settlement of the dispute which have already been adopted by the parties.

3. In making recommendations under this Article the Security Council should also take into consideration that legal disputes should as a general rule be referred by the parties to the International Court of Justice in accordance with the provisions of the Statute of the Court.

Article 37

1. Should the parties to a dispute of the nature referred to in Article 33 fail to settle it by the means indicated in that Article, they shall refer it to the Security Council.

2. If the Security Council deems that the continuance of the dispute is in fact likely to endanger the maintenance of international peace and security, it shall decide whether to take action under Article 36 or to recommend such terms of settlement as it may consider appropriate.

Article 38

Without prejudice to the provisions of Articles 33 to 37, the Security Council may, if all the parties to any dispute so request, make recommendations to the parties with a view of a pacific settlement of the dispute.

Chapter VII

Action with Respect to Threats to the Peace, Breaches of the Peace, and Acts of Aggression

Article 39

The Security Council shall determine the existence of any threat to the peace, breach of the peace, or act of aggression and shall make recommendations, or decide what measures shall be taken in accordance with Articles 41 and 42, to maintain or restore international peace and security.

Article 40

In order to prevent an aggravation of the situation, the Security Council may, before making the recommendations or deciding upon the measures provided for in Article 39, call upon the parties concerned to comply with such provisional measures as it deems necessary or desirable. Such provisional measures shall be without prejudice to the rights, claims, or position of the parties concerned. The Security Council shall duly take account of failure to comply with such provisional measures.

Article 41

The Security Council may decide what measures not involving the use of armed force are to be employed to give effect to its decisions, and it may call upon the Members of the United Nations to apply such measures. These may include complete or partial interruption of economic relations and of rail, sea, air, postal, telegraphic, radio, and other means of communication, and the severance of diplomatic relations.

Article 42

Should the Security Council consider that measures provided for the Article 41 would be inadequate or have proved to be inadequate, it may take such action by air, sea, or land forces as may be necessary to maintain or restore international peace and security. Such action may include demonstrations, blockade, and other operations by air, sea, or land forces of Members of the United Nations.

Article 43

1. All Members of the United Nations, in order to contribute to the maintenance of international peace and security, undertake to make available to the Security Council, on its call and in accordance with a special agreement or agreements, armed forces, assistance, and facilities, including rights of passage, necessary for the purpose of maintaining international peace and security.

2. Such agreement or agreements shall govern the numbers and types of forces, their degree of readiness and general location, and the nature of the facilities and assistance to be provided.

3. The agreement or agreements shall be negotiated as soon as possible on the initiative of the Security Council. They shall be concluded between the Security Council and Members or between the Security Council and groups of Members and shall be subject to ratification by the signatory states in accordance with their respective constitutional processes.

Article 44

When the Security Council has decided to use force it shall, before calling upon a Member not represented on it to provide armed forces in fulfilment of the obligations assumed under Article 43, invite that Member, if the Member so desires, to participate in the decisions of the Security Council concerning the employment of contingents of that Member's armed forces.

Article 45

In order to enable the United Nations to take urgent military measures, Members shall hold immediately available national air-force contingents for combined international enforcement action. The strength and degree of readiness of these contingents and plans for their combined action shall be determined within the limits laid down in the special agreement or agreements referred to in Article 43, by the Security Council with the assistance of the Military Staff Committee.

Article 46

Plans for the application of armed force shall be made by the Security Council with the assistance of the Military Staff Committee.

Article 47

1. There shall be established a Military Staff Committee to advise and assist the Security Council on all questions relating to the Security Council's military requirements for the maintenance of international peace and security, the employment and command of forces placed at its disposal, the regulation of armaments, and possible disarmament.

2. The Military Staff Committee shall consist of the Chiefs of Staff of the permanent members of the Security Council or their representatives. Any Members of the United Nations not permanently represented on the Committee shall be invited by the Committee to be associated with it when the efficient discharge of the Committee's responsibilities requires the participation of that Member in its work.

3. The Military Staff Committee shall be responsible under the Security Council for the strategic direction of any armed forces placed at the disposal of the Security Council. Questions relating to the command of such forces shall be worked out subsequently.

4. The Military Staff Committee, with the authorization of the Security Council and after consultation with appropriate regional agencies, may establish regional sub-committees.

Article 48

1. The action required to carry out the decisions of the Security Council for the maintenance of international peace and security shall be taken by all the Members of the United Nations or by some of them, as the Security Council may determine.

2. Such decisions shall be carried out by the Members of the United Nations directly and through their action in the appropriate international agencies of which they are members.

Article 49

The Members of the United Nations shall join in affording mutual assistance in carrying out the measures decided upon by the Security Council.

Article 50

If preventive or enforcement measures against any state are taken by the Security Council, any other state, whether a Member of the United Nations or not, which finds itself confronted with special economic problems arising from the carrying out of those measures shall have the right to consult the Security Council with regard to a solution of those problems.

Article 51

Nothing in the present Charter shall impair the inherent right of individual or collective self-defence if an armed attack occurs against a Member of the United Nations, until the Security Council has taken measures necessary to maintain international peace and security. Measures taken by Members in the exercise of this right of self-defence shall be immediately reported to the Security Council and shall not in any way affect the authority and responsibility of the Security Council under the present Charter to take at any time such action as it deems necessary in order to maintain or restore international peace and security.

Chapter VIII

Regional Arrangements

Article 52

1. Nothing in the present Charter precludes the existence of regional arrangements or agencies for dealing with such matters relating to the maintenance of international peace and security as are appropriate for regional action provided that such arrangements or agencies and their activities are consistent with the Purposes and Principles of the United Nations.

2. The Members of the United Nations entering into such arrangements or constituting such agencies shall make every effort to achieve pacific settlement of local disputes through such regional arrangements or by such regional agencies before referring them to the Security Council.

3. The Security Council shall encourage the development of pacific settlement of local disputes through such regional arrangements or by such regional agencies either on the initiative of the states concerned or by reference from the Security Council.

4. This Article in no way impairs the application of Articles 34 and 35.

Article 53

1. The Security Council shall, where appropriate, utilize such regional arrangements or agencies for enforcement action under its authority. But no enforcement action shall be taken under regional arrangements or by regional agencies without the authorization of the Security Council, with the exception of measures against any enemy state, as defined in paragraph 2 of this Article, provided for pursuant to Article 107 or in regional arrangements directed against renewal of aggressive policy on the part of any such state, until such time as the Organization may, on request of the Governments concerned, be charged with the responsibility for preventing further aggression by such a state.

2. The term enemy state as used in paragraph 1 of this Article applies to any state which during the Second World War has been an enemy of any signatory of the present Charter.

Article 54

The Security Council shall at all times be kept fully informed of activities undertaken or in contemplation under regional arrangements or by regional agencies for the maintenance of international peace and security.

Chapter IX

International Economic and Social Co-operation

Article 55

With a view to the creation of conditions of stability and well-being which are necessary for peaceful and friendly relations among nations based on respect for the principles of equal rights and self-determination of peoples, the United Nations shall promote:

a. higher standards of living, full employment, and conditions of economic and social progress and development;

b. solutions of international economic, social, health, and related problems; and international cultural and educational cooperation; and

c. universal respect for, and observance of, human rights and fundamental freedoms for all without distinction as to race, sex, language, or religion.

Article 56

All Members pledge themselves to take joint and separate action in co-operation with the Organization for the achievement of the purposes set forth in Article 55.

Article 57

1. The various specialized agencies, established by intergovernmental agreement and having wide international responsibilities, as defined in their basic instruments, in economic, social, cultural, educational, health, and related fields, shall be brought into relationship with the United Nations in accordance with the provisions of Article 63.

2. Such agencies thus brought into relationship with the United Nations are hereinafter referred to as specialized agencies.

Article 58

The Organization shall make recommendations for the co-ordination of the policies and activities of the specialized agencies.

Article 59

The Organization shall, where appropriate, initiate negotiations among the states concerned for the creation of any new specialized agencies required for the accomplishment of the purposes set forth in Article 55.

Article 60

Responsibility for the discharge of the functions of the Organization set forth in this Chapter shall be vested in the General Assembly and, under the authority of the General Assembly, in the Economic and Social Council, which have this purpose the powers set forth in Chapter X.

Chapter X

The Economic and Social Council

COMPOSITION

Article 61

1. The Economic and Social Council shall consist of fifty-four Members of the United Nations elected by the General Assembly.

2. Subject to the provisions of paragraph 3, eighteen members of the Economic and Social Council shall be elected each year for a term of three years. A retiring member shall be eligible for immediate re-election.

3. At the first election after the increase in the membership of the Economic and Social Council from twenty-seven to fifty-four members, in addition to the members elected in place of the nine members whose term of office expires at the end of that year, twenty-seven additional members shall be elected. Of these twenty-seven additional members, the term of office of nine members so elected shall expire at the end of one year, and of nine other members at the end of two years, in accordance with arrangements made by the General Assembly.

4. Each member of the Economic and Social Council shall have one representative.

FUNCTIONS AND POWERS

Article 62

1. The Economic and Social Council may make or initiate studies and reports with respect to international economic, social, cultural, educational, health, and related matters and may make recommendations with respect to any such matters to the General Assembly to the Members of the United Nations, and to the specialized agencies concerned.

2. It may make recommendations for the purpose of promoting respect for, and observance of, human rights and fundamental freedoms for all.

3. It may prepare draft conventions for submissions to the General Assembly, with respect to matters falling within its competence.

4. It may call, in accordance with the rules prescribed by the United Nations, international conferences on matters falling within its competence.

Article 63

1. The Economic and Social Council may enter into agreements with any of the agencies referred to in Article 57, defining the terms on which the agency concerned shall be brought into relationship with the United Nations. Such agreements shall be subject to approval by the General Assembly.

2. It may co-ordinate the activities of the specialized agencies through consultation with and recommendations to such agencies and through recommendations to the General Assembly and to the Members of the United Nations.

Article 64

1. The Economic and Social Council may take appropriate steps to obtain regular reports from the specialized agencies. It may make arrangements with the Members of the United Nations and with the specialized agencies to obtain reports on the steps taken to give effect to its own recommendations and to recommendations on matters falling within its competence made by the General Assembly.

2. It may communicate its observations on these reports to the General Assembly.

Article 65

The Economic and Social Council may furnish information to the Security Council and shall assist the Security Council upon its request.

Article 66

1. The Economic and Social Council shall perform such functions as fall within its competence in connexion with the carrying out of the recommendations of the General Assembly.

2. It may, with the approval of the General Assembly, perform services at the request of Members of the United Nations and at the request of specialized agencies.

3. It shall perform such other functions as are specified elsewhere in the present Charter or as may be assigned to it by the General Assembly.

VOTING

Article 67

1. Each member of the Economic and Social Council shall have one vote.

2. Decisions of the Economic and Social Council shall be made by a majority of the members present and voting.

PROCEDURE

Article 68

The Economic and Social Council shall set up commissions in economic and social fields and for the promotion of human rights, and such other commissions as may be required for the performance of its functions.

Article 69

The Economic and Social Council shall invite any Member of the United Nations to participate, without vote, in its deliberations on any matter of particular concern to that Member.

Article 70

The Economic and Social Council may make arrangements for representatives of the specialized agencies to participate, without vote, in its deliberations and in those of the commissions established by it, and for its representatives to participate in the deliberations of the specialized agencies.

Article 71

The Economic and Social Council make make suitable arrangements for consultation with non-governmental organizations which are concerned with matters within its competence. Such arrangements may be made with international organizations, and where appropriate, with national organizations after consultation with the Member of the United Nations concerned.

Article 72

1. The Economic and Social Council shall adopt its own rules of procedure, including the method of selecting its President.

2. The Economic and Social Council shall meet as required in accordance with its rules, which shall include provision for the convening of meetings on the request of a majority of its members.

Chapter XV

The Secretariat

Article 97

The Secretariat shall comprise a Secretary-General and such staff as the Organization may require. The Secretary-General shall be appointed by the General Assembly upon the recommendation of the Security Council. He shall be the chief administrative officer of the Organization.

Article 98

The Secretary-General shall act in that capacity in all meetings of the General Assembly, of the Security Council, of the Economic and Social Council, and of the

Trusteeship Council, and shall perform such other functions as are entrusted to him by these organs. The Secretary-General shall make an annual report to the General Assembly on the work of the Organization.

Article 99

The Secretary-General may bring to the attention of the Security Council any matter which in his opinion may threaten the maintenance of international peace and security.

Article 100

1. In the performance of their duties the Secretary-General and the staff shall not seek or receive instructions from any government or from any other authority external to the Organization. They shall refrain from any action which might reflect on their position as international officials responsible only to the Organization.

2. Each Member of the United Nations undertakes to respect the exclusively international character of the responsibilities of the Secretary-General and the staff and not to seek to influence them in the discharge of their responsibilities.

Article 101

1. The staff shall be appointed by the Secretary-General under regulations established by the General Assembly.

2. Appropriate staffs shall be permanently assigned to the Economic and Social Council, the Trusteeship Council, and, as required, to other organs of the United Nations. These staffs shall form a part of the Secretariat.

3. The paramount consideration in the employment of the staff and in the determination of the conditions of service shall be the necessity of securing the highest standards of efficiency, competence, and integrity. Due regard shall be paid to the importance of recruiting the staff on as wide a geographical basis as possible.

Chapter XVIII

Amendments

Article 108

Amendments to the present Charter shall come into force for all Members of the United Nations when they have been adopted by a vote of two thirds of the members of the General Assembly and ratified in accordance with their respective constitutional processes by two thirds of the Members of the United Nations, including all the permanent members of the Security Council.

Article 109

1. A General Conference of the Members of the United Nations for the purpose of reviewing the present Charter may be held at a date and place to be fixed by a

two-thirds vote of the members of the General Assembly and by a vote of any nine members of the Security Council. Each Member of the United Nations shall have one vote in the conference.

2. Any alteration of the present Charter recommended by a two-thirds vote of the conference shall take effect when ratified in accordance with their respective constitutional processes by two thirds of the Members of the United Nations including all the permanent members of the Security Council.

3. If such a conference has not be held before the tenth annual session of the General Assembly following the coming into force of the present Charter, the proposal to call such a conference shall be placed on the agenda of that session of the General Assembly, and the conference shall be held if so decided by a majority vote of the members of the General Assembly and by a vote of any seven members of the Security Council.

□ □ □

Discussion Questions

CHAPTER ONE

1. The post–Cold War world is being shaped by many developments. What are the most important issues and problems that deserve the attention of the world community?

2. Current civil conflicts, such as in Somalia, Rwanda, Haiti, and Bosnia, dramatize the tension between respecting states' sovereignty and intervening for humanitarian purposes. Should the United Nations move beyond humanitarian assistance and "take over" governing these countries?

3. How is state sovereignty being eroded? Do you regard that as a positive or a negative development and why? What examples can you cite of the continued strength of sovereignty?

4. Why have both integrative and disintegrative trends resulted in demands on the UN and other multilateral institutions? If states are making demands on the UN, why do you think they are unwilling or unable to provide the UN with the resources to meet those demands?

CHAPTER TWO

1. How did the predecessors of the United Nations, such as the public international unions, The Hague conferences, and the League of Nations, set precedents for the structure, scope, and membership of the United Nations?

2. The UN is based on the notion of the sovereign equality of member states, but inequality of states is also part of the UN framework, such as the veto power of the permanent members of the Security Council. Do you think the UN should be based strictly on equality of member states, or is it appropriate to grant some states special status and powers? How would you decide which states should have such status and powers? What do you think are the consequences for other states of this inequality?

3. If the UN is supposed to deal only with *international* problems, who decides what is an international versus a domestic problem? How do you think the scope of what is considered international has changed over time?

4. Over the UN's fifty years the definition of security has been continually broadened from an emphasis on threats or use of military force to economic and social well-being and respect for human rights. Do you agree with such a broadened definition of security? How do you think a broader definition conflicts with states' domestic authority and sovereignty?

5. Why is it important for members of the UN to have a smaller body such as the Security Council to deal primarily with threats to international peace and a larger one such as the General Assembly to deal with a broad range of issues? What is the value of the assembly for general debate with every member, large or small, having a voice and opportunity to form coalitions with other states?

6. If self-determination continues to lead to independent statehood for the nations and peoples who seek it, would the consequent increase in membership be beneficial, detrimental, or negligible to the UN's functioning?

7. Why do you think the United States has so often been concerned about politicization, administrative efficiency, and the U.S. share of UN contributions? Do you think other states would feel similarly or differently and why?

CHAPTER THREE

1. Can you identify ways in which the United States has used the UN and ways the UN has influenced the United States and its policies?

2. How do the changes in the former Soviet Union affect the United Nations and the influence of Russia in particular?

3. Why does the question of Germany's and Japan's role in the UN pose a major dilemma for them and for other UN members? What do you think should be the role of these two states?

4. China is becoming an important actor in multilateral institutions as a result of its economic development and large population. Yet China does not accept the concepts of universal human rights and liberal democracy. What, then, may be the consequences of China's playing a more active role in the UN system?

5. International politics has often been viewed solely from the perspective of the major powers. In what ways does the UN give middle powers and small states more influence in the global community? Is this a benefit or a liability for efforts to address international issues and problems?

6. Why have regional and special interest blocs played important roles in the functioning of the UN? How do you think these groups might evolve in the future, given changes that have accompanied the end of the Cold War and the breakdown in the G-77's former unity?

7. How does the trend of increasing numbers of NGOs affect the UN and international politics? Why can it be argued that this growing NGO activity represents the democratization of international relations? Do you think this is a positive or a negative development?

8. How can the UN secretary-general best use the power of persuasion to exert influence? Why is it important for the secretary-general to have sources of information on world events that are independent of what governments provide? Is it beneficial for the secretary-general to be an active, independent actor?

CHAPTER FOUR

1. Why has it proven more difficult for the UN to undertake enforcement actions rather than traditional peacekeeping? Why have many post–Cold War peacekeeping operations involved greater use of military force?

2. Why was the Gulf War *not* a peacekeeping operation, and why did many developing countries worry about the precedents it might set?

3. How do you explain why the UN has had success in some of its recent peacekeeping operations, such as in Namibia and Cambodia, but encountered severe difficulties in dealing with Bosnia and Somalia? What lessons would you draw for effective UN action in the future?

4. Do you think it is important for the UN always to seek the consent of conflicting parties to achieve successful peacekeeping or peacemaking? What are the implications if consent is a requirement?

5. The United States has generally refused to put its soldiers under UN command. Do you think it should continue or change this practice and why? If it continues, why should other countries put their own soldiers under UN command for peacekeeping operations?

6. Given current structure and resources, the UN cannot be involved in every international conflict and problem. On what basis should choices be made about where and when the UN gets involved?

7. An important UN peacemaking and peacebuilding activity in the post–Cold War era is the monitoring of elections. Why do you think this is so, and what do you think are the benefits of having outside observers for countries' elections?

CHAPTER FIVE

1. In what ways has the UN's approach to development been shaped by liberal economic thought? Why and how did developing countries challenge that approach and propose the New International Economic Order? Why did some women also challenge the assumptions of economic liberalism?

2. The North-South dialogue and demands by developing countries for the NIEO are generally considered to have failed. Why did they? Should these issues still be high on the UN's agenda? Why or why not?

3. How do the NIEO and women-in-development debates illustrate the ways issues can permeate different parts of the UN system? Do you think this process improves the chances of actions being taken to address the problems themselves?

4. What are the advantages and disadvantages of NGOs' participation in UN activities on the environment and development?

5. Which outcomes of UNCED should be priorities for further action by the United Nations and why?

6. How can the UN meet the need for environmentally sustainable development as well as for economic justice and equity? What problems may come from creating more institutions to address new needs?

7. In relation to the many aspects of development, do you think it is better to centralize programs and efforts through the UN or to decentralize responsibility to regional institutions? What are some advantages and disadvantages of each?

8. Efforts by UN-system institutions to address environmental and development-related issues increasingly amount to intervention in the domestic affairs of

states. Is it more important to respect state sovereignty or to take whatever steps seem most effective in addressing these issues? How might sovereignty be reinterpreted to take these changes into account?

CHAPTER SIX

1. Why is it so difficult, yet so important to reform the structure and operation of an organization like the UN? What are the main obstacles to change?
2. Currently the United Nations still accords a special status to the five members who hold permanent seats and veto powers in the Security Council. With all the changes that have taken place in the world since the UN was founded in 1945, do you think this structure should change? If so, in what ways?
3. Why is reform of ECOSOC to provide greater coordination of economic and social activities so important, yet so controversial?
4. Should the UN secretary-general be given more power and authority, for example, to coordinate systemwide development activities or to convene meetings of the Security Council, General Assembly, or specialized agencies? Would member states support such a change?
5. UN member states continue to vote for peacekeeping operations, development programs, and other activities but remain reluctant to provide the financial resources for the UN to implement these programs. What proposals have been made to provide more dependable funding for the UN? How could the UN develop sources of revenue that would be independent of states?
6. What do you think should be the role and contribution of the United States to the UN? If you think it should play a larger role and contribute more, why do you think this has not happened? How can U.S. citizens influence Congress and the president to undertake that role? How can other countries be sure that the United States will sustain the same level of commitment when the going gets difficult?
7. How does the failure of the United States to pay its full assessed contributions to the UN regular and peacekeeping budgets undermine that country's ability to exercise leadership? Why is "followership" so important to the exercise of leadership, and what is required to persuade other countries to follow U.S. leadership? What other states (or other actors, such as NGOs) might provide leadership in the UN?
8. The Cold War has ended, and the world is very different from what it was when the UN was founded in 1945. If we were to create a new global organization to replace the UN in the post–Cold War era, what should it look like? What lessons would the founders of a new organization draw from its predecessors, including the UN? Should the UN become more representative of the *peoples* of the world and of nongovernmental organizations? If so, why? How might that be accomplished?
9. Should we expect the three dilemmas—sovereignty versus its erosion, demands for global governance versus the limited capacity of states and the UN, and the need for leadership versus the proliferation of actors—to be resolved in the future? If not, why not? Are there other dilemmas you would add to these?

□ □ □

Notes

CHAPTER 1

1. Jarat Chopra and Thomas G. Weiss, "Sovereignty Is No Longer Sacrosanct: Codifying Humanitarian Intervention," *Ethics and International Affairs* 6 (1992):95–117.

2. See the chapters in James N. Rosenau and Ernst-Otto Czempiel, eds., *Governance Without Government: Order and Change in World Politics* (Cambridge: Cambridge University Press, 1992).

3. Joseph S. Nye Jr., *Bound to Lead: The Changing Nature of American Power* (New York: Basic Books, 1990).

4. John Bolton, "No Expansion for U.N. Security Council," *Wall Street Journal*, January 26, 1993, p. A14.

5. Leslie H. Gelb, "Tailoring a U.S. Role at the U.N.," *International Herald Tribune*, January 2–3, 1993, p. 4.

6. William H. McNeill, "Winds of Change," *Foreign Affairs* 69, no. 1 (Fall 1990):168.

7. Marshall McLuhan, *Understanding Media: The Extension of Man* (New York: McGraw-Hill, 1964).

8. Gerald B. Helman and Steven R. Ratner, "Saving Failed States," *Foreign Policy* 89 (Winter 1992–1993):3–30.

9. Gidon Gottlieb, "Nations Without States," *Foreign Affairs* 73, no. 3 (May-June 1994):112.

10. On the subject of multilateralism, see John Gerard Ruggie, ed., *Multilateralism Matters: The Theory and Praxis of an Institutional Form* (New York: Columbia University Press, 1993).

11. Hedley Bull, *The Anarchical Society: A Study of Order in World Politics* (New York: Columbia University Press, 1977), p. 13.

12. James N. Rosenau, *Turbulence in World Politics: A Theory of Change and Continuity* (Princeton: Princeton University Press, 1990).

CHAPTER 2

1. Hersch Lauterpacht, "The Grotian Tradition in International Law," in *The British Year Book of International Law* (London: Oxford University Press, 1946), pp. 1–56.

2. Inis L. Claude Jr., *Swords into Plowshares: The Problems and Progress of International Organization*, 3d rev. ed. (New York: Random House, 1964), esp. Chap. 2.

3. Ibid., p. 22.

4. On the League, see F. S. Northledge, *The League of Nations: Its Life and Times, 1920–1946* (New York: Holmes and Meier, 1986); and F. P. Walters, *A History of the League of Nations* (New York: Oxford University Press, 1952).

5. See Evan Luard, *A History of the United Nations: The Years of Western Domination, 1945–1955,* vol. 1 (New York: St. Martin's Press, 1982).

6. Classic works on the specific organs include Sydney D. Bailey, *The Procedure of the U.N. Security Council* (New York: Oxford University Press, 1975); Hayward R. Alker Jr. and Bruce Russett, *World Politics in the General Assembly* (New Haven: Yale University Press, 1965); Leon Gordenker, *The UN Secretary-General and the Maintenance of Peace* (New York: Columbia University Press, 1967); and M. J. Peterson, *The General Assembly in World Politics* (Boston: Unwin Hyman, 1986).

7. Miguel Marin-Bosch, "How Nations Vote in the General Assembly of the United Nations," *International Organization* 41:4 (Autumn 1987):705–724.

8. Brian Hall, "Blue Helmets," *New York Times Magazine,* January 2, 1994, p. 22.

9. International Peace Academy, *Peacekeeper's Handbook* (New York: Pergamon Press, 1984), p. 22.

10. Standard works describing the history of UN peacekeeping include Indar Jit Rikhye, *The Theory and Practice of Peacekeeping* (London: Hurst, 1984); Alan James, *Peacekeeping in International Politics* (London: Macmillan, 1990); Paul F. Diehl, *International Peacekeeping* (Baltimore: Johns Hopkins University Press, 1993); and United Nations, *The Blue Helmets: A Review of United Nations Peace-Keeping,* 2d ed. (New York: UNDPI, 1990).

11. Avi Beker, *The United Nations and Israel: From Recognition to Reprehension* (Lexington, Mass.: Lexington Books, 1988).

12. United Nations Association of the United States of America, *A Successor Vision: The United Nations of Tomorrow* (Lanham, Md.: University Press of America, 1988), p. xx.

13. For background on UN financing, consult John G. Stoessinger et al., *Financing the United Nations System* (Washington, D.C.: Brookings Institution, 1964).

CHAPTER 3

1. Ruth B. Russell, *The United Nations and United States Security Policy* (Washington, D.C.: Brookings Institution, 1968), p. 331.

2. Margaret P. Karns and Karen A. Mingst, eds., *The United States and Multilateral Institutions: Patterns of Changing Instrumentality and Influence* (Boston: Unwin Hyman, 1990).

3. Mikhail S. Gorbachev, "Secure World," in Foreign Broadcast Information Service, *Daily Report: Soviet Union,* September 17, 1987, pp. 23–28.

4. See Ken Matthews, *The Gulf Conflict and International Relations* (London: Routledge, 1993), p. 81.

5. Marie-Claude Smouts, "France and the United Nations System" (Paper prepared for the International Research Conference on the Future of the United Nations, Ottawa, Canada, January 5–7, 1990), p. 5.

6. For extensive treatment of the British position, see A.J.R. Groom, "Britain and the United Nations" (Paper prepared for the International Research Conference on the Future of the United Nations, Ottawa, Canada, January 5–7, 1990).

7. Martin Staniland, *Getting to No: The Diplomacy of the Gulf Conflict, August 2, 1990–January 15, 1991: Part 3: The Making of Resolution 678,* Pew Case Studies in International Affairs No. 449 (Washington, D.C.: Institute for the Study of Diplomacy, Georgetown University, 1992), p. 6.

8. See Sadako Ogata, "Japan's Policy Towards the United Nations" (Paper prepared for the International Research Conference on the Future of the United Nations, Ottawa, Canada, January 5–7, 1990).

9. See Eugene Brown, "Five on the Other Side of the River: Japan and the Persian Gulf War," in Robert O. Freedman, ed., *The Middle East After Iraq's Invasion of Kuwait* (Gainesville: University Press of Florida, 1993), pp. 137–164. See also Masaru Tamamoto, "Trial of an Ideal: Japan's Debate over the Gulf Crisis," *World Policy Journal* 8, no. 1 (Winter 1990–1991):89–106.

10. Quoted in David E. Sanger, "Japan's Parliament Votes to End Ban on Sending Troops Abroad," *New York Times International,* June 16, 1992, pp. 1, A15.

11. Okazaki Hisahiko, "Success in Cambodia, Time to Pull Out," *Japan Echo* 20, no. 3 (Autumn 1993):53–54.

12. Quoted in Paul Lewis, "Germany Asks Permanent UN Council Seat," *New York Times,* September 24, 1992, p. 1. For more extended discussion of Germany and the UN, see Wilfried von Bredow, "The Multilateral Obligation: German Perspectives on the UN System," in Keith Krause and W. Andy Knight, eds., *Changing State/Society Perspectives on the United Nations Systems* (Tokyo: United Nations University Press, forthcoming).

13. Laura Neack, "Beyond the Rhetoric of Peacekeeping and Peacemaking: Middle States in International Politics" (Ph.D. diss., University of Kentucky, 1991). See also Andrew F. Cooper, Richard A. Higgott, and Kim Richard Nossal, *Relocating Middle Powers: Australia and Canada in a Changing World Order* (Vancouver: University of British Columbia Press, 1993).

14. Keith Krause, David Dewitt, and W. Andy Knight, "Canada, the United Nations, and the Evolution of International Governance" (Paper prepared for the International Research Conference on the Future of the United Nations, Ottawa, Canada, January 5–7, 1990).

15. Quoted in J. L. Granatstein, "Peacekeeping: Did Canada Make a Difference? And What Difference Did Peacekeeping Make to Canada?" in John English and Norman Hillmer, eds., *Making a Difference? Canada's Foreign Policy in a Changing World Order* (Toronto: Lester Publishing, 1992), pp. 224–225.

16. Quoted in Elaine Sciolino, "How U.S. Got U.N. Backing for Use of Force in the Gulf," *New York Times,* August 30, 1990, pp. A1f.

17. Cooper, Higgott, and Nossal, *Relocating Middle Powers.*

18. Donald J. Puchala and Roger A. Coate, *The Challenge of Relevance: The United Nations in a Changing World Environment,* ACUNS Reports and Papers No. 5, 1989, p. 53.

19. Ibid.

20. Marin-Bosch, "How Nations Vote," p. 709.

21. Lynton Keith Caldwell, *International Environmental Policy: Emergence and Dimensions,* 2d ed. rev. (Durham, N.C.: Duke University Press, 1990), p. 94.

22. Robert W. Cox, "The Executive Head: An Essay on Leadership in International Organization," *International Organization* 23, no. 12 (Spring 1969):207.

23. Oran R. Young, *The Intermediaries: Third Parties in International Crises* (Princeton: Princeton University Press, 1967), p. 283.

24. Quoted in ibid., p. 284.

25. Javier Pérez de Cuéllar, "The Role of the UN Secretary-General," in Adam Roberts and Benedict Kingsbury, eds., *United Nations, Divided World: The UN's Role in International Relations* (Oxford: Clarendon Press, 1988), pp. 65–66.

26. U Thant, *View from the United Nations* (Garden City, N.Y.: Doubleday, 1978), p. 32.

27. Thomas M. Franck, "The Good Offices Function of the UN Secretary-General," in Adam Roberts and Benedict Kingsbury, eds., *United Nations, Divided World: The UN's Role in International Relations* (Oxford: Clarendon Press, 1988), pp. 85–86.

28. Julia Preston, "Boutros-Ghali Rushes in . . . in a Violent World: The U.N. Secretary General Has an Activist's Agenda," *Washington Post National Weekly Edition,* January 10–16, 1994, pp. 10–11.

CHAPTER 4

1. Substantial portions of this chapter previously appeared in *World Security: Challenges for a New Century,* by Michael T. Klare and Daniel C. Thomas. Copyright © 1994. Reprinted with permission of St. Martin's Press, Incorporated.

2. Charles Malik, *Man in the Struggle for Peace* (New York: Harper and Row, 1963), p. 124.

3. United Nations, *The Blue Helmets,* p. 4.

4. Brian Urquhart, *A Life in Peace and War* (New York: Harper and Row, 1987), p. 198.

5. Thomas G. Weiss and Jarat Chopra, *United Nations Peacekeeping: An ACUNS Teaching Text,* ACUNS Reports and Papers, 1992, p. 8.

6. Ibid.

7. Ibid., p. 23.

8. Address by the Secretary-General, "From Peace-Keeping to Peace-Building" (Delivered at the Ninth Annual David M. Abshire Lecture, Washington, D.C., May 13, 1992), p. 4.

9. Gorbachev, "Secure World," p. 25.

10. Margaret P. Karns and Karen A. Mingst, "The Past as Prologue: The United States and the Future of the UN System," in Chadwick R. Alger, Gene M. Lyons, and John E. Trent, eds., *The United Nations and the Politics of Member States* (Tokyo: United Nations University Press, forthcoming).

11. This section draws from Karen A. Mingst and Abdullah Mohammad, "Lessons from the Gulf War for the United Nations" (Paper presented at the International Conference on the Effects of the Iraqi Aggression on the State of Kuwait, Kuwait City, April 2–6, 1994).

12. See Weiss and Chopra, *United Nations Peacekeeping*, pp. 28–30, for a discussion of the U.S.-UN relationship.

13. Quoted in Kenneth R. Timmerman, "A Nuclear Iraq—Again," *Wall Street Journal*, November 12, 1993, p. A14.

14. Clovis Maksoud, "The Arab World's Quandry," *World Policy Journal* 8, no. 3 (Summer 1993):551.

15. Edward L. Luck and Tobi Trister Gati, "Where Collective Security," *Washington Quarterly* (Spring 1992):43.

16. McGeorge Bundy, "Nuclear Weapons and the Gulf," *Foreign Affairs* 70, no. 4 (Fall 1991):91.

17. John Gerard Ruggie, "Wandering in the Void: Charting the U.N.'s New Strategic Role," *Foreign Affairs* 72, no. 5 (November-December 1993):26.

18. "The 'Second Generation': Cambodia Elections 'Free and Fair,' but Challenges Remain," *UN Chronicle* 30, no. 3 (September 1993):32.

19. United Nations Security Council, "Letter Dated 29 November 1992 from the Secretary-General Addressed to the President of the Security Council," November 30, 1992 (S/24868), p. 2.

20. Richard Conroy, "Peacekeeping and Peace Enforcement in Somalia" (Paper presented at the Annual Meeting of the International Studies Association, Washington, D.C., March 30–April 2, 1994), p. 9.

21. Ibid., p. 12.

22. Ibid., p. 16.

23. Ibid., p. 22.

24. Larry Minear et al., *Humanitarian Action in the Former Yugoslavia: The U.N.'s Role in 1991–1993*, Occasional Paper No. 18 (Providence, R.I.: Thomas J. Watson Institute for International Studies and Refugee Policy Group, 1994), p. 89.

25. James B. Steinberg, "International Involvement in the Yugoslavia Conflict," in Lori Fischer Damrosch, ed., *Enforcing Restraint. Collective Intervention in International Conflicts* (New York: Council on Foreign Relations Press, 1993), pp. 68–69.

26. Weiss and Chopra, *United Nations Peacekeeping*, p. 31.

27. Report of the Secretary-General, "The Agenda for Peace," June 17, 1992 (S/24111), p. 4.

28. Tom Farer, "A Paradigm of Legitimate Intervention," in Lori Fischer Damrosch, ed., *Enforcing Restraint: Collective Intervention in Internal Conflicts* (New York: Council on Foreign Relations Press, 1993), p. 331.

29. UN Document A/44/605, pp. 19–20.

30. *New York Times*, December 12, 1993, p. 9.

31. Quoted in ibid.

CHAPTER 5

1. For a good overview, see Robert Gilpin, *The Political Economy of International Relations* (Princeton: Princeton University Press, 1987), Chapter 1.

2. Ibid., p. 33.

3. Robert L. Heilbroner, *Marxism: For and Against* (New York: Norton, 1980).

4. For early illustrations of the Latin American dependency approach, see Teotonio Dos Santos, "The Structure of Dependence," *American Economic Review* 60, no. 5 (1970):235–246; and Celso Furtado, *Development and Underdevelopment: A Structural View of the Problems of Developed and Underdeveloped Countries* (Berkeley and Los Angeles: University of California Press, 1964).

5. Norman Angell, *The Great Illusion: A Study of the Relation of Military Power in Nations to Their Economic and Social Advantage,* 3d ed. rev. (New York: Putnam, 1911).

6. For a historical overview of World Bank, see Edward Mason and Robert Asher, *The World Bank Since Bretton Woods* (Washington, D.C.: Brookings Institution, 1973); and Robert Ayres, *Banking on the Poor: The World Bank and World Poverty* (Cambridge, Mass.: MIT Press, 1983).

7. Consult J. Keith Horsefield, *The International Monetary Fund, 1945–1965,* vol. 1 (Washington, D.C.: IMF, 1969); and Margaret Garritsen DeVries, *The International Monetary Fund, 1972–1978: Cooperation on Trial* (Washington, D.C.: IMF, 1985).

8. For critical views of the IMF, see Martin Honeywell, ed., *The Poverty Brokers: The IMF and Latin America* (London: Latin America Bureau, 1983); and Cheryl Payer, *The Debt Trap: The IMF and the Third World* (New York: Monthly Review Press, 1974).

9. For background on the GATT, see Robert E. Hudec, *The GATT Legal System and World Trade Diplomacy* (New York: Praeger, 1975); and Gilbert R. Winham, *International Trade and the Tokyo Round Negotiations* (Princeton: Princeton University Press, 1986).

10. See Marc Williams, *Third World Cooperation: The Group of 77 in UNCTAD* (New York: St. Martin's Press, 1991); and Craig N. Murphy, *The Emergence of the NIEO Ideology* (Boulder: Westview Press, 1984).

11. Donald J. Puchala and Roger A. Coate, *The State of the United Nations, 1988,* ACUNS Reports and Papers, 1988, p. 31.

12. Esther Boserup, *Women's Role in Economic Development* (London: George Allen and Unwin, 1970).

13. Gareth Porter and Janet Welsh Brown, *Global Environmental Politics* (Boulder: Westview Press, 1991).

14. Peter R. Baehr and Leon Gordenker, *The United Nations in the 1990s* (New York: St. Martin's Press, 1992), p. 144.

15. For different disciplinary perspectives on sustainability, see the articles in *Finance and Development* 30, no. 4 (December 1993). For a critique, see S. M. Lele, "Sustainable Development: A Critical Review," *World Development* 19, no. 6 (1991):607–622.

16. World Commission on Environment and Development (Brundtland Commission Report), *Our Common Future* (Oxford: Oxford University Press, 1987), p. 8.

17. For details on the PrepCom process and documentation, see Shanna L. Halpern, "The United Nations Conference on Environment and Development: Process and Documentation," ACUNS Reports and Papers No. 2, 1993.

18. Observations on UNCED are from Catharine Tinker, "IGOs as Gatekeepers: Accreditation and Legitimation of Environmental NGOs" (Paper presented at the Annual Meeting of the International Studies Association, Washington, D.C., March 30–April 2, 1994).

19. Robert O. Matthews, "United Nations Reform in the 1990s," ACUNS Reports and Papers No. 5, 1993, p. 18.

20. Craig N. Murphy, "The United Nations' Capacity to Promote Sustainable Development: The Lessons of a Year that 'Eludes All Facile Judgment,'" in Albert Legault, Craig N. Murphy, and W. B. Ofuatey-Kodjoe, *The State of the United Nations: 1992*, ACUNS Reports and Papers No. 3, 1993, p. 60.

21. UN World Conference of the UN Decade for Women: Equality, Development, and Peace, August 13, 1980 (A/CONF.94/34).

22. Maureen O'Neill, "Men and Women Together," *Development* 1 (1991):49.

23. For useful suggestions, see Lawrence E. Suskind, *Environmental Diplomacy: Negotiating More Effective Global Agreements* (New York: Oxford University Press, 1994).

CHAPTER 6

1. Quoted in Larry Minear, "UN Coordination of the International Humanitarian Response to the Gulf Crisis, 1990–1992," Occasional Paper No. 13 (Providence, R.I.: Thomas J. Watson Institute for International Studies, 1992), p. 39.

2. Quoted in Nancy Seufert-Barr, "Towards a New Clarity for UN Work," *UN Chronicle* 30, no. 4 (December 1993):38.

3. Peter Wallensteen, "Representing the World: A Security Council for the 21st Century," *Security Dialogue* 25, no. 1 (1994):67.

4. Boutros Boutros-Ghali, *An Agenda for Peace* (New York: United Nations, 1992).

5. Jan Eliasson, "Keynote Address," in "Resolving Intra-National Conflicts: A Strengthened Role for Intergovernmental Organizations," Report Series vol. 5, no. 1 (Atlanta: Carter Center of Emory University, 1993), p. 18.

6. Quoted in Jacques Fomerand, "Strengthening the UN's Economic and Social Programs: A Documentary Essay," ACUNS System Report, 1990, p. 2.

7. Minear, "UN Coordination," pp. 8–9.

8. Ibid., p. 19.

9. Larry Minear, "Humanitarian Action in the Former Yugoslavia: The U.N.'s Role, 1991–1993," Occasional Paper No. 18, (Providence: Thomas J. Watson Institute for International Studies, 1994), p. 28.

10. UNA/USA, *A Successor Vision.*

11. The Nordic UN Project, *The United Nations in Development: Reform Issues in Economic and Social Fields* (Stockholm: Almqvist and Wiksell International, 1991).

12. Quoted in Seufert-Barr, "Towards a New Clarity," p. 39.

13. Urquhart, *A Life*, p. 352.

14. Shijuro Ogata and Paul Volcker, *Financing an Effective United Nations: A Report of the Independent Advisory Group on U.N. Financing* (New York: Ford Foundation, 1993).

15. Edward C. Luck, "Making Peace," *Foreign Policy* 90 (Winter 1992–1993):155.

16. Ken Matthews, *The Gulf Conflict and International Relations* (London: Routledge, 1993), pp. 87–88.

17. President Clinton address to UN General Assembly, September 27, 1993; excerpted in *New York Times*, September 28, 1993, p. A4.

18. Paul Lewis, "U.S. Plans Peacekeeping Guidelines," *New York Times*, November 18, 1993, p. A10.

19. Paul M. Kennedy, "The American Prospect," *New York Review of Books* 40 (March 4, 1993):42–43.

20. Gene M. Lyons, "Rethinking the United Nations," *Mershon International Studies Review* 38, supp. 1 (April 1994):98.

21. K. P. Saksena, *Reforming the United Nations: The Challenge of Relevance* (New Delhi: Sage, 1993), p. 194.

22. Lyons, "Rethinking the United Nations," p. 99.

23. Peter Wilenski, "Reforming the United Nations for the Post–Cold War Era," in M. R. Bustelo and P. Alson, eds., *Whose New World Order?* (Sydney: Federation Press, 1991), p. 125.

24. Lyons, "Rethinking the United Nations," p. 98.

□ □ □

Suggested Readings

HISTORY OF THE UNITED NATIONS

Claude, Inis L. Jr. *Swords into Plowshares: The Problems and Progress of International Organization*. 3d rev. ed. New York: Random House, 1964.

Luard, Evan. *A History of the United Nations: The Years of Western Domination, 1945–1955*. New York: St. Martin's Press, 1982.

GENERAL SOURCES ON THE UNITED NATIONS

Baehr, Peter R., and Leon Gordenker. *The United Nations in the 1990s*. New York: St. Martin's Press, 1992.

Bailey, Sydney D. *The Procedure of the U.N. Security Council*. New York: Oxford University Press, 1975.

———. *The Secretariat of the United Nations*. New York: Carnegie Endowment for International Peace, 1962.

Finkelstein, Lawrence S., ed. *Politics in the United Nations System*. Durham, N.C.: Duke University Press, 1988.

Gordenker, Leon. *The UN Secretary-General and the Maintenance of Peace*. New York: Columbia University Press, 1967.

Legault, Albert, Craig N. Murphy, and W. B. Ofuatey-Kodjoe. *The State of the United Nations: 1992*. ACUNS Reports and Papers No. 3. 1992.

Peterson, M. J. *The General Assembly in World Politics*. Boston: Unwin Hyman, 1986.

Puchala, Donald J., and Roger A. Coate. *The Challenge of Relevance: The United Nations in a Changing World Environment*. ACUNS Reports and Papers No. 5. 1989.

Riggs, Robert E., and Jack L. Plano. *The United Nations: International Organization and World Politics*. Chicago: Dorsey Press, 1988.

Roberts, Adam, and Benedict Kingsbury, eds. *United Nations, Divided World: The UN's Role in International Relations*. 2d ed. Oxford: Clarendon Press, 1993.

Stoessinger, John G. et al. *Financing the United Nations System*. Washington, D.C.: Brookings Institution, 1964.

Weiss, Thomas G., David P. Forsythe, and Roger A. Coate. *The United Nations and Changing World Politics*. Boulder: Westview Press, 1994.

Two general, excellent sources of material on the United Nations are the publications of the Academic Council on the United Nations System (ACUNS), headquartered at the Thomas J. Watson Institute for International

Studies, Brown University, Providence, Rhode Island, and *The United Nations Chronicle,* published by the UN Department of Public Information, New York.

MEMBER STATES AND THE UNITED NATIONS

Alger, Chadwick R., Gene M. Lyons, and John E. Trent, eds. *The United Nations and the Politics of Member States.* Tokyo: United Nations University Press, 1995.

Gregg, Robert W. *About Face? The United States and the United Nations.* Boulder: Lynne Rienner, 1993.

Karns, Margaret P., and Karen A. Mingst, eds. *The United States and Multilateral Institutions: Patterns of Changing Instrumentality and Influence.* Boston: Unwin Hyman, 1990.

Kay, David A. *The New Nations in the United Nations, 1960–1967.* New York: Columbia University Press, 1970.

Kim, Samuel S. *China, the United Nations, and World Order.* Princeton: Princeton University Press, 1979.

Moynihan, Daniel Patrick. *A Dangerous Place.* Boston: Little, Brown, 1978.

Nye, Joseph S. Jr., *Bound to Lead: The Changing Nature of American Power.* New York: Basic Books, 1990.

Russell, Ruth B. *The United Nations and United States Security Policy.* Washington, D.C.: Brookings Institution, 1968.

The U.S. Department of State publishes an annual volume, *United States Participation in the United Nations,* that is available from the U.S. Government Printing Office, Washington, D.C. Another excellent source on U.S. participation is the United Nations Association of the United States, headquartered in New York, and its bimonthly publication, *The Interdependent.*

COLLECTIVE SECURITY, PEACEKEEPING, AND ENFORCEMENT

Boutros-Ghali, Boutros. *An Agenda for Peace.* New York: United Nations, 1992.

Damrosch, Lori Fischer, ed. *Enforcing Restraint: Collective Intervention in International Conflicts.* New York: Council on Foreign Relations Press, 1993.

Diehl, Paul F. *International Peacekeeping.* Baltimore: Johns Hopkins University Press, 1993.

James, Alan. *Peacekeeping in International Politics.* London: Macmillan, 1990.

United Nations. *The Blue Helmets: A Review of United Nations Peace-Keeping.* 2d ed. New York: UNDPI, 1990.

Weiss, Thomas G. and Jarat Chopra. *United Nations Peacekeeping: An ACUNS Teaching Text.* ACUNS Reports and Papers. 1992.

ECONOMIC INSTITUTIONS AND SUSTAINABLE DEVELOPMENT

Ayres, Robert. *Banking on the Poor: The World Bank and World Poverty.* Cambridge, Mass.: MIT Press, 1983.

Caldwell, Lynton Keith. *International Environmental Policy: Emergence and Dimensions.* 2d ed. rev. Durham, N.C.: Duke University Press, 1990.

DeVries, Margaret Garritsen. *The International Monetary Fund, 1972–1978: Cooperation on Trial.* Washington, D.C.: IMF, 1985.

Halpern, Shanna L. "The United Nations Conference on Environment and Development: Process and Documentation," ACUNS Reports and Papers No. 2. 1993.

Honeywell, Martin, ed. *The Poverty Brokers: The IMF and Latin America.* London: Latin America Bureau, 1983.

Horsefield, J. Keith. *The International Monetary Fund, 1945–1965.* Vol. 1. Washington, D.C.: IMF, 1969.

Hudec, Robert E. *The GATT Legal System and World Trade Diplomacy.* New York: Praeger, 1975.

Mason, Edward, and Robert Asher. *The World Bank Since Bretton Woods.* Washington, D.C.: Brookings Institution, 1973.

Murphy, Craig N. *The Emergence of the NIEO Ideology.* Boulder: Westview Press, 1984.

Payer, Cheryl. *The Debt Trap: The IMF and the Third World.* New York: Monthly Review Press, 1974.

Pietila, Hilkka, and Jeanne Vickers. *Making Women Matter: The Role of the United Nations.* London: Zed Books, 1990.

Porter, Gareth, and Janet Welsh Brown. *Global Environmental Politics.* Boulder: Westview Press, 1991.

Suskind, Lawrence E. *Environmental Diplomacy: Negotiating More Effective Global Agreements.* New York: Oxford University Press, 1994.

Williams, Marc. *Third World Cooperation: The Group of 77 in UNCTAD.* New York: St. Martin's Press, 1991.

Winham, Gilbert R. *International Trade and the Tokyo Round Negotiations.* Princeton: Princeton University Press, 1986.

World Commission on Environment and Development (Brundtland Commission Report). *Our Common Future.* Oxford: Oxford University Press, 1987.

UN REFORM

Childers, Erskine, and Brian Urquhart. *Towards a More Effective United Nations.* Uppsala: Dag Hammarskjöld Foundation, 1990.

———. *Renewing the United Nations System.* Uppsala: Dag Hammarskjöld Foundation, 1994.

Matthews, Robert O. "United Nations Reform in the 1990s." ACUNS Reports and Papers No. 5. 1993.

Ogata, Shijuro and Paul Volcker. *Financing an Effective United Nations: A Report of the Independent Advisory Group on U.N. Financing.* New York: Ford Foundation, 1993.

United Nations Association of the United States of America. *A Successor Vision: The United Nations of Tomorrow.* Ed. Peter J. Fromuth. Lanham, Md.: University Press of America, 1988.

Urquhart, Brian and Erskine Childers. *A World in Need of Leadership: Tomorrow's United Nations.* Uppsala: Dag Hammarskjöld Foundation, 1990.

Glossary

Agenda 21: A document adopted as part of UNCED that presented detailed work plans, objectives, responsibilities, and financial estimates for achieving sustainable development.

Arrearages: Back payments of contributions to an international organization.

Balance of payments: The flow of money into and out of a country from trade, tourism, foreign aid, sale of services, profits, etc.

Basic human needs approach: Proposals in the development community to shift the orientation from growth to progress in meeting basic needs for the population, including better health care, education, and water supplies.

Bretton Woods: Generally refers to the international economic institutions, the World Bank and the International Monetary Fund, created in 1944, to ensure global monetary stability and economic growth.

Collective legitimation: The garnering of votes at the UN in support of a particular state's policy.

Collective security: The concept behind the League of Nations and United Nations, namely, that aggression by one state is aggression against all and should be defeated collectively.

Concert of Europe, or **Concert system:** The nineteenth-century practice of multilateral meetings among leaders of major European powers to settle problems.

Conditionality: A strategy by the IMF and World Bank to link further financial assistance to borrowers to the application of specified policy changes.

Democratization: The process whereby states become increasingly democratic, that is, where citizens vote for representatives who rule on behalf of the people.

Dependency theory: Derived from Marxism, an explanation of poverty and underdevelopment in less developed countries based on their historical dependence on and domination by rich countries.

Economic liberalism: A theory that posits that the free interplay of market forces leads to a more efficient allocation of resources to the benefit of the majority.

Enforcement measures: Direct military action by the UN to ensure compliance with Security Council directives.

Global governance: The rules, norms, and organizations that are designed to address international problems that states alone cannot solve.

Gross national product: The total of all goods and services produced by the nationals of a country at home and abroad.

Grotian tradition: Derived from the writings of Hugo Grotius, the idea that order in international relations is based on the rule of law.

Group of 77: A coalition of about 125 LDCs that pressed for reforms in economic relations between developing and developed countries; also referred to as the South.

Hague system: A system derived from conferences in 1897 and 1907 that established the principle of universality (all states should participate), rules for war, and dispute settlement mechanisms.

Humanitarian intervention: UN or individual states' actions to alleviate human suffering during violent conflicts without necessarily obtaining the consent of the "host" country.

International governmental organizations: International agencies or bodies set by states and controlled by member states that deal with areas of common interests.

Integration: The process by which societies or nations are economically and politically brought together.

Interdependence: The sensitivity and vulnerability of states to each other's actions resulting from increased interactions generated by trade, monetary flows, telecommunications, and shared interests.

League of states: A loose assembly of states joined for common purposes but in which each member retains sovereignty.

Marxism: A social theory formulated by Karl Marx according to which class conflict between owners and workers will cause the eventual demise of capitalism.

Mercantilism, or **statism:** The belief that world politics is influenced by a competition for wealth, resources, and power and that they should be mobilized to further states' interests and political goals.

Most-favored nation treatment: The equitable application of the lowest tariffs offered by one nation to other nations.

Multilateralism: The conduct of international activities by three or more states in accordance with shared general principles, often through international or multilateral institutions.

New International Economic Order: A list of demands by the G–77 to reform economic relations between the North and South, that is, between the developed countries and the less developed countries.

Noncompulsory dispute settlement: An arrangement whereby states are not obligated to bring disputes to a body for settlement.

Nongovernmental organizations: Private associations of individuals or groups that engage in political activity usually across national borders.

Nonintervention: The principle that obliges states and international organizations not to interfere in matters within the domestic jurisdiction of other sovereign states.

Peace building: Postconflict activities to strengthen and preserve peace settlements, such as development aid, civilian administration, and human rights monitoring.

Peacekeeping: The use of multilateral forces to achieve several different objectives: observation of cease-fire lines and cease-fires, separation of forces, promotion of law and order, offering of humanitarian aid and intervention.

Peacemaking: Efforts to bring parties to agreement.

Politicization: The linkage of different issues for political purposes, as in the introduction of a clearly political topic to an organization dealing with health problems.

Preferential treatment: The granting of special trade arrangements, usually giving trade advantages to less developed countries.

Preventive diplomacy: The practice of engaging in diplomatic actions before the outbreak of conflict; the monitoring of hot spots before conflict erupts.

Realist theory, or **realism:** A theory of world politics that emphasizes states' interest in accumulating power to ensure security in an anarchic world.

Self-determination: The principle according to which nationalities have the right to determine who will rule them; thought to minimize war for territorial expansion.

Sovereignty: The authority of the state, based on recognition by other states and nonstate actors, to govern matters within its own borders that affect its people, economy, security, and form of government.

Structural adjustment programs: IMF policies and recommendations to guide countries out of payment deficits and economic crises.

Sustainable development: An approach that tries to reconcile current economic growth and environmental protection with future needs.

Terms of trade: The ratio of the price of imports to the price of exports. (When import prices are greater than the value of exports, a state has an adverse or declining terms of trade.)

Transnational corporations: Private enterprises with production facilities, sales, or activity in more than one country.

Uniting for Peace Resolution: The resolution that enables the General Assembly to assume responsibility for peace and security issues if the Security Council is deadlocked.

Veto: A negative vote cast in the UN Security Council by one of the permanent members, which has the effect of defeating a decision.

Voting blocs: Group of states voting together in the UN General Assembly or other international bodies.

Weighted voting systems: Systems in which voting equality is waived so that states have unequal votes, based on financial contributions, population, or geographic representation.

Westphalian tradition: The tradition, dating to the Peace of Westphalia in 1648, that emphasizes state sovereignty within a territorial space.

□ □ □

About the Book and Authors

The United Nations faces unprecedented opportunities as well as heightened expectations in the wake of the Cold War. With as-yet-unmet challenges throughout the world, the limits to UN power and effectiveness are being realized.

From regional conflicts to areas of environmental degradation, the UN's success will depend on the way in which three dilemmas are resolved—the tensions between sovereignty and the reality of its erosion, between demands for global governance and the weakness of UN institutions (as well as the reluctance of states to commit), and between the need for leadership and the diffusion of power. The authors explore these dilemmas in the context of the UN's historical evolution, including its experience with peacekeeping, peacemaking, and environmentally sustainable development. They also consider the role of various actors in the UN system, from major powers (especially the United States), small and middle powers, coalitions, and nongovernmental organizations, to the six secretaries-general. The need for institutional reforms and specific proposals for reform are examined.

Because multilateral diplomacy is now the norm rather than the exception in world politics, the UN is more central than ever. This new text places the UN at the center of the entirely new set of dilemmas now emerging in world politics.

Karen A. Mingst is chair and professor of political science at the University of Kentucky. **Margaret P. Karns** is director of the Center for International Programs and professor of political science at the University of Dayton.

BOOKS IN THIS SERIES

Deborah J. Gerner
One Land, Two Peoples: The Conflict over Palestine, second edition

☐ ☐ ☐

Ted Robert Gurr and Barbara Harff
Ethnic Conflict in World Politics

☐ ☐ ☐

Kenneth W. Grundy
South Africa: Domestic Crisis and Global Challenge

☐ ☐ ☐

Gareth Porter and Janet Welsh Brown
Global Environmental Politics

☐ ☐ ☐

Davis S. Mason
Revolution in East-Central Europe and World Politics

☐ ☐ ☐

Georg Sørensen
Democracy and Democratization: Processes and Prospects in a Changing World

☐ ☐ ☐

Steve Chan
East Asian Dynamism: Growth, Order, and Security in the Pacific Region, second edition

☐ ☐ ☐

Barry B. Hughes
International Futures: Choices in the Creation of a New World Order

☐ ☐ ☐

Jack Donnelly
International Human Rights

☐ ☐ ☐

V. Spike Peterson and Anne Sisson Runyan
Global Gender Issues

□ □ □

Sarah J. Tisch and Michael B. Wallace
Dilemmas of Development Assistance:
The What, Why, and Who of Foreign Aid

□ □ □

Frederic S. Pearson
The Global Spread of Arms:
Political Economy of International Security

Index